rebecca robb benne

simon brown

jon hird

howard smith

nick witherick

# move

intermediate

teacher's book

MACMILLAN

Macmillan Education
Between Towns Road, Oxford OX4 3PP
A division of Macmillan Publishers Limited
Companies and representatives throughout the world

ISBN-13: 978-1-4050-0329-2
ISBN-10: 1-4050-0329-4

Text © Macmillan Publishers Limited 2006
Text by Rebecca Robb Benne
Resource materials by Simon Brown; Jon Hird; Howard Smith; Nick Witherick
Design and illustration © Macmillan Publishers Limited 2006

First published 2006

Designed by eMC Design
Illustrated by Kath Walker; Peter Richardson (Beehive Illustration); Pete Smith (Beehive
Illustration); Tim Kahane.

Author's acknowledgements:
Many thanks to Darina Richter for her invaluable input.

The publishers would like to thank the following for their help and advice with the test
material:
Nicola Seth and teachers at British Study Centre, Oxford; Steve Thomas at Regent, Oxford;
J Kaur and teachers at University Tutorial College, Reading.

The authors and publishers would like to thank the following for permission to reproduce
their material:
Quotation in 'See the world' by Cecil Rajendra, reprinted by permission of the author;
Extract from 'The world's most expensive house' taken from www.rediff.com/money/2004
27.04.04; Extract from 'After a Century, We've Produced The Stressed Out, Cooped Up
Battery Child' copyright © The Independent 1999 first published in The Independent
02.09.99, reprinted by permission of the publisher; Extract from 'Neighbours' taken from
http://en.wikipedia.org/wiki/Neighbours copyright © Wikipedia, the free encyclopedia;
Extract from 'How the Rules of War Work' taken http://people.howstuffworks.com/rules-of-
war1.htm; Extract from 'WTO reveals top ten tourist destinations in 2003' taken from
www.travelwirenews.com; Extract from Art by Yasmina Reza, translated by Christopher
Hamilton (Faber and Faber Limited, 1996), copyright © Yasmina Reza 1994; Translation
copyright © Yasmina Reza and Christopher Hamilton 1996, reprinted by permission of Faber
and Faber Ltd.

Whilst every effort has been made to locate the owners of copyright material in this book,
there may have been some cases when the publishers have been unable to contact the owners.
We should be grateful to hear from anyone who recognises copyright material and who is
unacknowledged. We shall be pleased to make the necessary amendments in future editions of
the book.

Printed and bound in Spain by Edelvives SA

2010 2009 2008 2007 2006
10 9 8 7 6 5 4 3 2 1

# Contents

# Introduction

## Welcome to *Move*

Adult learners have a wide variety of reasons for choosing to learn English. Some, for instance, do so as part of a foundation course for university or other course of studies; others do so for career reasons in order to gain promotion or perhaps to seek a new job. Yet others are planning to travel and wish to improve their English, or they are studying English as part of their holiday. Some students choose short, intensive courses of study, while others are studying perhaps two or three hours a week over a longer period.

*Move* recognises that to meet this wide variety of learning needs and teaching contexts, the key feature of a course for adults must be that it builds in a great deal of flexibility, allowing teachers to select from both core and optional material.

Each level of *Move* contains a core course of three modules, and with that there is an extensive range of optional materials, in the Coursebook and Class CD, and also in the CD-ROM and this Teacher's Book. There are five levels of *Move*, and it is suitable for use with adult students from an elementary level through to an advanced level of English.

The aim of this introduction is to explain both the methodological approach taken by *Move* as a language course, and the features that make up the core course and the optional materials.

## Methodology

*Move* recognises that the best way that most students learn is through a discovery approach. Throughout *Move* language is presented in context and students are encouraged to notice its use, meaning and form before plenty of practice is given.

*Move* attaches great importance to the accessibility of topics through engaging reading and listening texts. Throughout *Move* students are given the opportunity to present personalised and meaningful responses and to discuss their own ideas and opinions as a means of encouraging learning.

*Move* recognises that students are primarily looking to use their language in communicative situations. Therefore, central to *Move* are exercises and activities that encourage students to communicate their ideas in particular through speaking and listening.

*Move* recognises that learning a language means a lot more than studying tenses or other isolated grammatical features and individual lexical items. Just as important is the ability to recognise, for example, language chunks such as collocations and fixed phrases and to develop an awareness of the importance of naturalness and register. *Move* covers aspects of these language features throughout.

Each unit of *Move* has a Language study section, which focuses on a key area of language. The section starts with examples of the language in context taken from a preceding text or listening activity and then guides the students, encouraging them to notice its use and then work out meaning and form. Plenty of practice is then given through activities which allow the students to engage with the language on a personal level. Grammar reference pages support the Language study sections.

Each unit of *Move* has at least one Vocabulary section and many units have more than one. The students are encouraged to notice how the vocabulary is used in a preceding text or listening activity and it is then extended and practised, again allowing the students to engage with the language on a personal level.

Throughout *Move*, language is recycled and revised throughout each module. Additionally, the Review units at the end of each module bring language together from each of the preceding units and provide more overt revision. For further recycling and revision, *Move* has stimulating Extra practice material for each of the main units at the end of each module and the Teacher's Book includes photocopiable resource activities and end of unit and end of module tests. There are also CD-ROM activities for each unit (see below).

*Move* recognises the importance and value of self-study. The Extra practice activities are designed for use as homework or in class. The Grammar reference and Wordlist pages help students to review and keep a record of the language they have studied as they go through the course. The CD-ROM, which can be used on PC or Macintosh platforms, can be used either in school computer rooms or privately at home.

## Coursebook organisation

Each level of *Move* contains three stand-alone teaching modules, each of which focuses on one overall topic, such as 'Places' or 'Relationships'. The language is recycled and tested within the module. The main advantage of this is that students joining the course at a later stage are not disadvantaged if, for instance, they start their studies from the second module.

Each module contains four main teaching units and a review unit. The four main teaching units each take one aspect of the module's overall topic. So, for instance, the 'Relationships' module has topics that include family ties, partners, neighbours and troubles, which examines relationships within communities.

The key features of the main teaching units are:

A **Lead-in activity** at the start of every unit. The purpose of the Lead-in is to activate the topic by drawing on students' knowledge and curiosity.

Stimulating **reading texts**. These occur at least once in each unit and include a mixture of global, gist and detailed information tasks. Recognising the importance of authenticity, the texts are based on authentic sources such as magazine and internet articles and book extracts, and are chosen to be appropriate for use with Intermediate students. Students are encouraged to engage with and react to the texts on a personal level. The main reading texts in each unit are recorded to give you the flexibility to use an alternative means of presentation, or for the students to simultaneously listen and read. This can consolidate pronunciation features such as word and sentence stress and intonation, as well as helping students to adjust to the normal speed at which English is spoken.

Stimulating **listening activities**. These occur at least once in each unit and include carefully graded main listening tasks as well as student-to-student listening and speaking interaction. Skills covered include prediction, global and gist listening as well as listening for detail. The listening scripts are reproduced at the end of each module. There are also dedicated pronunciation tasks for all modules.

A **Language study section**. This draws from the reading and listening texts and follows a guided discovery approach. As well as work on traditional grammar such as tenses and word order, the Language study sections also cover broader language considerations such as politeness and register, how to express particular ideas or how to modify language. The sequence of tasks moves from more controlled to freer practice.

**Vocabulary input and practice sections**. These occur at least once in each unit and draw from the reading and listening texts. They include topic-based lexical sets and other useful language items such as phrasal verbs, phrases, expressions and collocations.

**Speaking activities**. These occur in a number of sections within every unit and include pairwork and small and larger group discussion opportunities. The speaking activities give the students the chance to respond personally to texts and issues. There are also more substantial speaking activities such as role-plays and presentations.

**Writing activities**. There is at least one major task in every module, and in most cases there are two. The writing tasks are integrated with other skills work in order to help students to plan and prepare for the written task. There is a variety of writing genres, which are chosen as practical examples of writing tasks students are likely to come across in everyday life. These include formal letters, emails, postcards and reviews.

**CD-ROM practice** at the end of each main teaching unit. This includes four corresponding activities for each unit. (For more details see below.)

The sequence of activity types within units varies to reflect the nature of the material.

The **Review units** focus on the main language presented in the preceding four main teaching units and recycle it through reading and listening texts, speaking activities and games. Review units also feature a song related to the module theme, with a short factfile about the singer / writer. There is also an extended production task, such as a role-play or discussion, using language from the module.

**Extra practice pages**, which are at the end of each module, offer a chance for further practice and consolidation of the grammar and vocabulary in each unit.

**Grammar reference** sections, which support each Language study section, are at the end of each module.

A **Wordlist** for each unit, with phonetic spellings, is at the end of each module.

## Flexibility

One of the key benefits of *Move* is that as teachers you can combine the core and additional course material to suit your teaching situation and the needs and interests of your students. Each module contains 15 hours of core teaching material (three hours per unit). Therefore using just the core material for each level provides a course of around 45 hours' study. But in addition, you can supplement this with the following additional materials and resources and potentially expand the course to over 90 hours:

**Extra practice pages**. These can be completed for homework or in class, during or at the end of each unit.

**CD-ROM** (see below).

**Teacher's Book optional activities**. Throughout this Teacher's Book there are suggestions for additional optional activities to consolidate and extend the language being taught.

**Teacher's Book resources**. For each of the main teaching units there are two photocopiable worksheets offering different kinds of practice (see below).

**Tests**. There are photocopiable progress tests for the end of each unit, and more substantial tests for the end of each module. There is also a placement test (see below).

## Common European Framework (CEF) links

There is a dedicated section in this Teacher's Book which explains how *Move* links to the CEF (see pages 7–18). Essentially, this section explains what the CEF is, introduces a photocopiable, detailed mapping document and photocopiable student checklists for each unit that students can use as part of their Biography. These checklists also draw on the 'Can do' learning aims which appear at the start of each unit of the Coursebook.

The CD-ROM contains one activity per unit which expressly links to the student checklists. Additionally, the Markbook feature allows marks for each of the activities to be recorded and printed so that students can add these to their dossiers, and you can also check progress. The bookmark feature also allows students to save their own wordlists or to access particular activities directly. Again, this can be used to contribute towards the student's Biography, and it encourages learner independence.

# Other components

## Class CD set

There are two CDs in the set. CD1 contains the listening material for the first and second modules, while CD2 contains material for the third module. All recorded listening material for the core course, which includes listening and pronunciation activities, is shown with the symbol, with the corresponding track number set out alongside the activity in the Coursebook. Optional listening activities, ie the main reading tasks, are shown by the symbol. The listening scripts are set out in the reference material at the end of each module in the Coursebook and, for convenience, in the teaching notes in this Teacher's Book.

## CD-ROM

There are four activities for each of the main units. These provide further practice of language presented in the unit:

Language study activity – focusing on language presented in the Language study.

Vocabulary – recycling language presented in the Vocabulary sections.

'Can do' activity – focusing on one of the main 'Can do' statements in the Common European Framework student checklists. These include reading, listening and writing activities.

Language game – drawing on language from the unit, these are highly interactive fun activities in which students have to perform tasks such as beating the clock, chasing a villain, or saving someone from meeting a terrible fate.

The CD-ROM contains a useful Help section which shows students how to use it. Additionally, the Markbook feature allows students to record and update their results, as well as to print them out. The Bookmark feature is a space for students to create their own wordlists, revision notes, or shortcuts to their favourite activities. The Help section shows students how to create bookmarks and build their own learning resource.

## Teacher's Book

This Teacher's Book contains a range of useful sections:

The Common European Framework section sets out how *Move* links with the CEF (see page 7).

The Teaching tips is an invaluable four-page section providing useful teaching ideas. These include suggestions for five-minute lesson warmers before opening the Coursebook, lesson closing activities, and five-minute revision activities. Tips include ideas for varying speaking activities such as different ways of organising pairwork, how to lead whole class discussions and lots more.

The Teaching notes provide straightforward and clear procedural notes, with answer keys and listening scripts inserted in the body of the notes for easy reference. You'll also find useful optional activities to add extra practice, alternative ways of presenting new language, cultural background notes and help with pronunciation of difficult words and phrases. The summary at the start of each unit sets out the main learning aims and content of each unit, as well as a preparation checklist for some of the optional activities. The reference section at the end of each unit shows where to find additional study material in the Coursebook and this Teacher's Book.

The Teacher's resource section comprises two parts: a Resource pack section, and a Test section:

The Resource pack contains 24 photocopiable worksheets, two for each of the main teaching units. These comprise a stand-alone discussion lesson based on the topic of the unit, and a language-oriented activity, which consolidates and extends the language presented in the unit.

The Test section comprises three kinds of tests. The pre-course placement test is flexible and contains a half-hour multiple-choice grammar and vocabulary test, which is easily marked. It includes a suggested, additional spoken interview and written task for a more comprehensive assessment of a student's level. The complete test can be administered in under one and a half hours, and is the same test for all levels of *Move*. The end of unit tests are flexible, quick tests which contain grammar, vocabulary and reading skill elements drawn from the unit. The three end of module tests are more substantial tests which assess students' progress against the main learning points in each of the preceding four units. These can be used instead of the end of unit tests or in addition to them. The end of module test also contains a listening element. All of the tests are easily marked.

We very much hope you and your students enjoy using *Move*. The range of material and resources it offers make it a unique course with enough space within each unit for students to get an impressive range of practice, and plenty of variety in their learning experience.

**Jon Hird**

# The Common European Framework and *Move*

## Introduction

The Common European Framework (CEF) is a document which has been drawn up by the Council of Europe. Its main purpose is to provide an 'open, neutral framework of reference' to help students, teachers, institutions and employers describe the stages of learning that students typically go through when they are learning a foreign language, and to establish benchmark levels of language proficiency. A range of international language qualifications can also be mapped against these benchmark levels of proficiency.

The Framework sets out six levels of language proficiency. These are A1, A2, B1, B2, C1, and C2. A1 learners are just starting to learn a language. The B1 level represents the threshold level of English and C2 learners are at a very advanced level of proficiency. Each of these levels incorporates a series of statements that describe a wide range of language skills and sub-skills. The main advantage of this is that it enables the individual student to assess their own progress in order to build up a profile of their own learning, and to set learning objectives for the future.

The series of level statements can be made more specific to the course of learning by generating a series of language descriptors that correlate to the level statements. The CEF sets out clear guidelines about how these descriptors should be formulated in Chapter 9, Assessment (pp177–196) of the *Common European Framework of Reference*, and in Appendix A: developing proficiency descriptors (pp205–216). This document can be downloaded in all European languages from: www.coe.int.

The three criteria of assessment that the guidelines set out are:

1 Validity: what is actually assessed is what should be assessed;
2 Reliability: the accuracy of decisions; and
3 Feasibility: the assessment has to be practical.

Additionally, the guidelines advise that descriptors should be set out as follows:

- Positiveness: although it is easier, particularly at low levels, to describe what a learner can't do, rather than what they can do; if levels of proficiency are to serve as objectives rather than just an instrument for screening candidates, then it is desirable to use positive descriptors.
- Definiteness: descriptors should describe concrete tasks and / or degrees of skill in performing tasks.
- Clarity: descriptors should be transparent, not jargon laden.
- Brevity: no individual student is typical. A range of shorter descriptors helps both students and teachers to identify what is being assessed. Descriptors that are longer than a two-clause sentence cannot realistically be used accurately. Teachers also consistently prefer short descriptors.
- Independence: descriptors that are likely to describe a behaviour about which one can say 'Yes, this person can do this' can be used as independent criteria statements in checklists, self assessment or teacher continuous assessment. Independent descriptors offer greater integrity to those forms of assessment.

The CEF also introduces the concept of a student portfolio. A student portfolio can consist of three strands. Firstly, a language 'Passport' will incorporate the formal qualifications that a student has successfully completed, along with details of courses completed. Secondly, the portfolio contains a personal 'Biography' which can contain notes about what the student found easy or difficult and a record of his or her learning experience. The third element is a 'Dossier', which can contain individual pieces of student's writing in a foreign language as well as recordings of the student speaking it.

## The approach used in *Move*

The key point is that no coursebook can accurately claim that by completing the activities contained within it a student will have attained a given level of the CEF. *Move* is a short course which has been comprehensively mapped against appropriate levels of the Framework. In completing the course, students are offered a range of activities that are consistent with the aims of the Framework, and which contribute significantly towards the learning progress that a student will make.

### CEF mapping document

In the case of *Move Intermediate*, the course has been mapped against statements at the B1 (threshold) level of attainment. The photocopiable mapping document which follows this introduction uses statements taken from the CEF and provides instances from the course where each skill and sub-skill is presented and practised. The main purpose of this is to provide teachers with a detailed overview of how *Move* relates to the various skills and sub-skills identified in the CEF.

### CEF student portfolio checklists

The second set of documents is a series of photocopiable student portfolio checklists, one for each of the main teaching units of the course. We have followed the guidelines contained within the CEF to generate the descriptors within each of these checklists, and these are linked in turn to the level statements. The purpose of these checklists is to enable students to reflect at the end of each unit in the Coursebook, and related CD-ROM activities, on the level of proficiency that they have reached for each of the skills and sub-skills that are set out. The main purpose of the checklists is to provide the students with a record of their ongoing self-assessment, as part of their portfolio Biography.

In completing the student portfolio checklists students can assess how successful they have been, what they need more practice in, and what specific help they could ask their teacher for.

Levels of learning:
1  = a very low level of understanding. The student may recognise the item but not be able to use it at all.
2  = understands and can use a little.
3  = understands and can manipulate the item fairly well.
4  = understands, can self-correct and manipulate the item appropriately most of the time.
5  = the learner has passive understanding, appropriate selection and accurate active use of the item.

How to use the checklists:
1  Once you have completed a unit, give your students a photocopy of the relevant checklist. Avoid giving the impression that you are testing them.
2  Ask students to take the list home and think it over.
3  In the following lesson discuss any points that the students raise.
4  After each review unit ask students to look at the four checklists for that module again and update their assessments.
5  Ask students to keep their checklists and file them with their self-assessment documentation as part of their portfolio.

## Coursebook links to the CEF

As well as the photocopiable material contained within this section of the Teacher's Book, there are a number of other 'tools' that *Move* incorporates as part of an integrated approach towards the European Framework. Each module of the course begins with a Contents map which sets out the content of each of the syllabus strands of the course. *Move* has a multi-stranded syllabus which is consistent with the range of skills and sub-skills set out in the CEF.

Additionally, the main learning aims of each of the teaching units are expressed as 'Can do' descriptors. These are replicated in the student portfolio checklists, thus ensuring that what is presented is also what is being assessed.

## Revision and testing

The importance of revision work in recycling new language cannot be underestimated. Each module of *Move* contains a review unit, and we recommend that as part of the review process students revisit their student portfolio checklists and re-evaluate their self-assessment after completing each review unit.

This Teacher's Book also contains a comprehensive, photocopiable test section. The placement test provides a benchmark pre-course record of attainment, and there are end of unit and end of module progress tests which can contribute either towards an overall end of course grade, as part of the student portfolio Passport, or alternatively, be integrated into the student's Dossier.

## CD-ROM links to the CEF

The CD-ROM contains at least one activity for each unit which has been specifically written to provide further support for one of the descriptors set out in the student portfolio checklists. Other activities for each unit are also consistent with the learning aims recorded on the checklists.

The Markbook feature of the CD-ROM allows students to print out their end scores for the activities, and provides a further record of how the student is performing against the descriptors set out in the student portfolio checklist. This becomes an invaluable document for the student's Dossier.

## Concluding remarks

The comprehensive approach in *Move* to the Common European Framework reflects the overall aim of the Framework to provide an ongoing practical and accurate assessment of the level of language proficiency that a student has attained. The 'tools' provided for both teachers and students to record progress allow for a flexible approach which can be tailored to reflect the level of detail needed by individual students and educational institutions.

# CEF mapping

| Descriptor | Page of CEF | Pages of *Move Intermediate* containing practice for this descriptor |
|---|---|---|
| **GLOBAL** | | |
| *Range (vocabulary)* | | |
| Has enough language to get by, with sufficient vocabulary to express himself / herself with some hesitation and circumlocutions on topics such as family, hobbies and interests, work, travel and current events, but lexical limitations cause repetition and even difficulty with formulation at times. | 110 | 9, 10, 13, 15, 16, 19, 23, 24, 36, 38, 42, 47, 48, 50, 57, 68, 70, 72, 74, 77, 81, 83, 87, 89 |
| Shows good control of elementary vocabulary but major errors still occur when expressing more complex thoughts or handling unfamiliar topics and situations. | 112 | 12, 16, 22, 23, 25, 36, 37, 39, 42, 48, 54, 55, 56, 57, 71, 86, 87, 88, 89 |
| *Accuracy (grammar)* | | |
| Uses reasonably accurately a repertoire of frequently used 'routines' and patterns associated with more predictable situations. | 29 | 4, 12, 16, 22, 24, 25, 36, 44, 48, 54, 55, 57, 68, 71, 76, 80, 81, 82, 86, 87 |
| *Pronunciation* | | |
| Pronunciation is clearly intelligible even if a foreign accent is sometimes evident and occasional mispronunciations occur. | 117 | 6, 16, 23, 41, 73 |
| *Sociolinguistic appropriateness (function / register)* | | |
| Can perform and respond to a wide range of language functions, using their most common exponents in a neutral register. | 122 | 4, 44, 56 |
| Is aware of the salient politeness conventions and acts appropriately. | 122 | 39 |
| Is aware of, and looks out for signs of, the most significant differences between the customs, usages, attitudes, values and beliefs prevalent in the community concerned and those of his or her own. | 122 | 39, 73 |
| *Fluency* | | |
| Can keep going comprehensibly, even though pausing for grammatical and lexical planning and repair is very evident, especially in longer stretches of free production. | 29 | 9, 34, 72, 73 |
| Can exploit a wide range of simple language flexibly to express much of what he / she wants. | 124 | 9, 16, 25, 51, 73, 76, 88 |
| *Interaction* | | |
| Can initiate, maintain and close simple face to face conversation on topics that are familiar or of personal interest. | 29 | 34, 41 |
| *Coherence* | | |
| Can link a series of shorter, discrete simple elements into a connected, linear sequence of points. | 29 | 8, 19, 23, 76, 88, 89 |
| Can reasonably fluently relate a straightforward narrative or description as a linear sequence of points. | 125 | 8, 19, 23, 76 |
| Can convey simple, straightforward information of immediate relevance, getting across which point he / she feels is most important. | 129 | 25 |
| Can express the main point he / she wants to make comprehensibly. | 129 | 25, 34, 73 |
| **LISTENING** | | |
| *General* | | |
| Can understand the main point of many radio or TV programmes on current affairs or topics of personal and professional interest when the delivery is relatively slow and clear. | 26 | 6, 18, 43, 70, 71, 73, 81 |
| Can understand the main points of clear standard speech on familiar matters regularly encountered in work, school, leisure etc, including short narratives. | 66 | 5, 6, 13, 15, 18, 37, 38, 43, 49, 50, 69, 77 |
| Can identify unfamiliar words from the context on topics related to his / her field and interests. | 72 | 6, 18, 77 |
| Can extrapolate the meaning of occasional unknown words from the context and deduce sentence meaning provided the topic discussed is familiar. | 72 | 6, 18, 43, 50, 71 |
| *Conversation between native speakers* | | |
| Can generally follow the main points of extended discussion around him / her, provided speech is clearly articulated in standard dialect. | 66 | 5, 50, 69, 71 |
| *As member of live audience* | | |
| Can follow in outline straightforward short talks on familiar topics provided these are delivered in clearly articulated standard speech. | 67 | 6, 21, 49, 73, 81, 85 |

| Descriptor | Page of CEF | Pages of *Move Intermediate* containing practice for this descriptor |
|---|---|---|
| *Audio media and recordings* | | |
| Can understand the main points of radio news bulletins and simpler recorded material about familiar subjects delivered relatively slowly and clearly. | 68 | 5, 6, 18, 37, 38, 43, 49, 70, 71, 81 |
| *Watching TV and film (sample of category 'audio-visual reception')* | | |
| Can follow many films in which visuals and action carry much of the storyline, and which are delivered clearly in straightforward language. | 71 | 73 |
| Can catch the main points in TV programmes on familiar topics when the delivery is relatively slow and clear. | 71 | 21, 69 |
| **READING** | | |
| *General* | | |
| Can understand texts that consist mainly of high-frequency everyday or job-related language. | 26 | 2-3, 7, 10, 14, 20, 22, 40, 42, 53, 66, 78 |
| Can understand the description of events, feelings and wishes in personal letters. | 26 | 7, 10, 14, 40, 42, 66 |
| Can read straightforward factual texts on subjects related to his / her field and interest with a satisfactory level of comprehension. | 69 | 2-3, 9, 10, 14, 20, 35, 53, 66, 74, 84 |
| Can identify unfamiliar words from the context on topics related to his / her field and interests. | 72 | 3, 35, 42, 46, 47, 66, 74, 79 |
| Can extrapolate the meaning of occasional unknown words from the context and deduce sentence meaning provided the topic discussed is familiar. | 72 | 7, 9, 35, 40, 42, 46, 47, 52, 66, 78 |
| *Correspondence* | | |
| Can understand the description of events, feelings and wishes in personal letters well enough to correspond regularly with a pen friend. | 69 | 7, 10, 20 |
| *For orientation* | | |
| Can find and understand relevant information in everyday material, such as letters, brochures and short official documents. | 70 | 10, 14, 24, 49 |
| *For information and argument* | | |
| Can recognise significant points in straightforward newspaper articles on familiar subjects. | 70 | 7, 35, 46, 49, 66, 78 |
| *Instructions* | | |
| Can understand clearly written, straightforward instructions for a piece of equipment. | 71 | 51, 53, 83 |
| **SPOKEN INTERACTION** | | |
| *General* | | |
| Can deal with most situations likely to arise whilst travelling in an area where the language is spoken. | 26 | 13, 46, 66 |
| Can initiate, maintain and close simple face to face conversation on topics that are familiar or of personal interest. | 29 | 5, 10, 14, 15, 34, 37, 38, 40, 41, 42, 43, 66, 74, 75 |
| Can repeat back part of what someone has said to confirm mutual understanding. | 29 | 5, 72 |
| Can work out how to communicate the main point(s) he / she wants to get across, exploiting any resources available and limiting the message to what he / she can recall or find the means to express. | 64 | 5, 11, 13, 14, 21, 34, 38, 40, 41, 73, 74 |
| Can use a simple word meaning something similar to the concept he / she wants to convey and invites 'correction'. | 64 | 16, 44 |
| Can foreignise a mother tongue word and ask for confirmation. | 64 | 16 |
| Can ask for confirmation that a form used is correct. | 65 | 51 |
| Can start again using a different tactic when communication breaks down. | 65 | 72 |
| Can exploit a wide range of simple language to deal with most situations likely to arise whilst travelling. | 74 | 13, 51 |
| *Understanding a native speaker* | | |
| Can follow clearly articulated speech directed at him / her in everyday conversation, though will sometimes have to ask for repetition of particular words and phrases. | 75 | 13 |
| *Conversation* | | |
| Can enter unprepared into conversations on familiar topics. | 76 | 5, 9, 11, 12, 14, 15, 34, 37, 38, 42, 50, 70, 75, 78, 79 |
| Can follow clearly articulated speech directed at him / her in everyday conversation, though will sometimes have to ask for repetition of particular words and phrases. | 76 | 5 |
| Can maintain a conversation or discussion but may sometimes be difficult to follow when trying to say exactly what he / she would like to. | 76 | 5, 9, 11, 14, 15, 34, 37, 41, 42, 43, 46, 66, 71 |

Move Intermediate Teacher's Book © Macmillan Publishers Limited 2006

| Descriptor | Page of CEF | Pages of *Move Intermediate* containing practice for this descriptor |
|---|---|---|
| Can express and respond to feelings such as surprise, happiness, sadness, interest and indifference. | 76 | 9, 44, 46, 66 |
| *Informal discussion (with friends)* | | |
| Can generally follow the main points in an informal discussion with friends provided speech is clearly articulated in standard dialect. | 77 | 5, 42, 44, 46, 50 |
| Can give or seek personal views and opinions in discussing topics of interest. | 77 | 8, 9, 14, 15, 17, 34, 37, 42, 43, 50 |
| Can make his / her opinions and reactions understood as regards solutions to problems or practical questions of where to go, what to do, how to organise an event (eg an outing). | 77 | 5, 44 |
| Can express belief, opinion, agreement and disagreement politely. | 77 | 8, 9, 14, 34, 41, 42, 44 |
| *Formal discussion and meetings* | | |
| Can put over a point of view clearly, but has difficulty engaging in debate. | 78 | 5, 72 |
| *Goal-oriented co-operation* | | |
| Can generally follow what is said and, when necessary, can repeat back part of what someone has said to confirm mutual understanding. | 79 | 5, 73, 77 |
| Can make his / her opinions and reactions understood as regards possible solutions or the question of what to do next, giving brief reasons and explanations. | 79 | 5, 44, 45, 77 |
| Can invite others to give their views on how to proceed. | 79 | 5, 72, 77 |
| *Transactions for goods and services* | | |
| Can deal with most transactions likely to arise whilst travelling, arranging travel or accommodation, or dealing with authorities during a foreign visit. | 80 | 13 |
| Can cope with less routine situations in shops, post offices, banks, eg returning an unsatisfactory purchase. | 80 | 13, 72, 73 |
| Can make a complaint. | 80 | 72 |
| Can deal with most situations likely to arise when making travel arrangements through an agent or when actually travelling, eg asking a passenger where to get off for an unfamiliar destination. | 80 | 13 |
| *Information exchange* | | |
| Can find out and pass on straightforward factual information. | 81 | 5, 10, 17, 21 |
| Can obtain more detailed information. | 81 | 11, 21, 45 |
| *Interviews* | | |
| Can take some initiatives in an interview / consultation (eg to bring up a new subject) but is very dependent on interviewer in the interaction. | 82 | 11, 15, 18, 21, 77 |
| Can use a prepared questionnaire to carry out a structured interview, with some spontaneous follow up questions. | 82 | 13, 17, 21, 77 |
| *Turntaking* | | |
| Can initiate, maintain and close simple, face to face conversation on topics that are familiar or of personal interest. | 86 | 5, 11, 43, 72, 77 |
| *Clarification* | | |
| Can ask someone to clarify or elaborate what they have just said. | 87 | 45 |
| **SPOKEN PRODUCTION** | | |
| *General* | | |
| Can connect phrases in a simple way in order to describe experiences and events, his / her dreams, hopes and ambitions. | 26 | 4, 10, 11 |
| Can briefly give reasons and explanations for opinions and plans. | 26 | 5, 73 |
| Can narrate a story or relate the plot of a book or film and describe his / her reactions. | 26 | 43 |
| Can reasonably fluently sustain a straightforward description of one of a variety of subjects within his / her field of interest, presenting it as a linear sequence of points. | 58 | 5, 10, 11, 69, 81 |
| Can keep going comprehensibly, even though pausing for grammatical and lexical planning and repair is very evident, especially in longer stretches of free production. | 129 | 5, 11, 53, 69 |
| *Sustained monologue* | | |
| Can give straightforward descriptions on a variety of familiar subjects within his / her field of interest. | 59 | 4, 10, 69 |
| Can reasonably fluently relate a straightforward narrative or description as a linear sequence of points. | 59 | 17, 43, 69, 73, 81 |

| Descriptor | Page of CEF | Pages of *Move Intermediate* containing practice for this descriptor |
|---|---|---|
| Can give detailed accounts of experiences, describing feelings and reactions. | 59 | 43, 81 |
| Can relate details of unpredictable occurrences, eg an accident. | 59 | 17, 53, 81 |
| Can relate the plot of a book or film and describe his / her reactions. | 59 | 43 |
| Can describe dreams, hopes and ambitions. | 59 | 11, 84 |
| Can describe events, real or imagined. | 59 | 4, 17, 43 |
| Can narrate a story. | 59 | 18, 19, 43 |
| Can briefly give reasons and explanations for opinions, plans and actions. | 59 | 5, 10, 53, 69, 73, 84 |
| *Addressing Audiences* | | |
| Can give a prepared straightforward presentation on a familiar topic within his / her field which is clear enough to be followed without difficulty most of the time, and in which the main points are explained with reasonable precision. | 60 | 5, 17, 69, 84 |
| Can take follow up questions, but may have to ask for repetition if the speech was rapid. | 60 | 10, 73, 84 |
| **WRITING** | | |
| *General* | | |
| Can write simple connected text on topics which are familiar or of personal interest. | 26 | 17, 23, 41, 54 |
| Can write personal letters describing experiences and impressions. | 26 | 17, 54 |
| Can write straightforward connected texts on a range of familiar subjects within his field of interest, by linking a series of shorter discrete elements into a linear sequence. | 61 | 5, 41, 45, 69 |
| Can write straightforward, detailed descriptions on a range of familiar subjects within his / her field of interest. | 62 | 5, 22 |
| Can write accounts of experiences, describing feelings and reactions in simple connected text. | 62 | 25, 47, 81 |
| Can write a description of an event, a recent trip – real or imagined. | 62 | 81 |
| Can narrate a story. | 62 | 8, 18, 23, 81 |
| Can write very brief reports to a standard conventionalised format, which pass on routine factual information and state reasons for actions. | 62 | 17, 24, 69, 81 |
| Can work out how to communicate the main point(s) he / she wants to get across, exploiting any resources available and limiting the message to what he / she can recall or find the means to express. | 64 | 5, 45, 69, 81 |
| *Written interaction* | | |
| Can convey information and ideas on abstract as well as concrete topics, check information and ask about or explain problems with reasonable precision. | 83 | 5, 17, 24, 25, 45, 53, 69, 81 |
| Can write personal letters and notes asking for or conveying simple information of immediate relevance, getting across the point he / she feels to be important. | 83 | 17, 25, 41, 45 |
| *Correspondence* | | |
| Can write personal letters describing experiences, feelings and events in some detail. | 83 | 17, 25, 45, 82 |
| *Notes, messages and forms* | | |
| Can write notes conveying simple information of immediate relevance to friends, service people, teachers and others who feature in his / her everyday life, getting across comprehensibly the points he / she feels are important. | 84 | 17, 41 |
| *Note-taking* | | |
| Can take notes as a list of key points during a straightforward lecture, provided the topic is familiar, and the talk is both formulated in simple language and delivered in clearly articulated standard speech. | 96 | 10, 35, 50 |
| *Processing text* | | |
| Can collate short pieces of information from several sources and summarise them for somebody else. | 96 | 17 |
| Can paraphrase short written passages in a simple fashion, using the original text wording and ordering. | 96 | 35 |
| *Spelling* | | |
| Can produce continuous writing which is generally intelligible throughout. | 118 | 23, 52, 82 |
| Spelling, punctuation and layout are accurate enough to be followed most of the time. | 118 | 23, 82 |

# CEF student checklists

## Module 1 Unit 1 My life

Complete the checklist. Add an extra activity you have done in class or at home.

1 = I can do this with a lot of help from my teacher 2 = I can do this with a little help
3 = I can do this fairly well 4 = I can do this really well 5 = I can do this almost perfectly

| Competences | Page | Exercise | Your score |
|---|---|---|---|
| **Language quality** | | | |
| I can use adverbs of frequency. | 4 | Language study 1–6 | 1  2  3  4  5 |
| I can ask questions about routines and habits. | 4–5 | Speaking 1–4 | 1  2  3  4  5 |
| **Spoken interaction** | | | |
| I can discuss routines and habits. | 4–5 | Speaking 1–4 | 1  2  3  4  5 |
| I can discuss daily activities. | 4 | Speaking 1 / CD-ROM | 1  2  3  4  5 |
| **Spoken production** | | | |
| I can talk about mine and other people's lifestyle. | 3 | Speaking 1, 4 | 1  2  3  4  5 |
| I can give opinions on a reading text. | 3 | Speaking 2 | 1  2  3  4  5 |
| I can give a short presentation of a project. | 5 | Listening and writing 5 | 1  2  3  4  5 |
| **Reading** | | | |
| I can understand the main information in an article. | 3 | Speaking 1 | 1  2  3  4  5 |
| I can summarise the main message of a text. | 2 | Reading and vocabulary 3 | 1  2  3  4  5 |
| I can guess the meaning of words from the context. | 3 | Reading and vocabulary 5 | 1  2  3  4  5 |
| **Listening** | | | |
| I can understand the main information of a phone conversation between two friends. | 5 | Listening and writing 2 | 1  2  3  4  5 |
| **Writing** | | | |
| I can write a leaflet. | 5 | Listening and writing 3–4 | 1  2  3  4  5 |
| **Strategies** | | | |
| I can find specific information in a reading text. | 2 | Reading and vocabulary 4 | 1  2  3  4  5 |
| **Your own extra activity** | | | |
| | | | 1  2  3  4  5 |

## Module 1 Unit 2 Who needs fame?

Complete the checklist. Add an extra activity you have done in class or at home.

1 = I can do this with a lot of help from my teacher 2 = I can do this a little
3 = I can do this fairly well 4 = I can do this really well 5 = I can do this almost perfectly

| Competences | Page | Exercise | Your score |
|---|---|---|---|
| **Language quality** | | | |
| I can sequence events. | 8 | Language study 1–5 | 1  2  3  4  5 |
| I can use *before / after / while / later / earlier / beforehand / afterwards*. | 8 | Language study 6 / CD-ROM | 1  2  3  4  5 |
| **Spoken interaction** | | | |
| I can discuss the advantages and disadvantages of fame. | 6 | Lead-in | 1  2  3  4  5 |
| I can reach agreement with other students. | 9 | Speaking 1–2 | 1  2  3  4  5 |
| I can discuss celebrity and privacy. | 9 | Speaking 3 | 1  2  3  4  5 |
| **Spoken production** | | | |
| I can present my ideas on privacy rules. | 9 | Speaking 3 | 1  2  3  4  5 |
| **Reading** | | | |
| I can use pictures and words to help me predict the content of an article. | 7 | Reading 2 | 1  2  3  4  5 |
| I can find specific information in an article. | 7 | Reading 4 | 1  2  3  4  5 |
| **Listening** | | | |
| I can understand the main information from an interview with a journalist. | 6 | Listening and vocabulary 2 | 1  2  3  4  5 |
| I can identify correct word stress. | 6 | Pronunciation 2 | 1  2  3  4  5 |
| I can explain the meaning of words from an interview. | 6 | Listening and vocabulary 4 | 1  2  3  4  5 |
| **Strategies** | | | |
| I can take part in a group discussion to reach an agreement. | 9 | Speaking 2 | 1  2  3  4  5 |
| **Your own extra activity** | | | |
| | | | 1  2  3  4  5 |

Move Intermediate Teacher's Book © Macmillan Publishers Limited 2006

# Module 1 Unit 3 A place to live

Complete the checklist. Add an extra activity you have done in class or at home.

1 = I can do this with a lot of help from my teacher 2 = I can do this a little
3 = I can do this fairly well 4 = I can do this really well 5 = I can do this almost perfectly

| Competences | Page | Exercise | Your score |
|---|---|---|---|
| **Language quality** | | | |
| I can use vocabulary for renting accommodation. | 13 | Vocabulary and listening 1 / Speaking 1 | 1  2  3  4  5 |
| I can modify comparisons. | 12 | Language study 1–3 | 1  2  3  4  5 |
| **Spoken interaction** | | | |
| I can describe houses. | 10 | Lead-in 2 | 1  2  3  4  5 |
| I can have a telephone conversation about suitable accommodation. | 13 | Speaking 1 | 1  2  3  4  5 |
| I can discuss preferences in places to live. | 10 | Reading 5 | 1  2  3  4  5 |
| I can compare countries, people, buildings, food, and hobbies. | 12 | Language study 5 | 1  2  3  4  5 |
| **Spoken production** | | | |
| I can describe unusual houses. | 10 | Reading 4 | 1  2  3  4  5 |
| I can describe my ideal home. | 11 | Reading 6.2 | 1  2  3  4  5 |
| **Reading** | | | |
| I can read a short text and summarise it by noting down the main ideas. | 10–11 | Reading 3 | 1  2  3  4  5 |
| **Listening** | | | |
| I can identify key information in a conversation. | 13 | Vocabulary and listening 3 | 1  2  3  4  5 |
| I can listen for details about a flat. | 13 | Vocabulary and listening 4 / CD-ROM | 1  2  3  4  5 |
| **Writing** | | | |
| I can complete a table with notes from a reading text. | 10 | Reading 3 | 1  2  3  4  5 |
| **Strategies** | | | |
| I can share my opinion with others. | 10 | Reading 5 | 1  2  3  4  5 |
| **Your own extra activity** | | | 1  2  3  4  5 |

✂ - - - - - - - - - - - - - - - - - - - - - - - - - - - - - - - - - - - - - - - - - - - - - - - - - - - - - - - - - - - - - - - - - - - -

# Module 1 Unit 4 Life changes

Complete the checklist. Add an extra activity you have done in class or at home.

1 = I can do this with a lot of help from my teacher 2 = I can do this a little
3 = I can do this fairly well 4 = I can do this really well 5 = I can do this almost perfectly

| Competences | Page | Exercise | Your score |
|---|---|---|---|
| **Language quality** | | | |
| I can use verbs for talking about the future. | 16 | Language study 1–4 | 1  2  3  4  5 |
| I can use phrasal verbs for life changes. | 15 | Vocabulary 1–2 | 1  2  3  4  5 |
| I can show how sure or unsure I am about future ideas. | 16 | Language study 2–3 | 1  2  3  4  5 |
| **Spoken interaction** | | | |
| I can discuss the main ideas in a text. | 14 | Reading 3.1 / CD-ROM | 1  2  3  4  5 |
| I can discuss my hopes and plans. | 15 / 16 | Vocabulary 2 / Language study 4 | 1  2  3  4  5 |
| I can discuss and compare people's lives. | 15 | Listening 3 | 1  2  3  4  5 |
| I can discuss jobs. | 16 | Vocabulary and pronunciation 4 | 1  2  3  4  5 |
| **Spoken production** | | | |
| I can predict people's life changes. | 14 | Reading 3.3 | 1  2  3  4  5 |
| I can conduct a series of short interviews for a questionnaire. | 17 | Speaking 5 | 1  2  3  4  5 |
| I can present the results of a questionnaire. | 17 | Speaking 6 | 1  2  3  4  5 |
| **Reading** | | | |
| I can predict content and scan a short text for specific information. | 14 | Reading 1–2 | 1  2  3  4  5 |
| I can complete a personality questionnaire. | 17 | Speaking 1 | 1  2  3  4  5 |
| **Listening** | | | |
| I can follow a conversation with four people about their life changes. | 15 | Listening 1 | 1  2  3  4  5 |
| I can identify the correct word stress of nouns. | 16 | Vocabulary and pronunciation 2 | 1  2  3  4  5 |
| **Writing** | | | |
| I can write a short questionnaire. | 17 | Speaking 4 | 1  2  3  4  5 |
| I can write a letter to myself. | 17 | Writing 1 | 1  2  3  4  5 |
| **Strategies** | | | |
| I can create and conduct a survey. | 17 | Speaking 3–6 | 1  2  3  4  5 |
| **Your own extra activity** | | | 1  2  3  4  5 |

# Module 2 Unit 1 Family ties

Complete the checklist. Add an extra activity you have done in class or at home.

1 = I can do this with a lot of help from my teacher 2 = I can do this with a little help

3 = I can do this fairly well 4 = I can do this really well 5 = I can do this almost perfectly

| Competences | Page | Exercise | Your score |
|---|---|---|---|
| **Language quality**<br>I can talk about the past and the present.<br>I can use time phrases for the past simple and present perfect. | 36<br>36 | Language study 1, 3, 4<br>Language study 2 | 1 2 3 4 5<br>1 2 3 4 5 |
| **Spoken interaction**<br>I can discuss opinion statements about families.<br>I can discuss the personal relevance of reading text information.<br>I can personalise general statements.<br><br>**Spoken production**<br>I can describe family and friendship networks.<br>I can describe character. | 34<br>35<br>36<br><br>37<br>36 | Lead-in 1–2<br>Reading 6<br>Language study 4<br><br>Listening and speaking 4 / CD-ROM<br>Vocabulary 1–3 | 1 2 3 4 5<br>1 2 3 4 5<br>1 2 3 4 5<br><br>1 2 3 4 5<br>1 2 3 4 5 |
| **Reading**<br>I can identify the main meaning in an article.<br>I can summarise the main information in an article. | 34<br>34 | Reading 1<br>Reading 2 | 1 2 3 4 5<br>1 2 3 4 5 |
| **Listening**<br>I can listen for specific information and complete a family and friend network. | 5 | Listening and speaking 2 | 1 2 3 4 5 |
| **Strategies**<br>I can guess the meaning of words from the context. | 35 | Reading 4 | 1 2 3 4 5 |
| **Your own extra activity** | | | 1 2 3 4 5 |

# Module 2 Unit 2 Neighbours

Complete the checklist. Add an extra activity you have done in class or at home.

1 = I can do this with a lot of help from my teacher 2 = I can do this a little

3 = I can do this fairly well 4 = I can do this really well 5 = I can do this almost perfectly

| Competences | Page | Exercise | Your score |
|---|---|---|---|
| **Language quality**<br>I can understand degrees of politeness and formality.<br>I can use polite language with the right degree of formality. | 39<br>39 | Language study 1–4<br>Language study 5–7 | 1 2 3 4 5<br>1 2 3 4 5 |
| **Spoken interaction**<br>I can discuss a complaint.<br>I can give advice on resolving disputes.<br><br>**Spoken production**<br>I can describe my neighbours.<br>I can describe antisocial behaviour.<br>I can use stress to indicate the importance of words. | 41<br>38<br><br>38<br>41<br>41 | Pronunciation and Speaking 3<br>Listening and vocabulary 6<br><br>Lead-in 1<br>Reading 4 / CD-ROM<br>Pronunciation and speaking 1 | 1 2 3 4 5<br>1 2 3 4 5<br><br>1 2 3 4 5<br>1 2 3 4 5<br>1 2 3 4 5 |
| **Reading**<br>I can identify the main information in a text.<br>I can list information from a text. | 40<br>40 | Reading 1<br>Reading 2 | 1 2 3 4 5<br>1 2 3 4 5 |
| **Listening**<br>I can understand the main information in a radio news item. | 38 | Listening and vocabulary 3, 5 | 1 2 3 4 5 |
| **Writing**<br>I can write a note to a friend to explain a problem. | 41 | Writing 1 | 1 2 3 4 5 |
| **Strategies**<br>I can predict the content of a listening passage from a photo. | 38 | Listening and vocabulary 2 | 1 2 3 4 5 |
| **Your own extra activity** | | | 1 2 3 4 5 |

# Module 2 Unit 3 Partners

Complete the checklist. Add an extra activity you have done in class or at home.

1 = I can do this with a lot of help from my teacher 2 = I can do this a little

3 = I can do this fairly well 4 = I can do this really well 5 = I can do this almost perfectly

| Competences | Page | Exercise | Your score |
|---|---|---|---|
| **Language quality**<br>I can use phrasal verbs for relationships.<br>I can give advice. | 43<br>44 | Vocabulary 1–2 / CD-ROM<br>Language study 1–3 | 1 2 3 4 5<br>1 2 3 4 5 |
| **Spoken interaction**<br>I can discuss statements about relationships.<br>I can agree / disagree and give reasons for my opinion. | 42<br>43 | Lead-in 1–2<br>Listening 2 | 1 2 3 4 5<br>1 2 3 4 5 |
| **Spoken production**<br>I can use notes to tell a story about a relationship. | 43 | Vocabulary 3 | 1 2 3 4 5 |
| **Reading**<br>I can identify the main meaning of a text.<br>I can sequence events correctly.<br>I can read an email and understand the purpose of each paragraph. | 42<br>43<br>45 | Reading 1<br>Vocabulary 2<br>Writing 2 | 1 2 3 4 5<br>1 2 3 4 5<br>1 2 3 4 5 |
| **Listening**<br>I can understand specific information in a radio problem phone-in. | 43 | Listening 1 | 1 2 3 4 5 |
| **Writing**<br>I can make notes to tell a story about a relationship.<br>I can write an email giving advice to a friend. | 43<br>45 | Vocabulary 3<br>Writing 3 | 1 2 3 4 5 |
| **Strategies**<br>I can lay out an email to communicate effectively. | 45 | Writing 1–4 | 1 2 3 4 5 |
| **Your own extra activity** | | | 1 2 3 4 5 |

# Module 2 Unit 4 Troubles

Complete the checklist. Add an extra activity you have done in class or at home.

1 = I can do this with a lot of help from my teacher 2 = I can do this with a little help

3 = I can do this fairly well 4 = I can do this really well 5 = I can do this almost perfectly

| Competences | Page | Exercise | Your score |
|---|---|---|---|
| **Language quality**<br>I can recognise verb + preposition patterns.<br>I can understand vocabulary to describe conflict. | 48<br>47 | Language study 1–3<br>Reading and Vocabulary 4 | 1 2 3 4 5<br>1 2 3 4 5 |
| **Spoken interaction**<br>I can discuss my opinions on a reading text.<br>I can discuss the results of a questionnaire. | 46<br>49 | Reading and vocabulary 3<br>Speaking and listening 3 | 1 2 3 4 5<br>1 2 3 4 5 |
| **Spoken production**<br>I can talk about my reactions when I disagree with someone. | 49 | Speaking and listening 7 | 1 2 3 4 5 |
| **Reading**<br>I can read a historical timeline and understand the main meaning.<br>I can identify the main information in a text.<br>I can find specific words in a text.<br>I can read and complete a personality questionnaire. | 46<br>46<br>47<br>49 | Lead-in 2<br>Reading and vocabulary 1–2<br>Reading and vocabulary 4<br>Speaking and listening 1 / CD-ROM | 1 2 3 4 5<br>1 2 3 4 5<br>1 2 3 4 5<br>1 2 3 4 5 |
| **Listening**<br>I can identify the main ideas in a talk about conflict.<br>I can complete a list of detailed information from a talk. | 49<br>49 | Speaking and listening 4<br>Speaking and listening 5 | 1 2 3 4 5<br>1 2 3 4 5 |
| **Writing**<br>I can complete notes on a talk. | 49 | Speaking and listening 4 | 1 2 3 4 5 |
| **Strategies**<br>I can use a glossary to read and understand a text faster. | 47 | Reading text | 1 2 3 4 5 |
| **Your own extra activity** | | | 1 2 3 4 5 |

Move Intermediate Teacher's Book © Macmillan Publishers Limited 2006 **Photocopiable**

# Module 3 Unit 1 Crossing the line

Complete the checklist. Add an extra activity you have done in class or at home.
1 = I can do this with a lot of help from my teacher 2 = I can do this with a little help
3 = I can do this fairly well 4 = I can do this really well 5 = I can do this almost perfectly

| Competences | Page | Exercise | Your score |
|---|---|---|---|
| **Language quality** <br> I can use sports vocabulary. <br> I can describe past events. | <br> 68 <br> 68 | <br> Vocabulary and listening 1 <br> Language study 1–4 | <br> 1  2  3  4  5 <br> 1  2  3  4  5 |
| **Spoken interaction** <br> I can discuss sport. <br> I can discuss my opinions on a reading text. | <br> 66 <br> 66 | <br> Lead-in 1 <br> Reading 4.1 | <br> 1  2  3  4  5 <br> 1  2  3  4  5 |
| **Spoken production** <br> I can describe a violent incident. <br> I can talk about myself and my temper. <br> I can present an argument. | <br> 66 <br> 66 <br> 69 | <br> Language study 4 <br> Reading 4.2–3 <br> Speaking 1–2 | <br> 1  2  3  4  5 <br> 1  2  3  4  5 <br> 1  2  3  4  5 |
| **Reading** <br> I can sequence events from a reading text. | <br> 66 | <br> Reading 2 | <br> 1  2  3  4  5 |
| **Listening** <br> I can understand and identify the main information in a discussion about sport. | <br> 69 | <br> Vocabulary and listening 2–3 | <br> 1  2  3  4  5 |
| **Writing** <br> I can write a formal letter giving my views and reasons. | <br> 69 | <br> Writing 1 / CD-ROM | <br> 1  2  3  4  5 |
| **Strategies** <br> I can use my general knowledge to predict the content of a text. | <br> 66 | <br> Reading 1 | <br> 1  2  3  4  5 |
| **Your own extra activity** | | | 1  2  3  4  5 |

# Module 3 Unit 2 Is it art?

Complete the checklist. Add an extra activity you have done in class or at home.
1 = I can do this with a lot of help from my teacher 2 = I can do this a little
3 = I can do this fairly well 4 = I can do this really well 5 = I can do this almost perfectly

| Competences | Page | Exercise | Your score |
|---|---|---|---|
| **Language quality** <br> I can qualify adjectives. <br> I can use common expressions to give my opinions. | <br> 71 <br> 72 | <br> Language study 1–6 <br> Vocabulary 4 | <br> 1  2  3  4  5 <br> 1  2  3  4  5 |
| **Spoken interaction** <br> I express and discuss opinions about art. <br> I can discuss different types of art. | <br> 72 <br> 70 | <br> Vocabulary 3 <br> Lead-in 1–2 | <br> 1  2  3  4  5 <br> 1  2  3  4  5 |
| **Spoken production** <br> I can give opinions using intonation. <br> I can give a short, persuasive sales presentation. | <br> 73 <br> 73 | <br> Pronunciation 1–2 / CD-ROM <br> Speaking 1–2 | <br> 1  2  3  4  5 <br> 1  2  3  4  5 |
| **Reading** <br> I can understand opinion expressions from short texts. <br> I can match a description to an artwork. | <br> 72 <br> 72 | <br> Vocabulary 4 <br> Vocabulary 3 | <br> 1  2  3  4  5 <br> 1  2  3  4  5 |
| **Listening** <br> I can put information based on an interview in the correct order. <br> I can check information based on an interview with an artist. <br> I can hear the difference between strong and weak opinions. | <br> 70 <br> 71 <br> 73 | <br> Listening 2 <br> Listening 3 <br> Reading and listening 1 | <br> 1  2  3  4  5 <br> 1  2  3  4  5 <br> 1  2  3  4  5 |
| **Strategies** <br> When I don't know the precise word I can use a definition to explain myself. | <br> 70 | <br> Listening 1 | <br> 1  2  3  4  5 |
| **Your own extra activity** | | | 1  2  3  4  5 |

# Module 3 Unit 3 Fashion victims

Complete the checklist. Add an extra activity you have done in class or at home.
1 = I can do this with a lot of help from my teacher 2 = I can do this a little
3 = I can do this fairly well 4 = I can do this really well 5 = I can do this almost perfectly

| Competences | Page | Exercise | Your score |
|---|---|---|---|
| **Language quality** | | | |
| I can link ideas. | 76 | Language study 1–5 | 1 2 3 4 5 |
| I can use adjectives in the correct order. | 74 | Language study 6–7 / CD-ROM | 1 2 3 4 5 |
| **Spoken interaction** | | | |
| I can discuss clothes and fashion. | 74 | Lead-in 1–2 | 1 2 3 4 5 |
| I can discuss my likes and dislikes in clothes. | 75 | Reading and vocabulary 5 | 1 2 3 4 5 |
| I can make a request, agree and refuse. | 77 | Language study 9 | 1 2 3 4 5 |
| I can ask questions about fashion habits and clothes. | 77 | Listening and speaking 4–5 | 1 2 3 4 5 |
| I can compare the results of a questionnaire. | 77 | Listening and speaking 6 | 1 2 3 4 5 |
| **Spoken production** | | | |
| I can describe my partner's clothes. | 77 | Language study 8 | 1 2 3 4 5 |
| **Reading** | | | |
| I can read a magazine article to find the main information. | 74 | Reading and vocabulary 1 | 1 2 3 4 5 |
| I can explain what some adjectives refer to in an article. | 74 | Reading and vocabulary 2 | 1 2 3 4 5 |
| **Listening** | | | |
| I can understand the main information in an interview with a shopaholic. | 77 | Listening and speaking 3 | 1 2 3 4 5 |
| I can get specific information from an interview. | 77 | Listening and speaking 4 | 1 2 3 4 5 |
| **Strategies** | | | |
| I can initiate and build a conversation with a partner. | 77 | Listening and speaking 2, 5 | 1 2 3 4 5 |
| **Your own extra activity** | | | |
| | | | 1 2 3 4 5 |

# Module 3 Unit 4 Globetrotting

Complete the checklist. Add an extra activity you have done in class or at home.
1 = I can do this with a lot of help from my teacher 2 = I can do this with a little help
3 = I can do this fairly well 4 = I can do this really well 5 = I can do this almost perfectly

| Competences | Page | Exercise | Your score |
|---|---|---|---|
| **Language quality** | | | |
| I can recognise verb + infinitive or -ing patterns. | 80 | Language study 1–6 | 1 2 3 4 5 |
| I can use phrasal verbs for travel. | 81 | Vocabulary and listening 1 | 1 2 3 4 5 |
| **Spoken interaction** | | | |
| I can discuss travel experiences. | 81 | Speaking 4 | 1 2 3 4 5 |
| I can discuss the advantages and disadvantages of being a travel guidebook writer. | 79 | Reading 4 | 1 2 3 4 5 |
| **Spoken production** | | | |
| I can describe trips I would like to go on. | 78 | Lead-in 1–2 | 1 2 3 4 5 |
| I can tell a story about a difficult journey. | 81 | Speaking 4 | 1 2 3 4 5 |
| **Reading** | | | |
| I can read an interview for general information. | 78 | Reading 1 / CD-ROM | 1 2 3 4 5 |
| I can read an interview for specific information. | 78 | Reading 2 / CD-ROM | 1 2 3 4 5 |
| **Listening** | | | |
| I can understand the main references from a personal story. | 81 | Vocabulary and listening 3 | 1 2 3 4 5 |
| **Writing** | | | |
| I can write a negative review about a holiday destination. | 81 | Writing 1–2 | 1 2 3 4 5 |
| **Strategies** | | | |
| I can solve multiple choice questions about a text. | 78 | Reading 2 | 1 2 3 4 5 |
| I can plan a piece of writing. | 81 | Writing 1–2 | 1 2 3 4 5 |
| **Your own extra activity** | | | |
| | | | 1 2 3 4 5 |

 **Photocopiable**

# Teaching tips

## Starting lessons

Start the lesson with an interesting opener related to the topic of your lesson, before students open their books. The teacher's notes give ideas for lesson warmers, usually using an opening discussion question. You could also use one of these ideas:

- Show students realia (everyday objects) related to the topic but not too obvious. Ask students to guess the topic of the lesson. For example, for Module 1, Unit 1, daily activities, you could bring in a toothbrush, a shopping bag and a pair of trainers.
- Ask students to describe and speculate about a magazine picture that is related to the subject of the lesson in some way.
- Write the unit title or the subject of the lesson on the board and ask students to brainstorm words connected to it. You can do this with the class for more control, or with teams of students as a competition for more fun.
- Write a word related to the unit topic on the board (for example: *home, mother, health*) and ask students what they associate with that word. This is a good way to discuss how things are seen in different cultures and the differing importance attached to them.
- Write one or two controversial statements relating to the topic on the board (for example, for Module 1, Unit 4: *Earning lots of money is the most important thing in life*). Ask students to discuss the statement(s).
- Write a jumbled list of topic-related verb–noun collocations (for example, for Module 1, Unit 1: *play – chess, do – sport*), or adjective–noun collocations (*daily – activity, healthy – lifestyle*) on the board and ask students to match them.

## Whole class work

Whole class work needs to address the needs of each student as far as possible. Here are some tips for large or mixed ability classes.

- Make sure that you know the names of everybody in the class! Ask students to make a desk name card.
- The best classroom layout of desks is usually a horseshoe shape so that all students can see and be seen.
- Ensure that every student has the chance to speak. Most students are quite happy to contribute when asked directly but some students will not offer information voluntarily.
- Make sure that everyone has understood the instructions. For more complex tasks, demonstrate the steps with a stronger student. Allow students thinking time before answering or performing a task.
- Ask weaker students easier questions so that they feel encouraged to participate in discussions.
- Do not allow stronger or more outgoing students to dominate. Encourage students to listen and show respect for each other.

- Ensure whatever you write on the board is clear and clearly visible to everybody in the class.
- Try to provide a variety of tasks that will appeal to all learning styles: visual tasks (for example, picture description and speculation, TV and video extracts, newspaper cartoons); physical response tasks (mime, drawing, acting out); audio tasks (songs, sound recognition, dictations, pronunciation tasks, rhymes); mechanical tasks (comprehension questions, gap-fills, rewriting sentences); problem-solving tasks (ranking activities, group discussion tasks requiring agreement, logic puzzles); tasks requiring creativity and imagination (role-plays, writing brochures, making posters, interpreting poems).
- If you have a wide range of ability, make sure that you have prepared extension tasks for students who work more quickly (extra questions, extra tasks, checking tasks etc) and provide extra support for weaker students while they are doing tasks (checking, offering help etc).

## Pairwork and groupwork

Pairwork and groupwork allow students to speak more and exchange ideas and information with other students. Use these tips to ensure that students work effectively in pairs and groups.

- It is usually easier to let students work with their neighbour or neighbours. However, you can swap pairs and groups round for variety now and then by getting them to work with someone else in the class.
- To randomly pair two students: make cards with pairs of words and distribute them at random. Students have to find their partner by asking questions or showing their card. You can use for example, two words that make a compound word (*foot, ball*); pairs of names (*Jekyll, Hyde / David, Beckham*), synonyms (*rich, wealthy*) or opposites (*rich, poor*).
  For group work: give every student a letter from a set of, say, four letters (*A, B, C, D*) and then ask all *A*s to work together, all *B*s etc.
- Always make sure students know what they have to do. Present the task clearly, using an example. You can demonstrate the tasks using open pairs: ask two students to perform the task or part of the task to the class. Check students have understood the task and allow time for questions.
- Set a time limit for the task. Make sure students know they have to stop when the time limit has been reached, even if they have not quite finished. About a minute before time runs out, warn students to try and complete their task.
- Monitor discussions. Sort out any problems, praise students and make a note of recurring errors for later discussion and correction.

Always ensure whole class feedback so that students feel their activity had a point or an end result. Ask students to report back to the class, discuss their results or ask individual pairs or groups to perform their role-play etc to the class.

# Correcting and praising

Students need to feel that they are making progress and achieving something. Encourage students as much as possible by praising them both for effort and for achievement:

- Smile and make positive comments.
- Always begin by focusing on what students have done well before correcting mistakes.

The level of language correction necessary will depend on the type of activity you are using. Explicit and frequent correction will be necessary in accuracy tasks such as controlled grammar, pronunciation and vocabulary activities. In fluency activities and warmers, it is unnecessary to correct every mistake if students are able to convey their message. In these cases, you can correct indirectly as follows:

- Correct students by adding a comment which repeats the correct formulation or pronunciation, rather than drawing attention to the mistake directly.
- Make a note of frequent mistakes and correct them on the board with the whole class after the activity has finished.
- Ignore minor mistakes completely!

# Dealing with cultural differences

The huge advantage of having multilingual or multicultural classes is that students bring a wealth of different experiences and opinions to the language class. Exploit this by:

- asking students to compare the material in their Coursebook with their own country and customs as much as possible. Ask, for example: *Do you have this tradition / type of house etc in your country? How is the further education system different in your country?* Discussing idioms and popular sayings is often a good way to discuss the importance of things in different cultures.
- asking students to reflect on their own experiences and compare them with those of students from different countries. Ask in Module 1, Unit 1, for example: *Do you have a mobile phone like Rachel? When did you get it? Do most young people in your country have mobile phones?*

However, be aware that not all students will possess the same degree of awareness about popular culture, such as famous people, famous buildings and places, music, sports, technology etc. You can get students to share knowledge by:

- mixing students from different countries and backgrounds when doing pairwork and groupwork.
- asking the class to define potentially problematic terms or explain proper names that come up in the Coursebook material. Scan texts for these in advance.
- doing specific cultural recognition activities (for example, in Module 1, Unit 2, by asking students to guess the names of famous people or in Module 3, Unit 4, by doing a quiz on famous monuments).

# Using reading materials

- Before reading a text, students can use the photos, the title and the general look of the text to predict the content of the text and the text type. If students already have some ideas about the text before they read it, they will be able to deal with it more confidently. Predicting also motivates students to read the text to find out if their ideas are correct. Ask questions such as: *Look at the title: what does it tell you about the subject of the text? Look at the photos: who is the text about? Where does this text come from – a teenage magazine, a newspaper, a travel brochure?*
- Pre-teaching vocabulary can give students extra support when reading a text. You can pre-teach particular items from the text by deciding in advance which items might cause difficulty and writing them on the board. Or you can choose a vocabulary set which covers several items in the text (for example, in Module 1, Unit 2 there is a text on flying which includes the words *engine* and *runway*, you could pre-teach / elicit a 'plane' set which includes things like *cockpit, engine, wing, tail, runway, airport*). You can also do word building exercises (focusing on verbs, nouns, adjectives) which include words from the text (for example, in Module 1, Unit 2: *arrive – arrival, achieve – achievement*, where *arrival* and *achievement* are the words in the text.)
- All *Move* reading texts are recorded on the CD which means that students can listen to the text while they read it. This helps learners who prefer learning orally rather than visually and is a good pronunciation aid for all students. It also means that learners have to read at a certain speed; it is therefore sometimes a good idea to let students listen and read the first time they read a text and have to perform a gist-reading task. Simply listening to a reading text can also be a useful alternative, particularly for 'spoken' texts such as interviews.
- Jigsaw reading tasks are a good way of exploiting reading texts in pairs and groups. Divide a text into sections; ask students to read one section, find out information and then share this information orally with their partner or group members.

- Reading texts often contain a lot of unknown vocabulary. Emphasise again and again that students don't have to understand every word! Students need to understand enough to complete the main task. Advise students to always try and work out the meaning of the word from the context if they can – by looking at the type of word (adjective, noun, verb etc) and 'clues' about the meaning of the word in the lines before and after.
- If students need to look up the meanings of unknown words, encourage them to use a good monolingual learner dictionary. This type of dictionary gives a simple definition in English as well as an example, making the meaning clearer than a translation – which may well have several meanings. You can build dictionary work into your class (finding definitions, discussing different forms of a word, explaining dictionary abbreviations etc) so that students can get the maximum help out of their dictionaries and become more independent learners.

## Speaking

- Encourage students to speak as much as possible and stress that they should not worry about making mistakes.
- Make sure students speak with correct pronunciation and intonation. Ask students to repeat new words in class, in chorus and individually; ask students to repeat sentences from listening and reading texts or their own sentences, with correct rhythm and sentence stress.
- Speaking about concrete, personal topics is easier than discussing abstract situations. Personalise tasks as much as possible, so that all students have the chance to say something.
- Train students to use strategies to help them make the best use of the language they have. For example, you can train students to describe things when they don't know an English word using phrases such as '*It looks like a …, It's made of …, It's used for …*' (practice task: *You are in a chemist's and want to buy plasters and mouthwash, but you don't know the English words. Explain to the chemist what you need*). Teach the use of fillers such as '*Well, Actually, Anyway, What I mean to say is …*' which allow students to keep a conversation going while looking for the language to express something.
- Use pairwork for checking and comparing answers to tasks, so that students have more opportunities to speak.

## Using listening materials

- Before listening, as before reading, exploit the pictures in the book and any other clues to the content of the listening text.
- Tell students not to panic if they can't understand some of what they hear. Make sure students understand that they are listening to perform a task and if they can complete the task, they have been successful.

- Encourage students to use clues in people's voices which show their feelings, age, attitudes etc, to reinforce understanding of the content.
- Allow students to listen to the material more than once, if they wish.
- You can direct students to use the Listening scripts in the Coursebook to support their understanding and check answers.
- Encourage students to watch English TV, listen to the radio and interact in English as much as possible outside their classes in order to 'tune their ear' to the English language.

## Writing

- Brainstorm ideas on the board before students write to make sure all students have something to write about.
- Tell students to use any similar texts in the Coursebook as models.
- Tell students to think carefully about what they write and revise their work when they have finished: *Is it interesting? Are there any repetitions or unclear parts? Is it grammatically correct?*
- Make sure somebody reads or listens to written work: check writing tasks individually yourself; ask students to read a partner's work and check it; ask students to read out an answer or task to the whole class and the class to comment.
- The Optional activities in the Teacher's notes contain several extra writing tasks which can be used both for language consolidation and for practising writing skills.

## Reviewing and revising

Build in regular revision of structures and vocabulary. The Teacher's notes contain suggestions for unit-related revision activities at the end of each unit. Students can use the Grammar reference to revise or check structures at any time. They can revise vocabulary by studying the Wordlist and playing these word games:

- **Explain it:** Students work in teams of four. They write out all the nouns / adjectives / verbs in the Wordlist on small pieces of paper. They then work with another team. Teams take turns explaining words. Each member of a team must pick up a word and explain it to their team while the other team times them (1 minute). If the team gets the word in time, they get a point.
- **Categories:** Write umbrella nouns from the Wordlist on the board (for example: *furniture, emotions*). Students work individually or in teams and make a list of as many words as possible which fit this category.
- **Countdown:** Write a (long) word from the Wordlist in jumbled form on the board. Teams of students try and make a word using all the letters. Follow up with students making a new word with the same letters (the team with the longest word wins).

- **Collocations:** Write a noun from the Wordlist on the board. Teams of students make lists of verbs that go with the noun (set a time limit for this). Check the collocations on the board, the team with the most correct ones wins (for example: *chess: play, watch, understand, practise, compete at, win at, lose at, like, dislike, hate, enjoy …*). You can also practise other collocations, such as noun–noun (*chess board, chess champion, chess match, chess set …*).
- **Pictionary:** Students choose a word from the Wordlist and draw a picture on the board. The class or their team guesses.
- **Comparisons:** Write two nouns from the Wordlist on the board. Students work individually or in teams. They have to compare the two things (for example, in Module 1, Unit 2: *cottage, warehouse – A cottage is cosier than a warehouse*. Or in Module 1, Unit 4: *ambition, statistician – Ambition is easier to spell than statistician*).
- **Crosswords:** Students work in pairs. They make a completed crossword grid using ten words from the Wordlist. Then they make an empty, numbered grid and write clues for the words. Pairs exchange their crosswords with another pair and complete them.
- **Headlines:** Students make headlines using only the words in the Wordlist and prepositions (for example, in Module 1, Unit 1: *Couch potatoes gossip in health farm*). They then write a short story for the headline.

# Ending or filling in lessons

Sometimes you will need a short activity or game to change the pace of the lesson, end a lesson on a positive note or just provide a bit of fun. Here are a few ideas that can be used with different topic and language areas:
- **Charades:** Students mime a film, book, item of vocabulary or phrase for the class or their team to guess.
- **Bingo:** Write 20 large numbers (over 100) on the board. Students choose five and write them down. Call out the numbers on the board at random. The first student to tick off their numbers is the winner. You can also play this with categories of words or a list of unit-related words.
- **Find someone who …:** Write a list of questions on the board (*find someone who was born in the same month as you, find someone who likes cats, find someone who knows what (a word from the Wordlist) means*, etc). Students move around the class asking questions, and find at least one name for each question.
- **Picture dictation and drawing:** Describe a scene or a person. Students draw a picture. Students then compare pictures with a partner and discuss any differences. Students can also dictate pictures to each other.
- **Coursebook picture dictation:** Students choose a picture in one of the units already covered in their Coursebook and describe it to the class or to a partner without showing them the picture. The class or their partner listens and then has to find the correct picture in their book.

- **Five things:** Ask students to think of five things …
  - they do well / badly
  - they hate to eat / love to do
  - that are small / disgusting / beautiful / blue / …
  - that make people embarrassed / angry / happy / … etc
  Students discuss their ideas with a partner.
- **Memory game:** Bring ten objects from home or collect ten things from students in class. Hold the objects up to the class to memorise first and then put them in a dark bag or put them on the teacher's desk and cover them with a blanket. Students have to say what is in the bag or under the blanket, giving a description of each object.
- **Chinese whispers:** Whisper a fairly complex sentence to a student at the front of the class. Students take it in turns to whisper the sentence to another student. The last student writes it on the board. Whisper different sentences at intervals, so about five sentences are circulating in a clear progression. Compare the sentences on the board to the original sentences.
- **Stand in line:** Write the words of a long sentence on individual cards. Give out the cards at random to students. Students with cards go to the front of the class in turn. They show the class their word and take their place in the sentence, moving around until students form the correct sentence.
- **General knowledge quiz:** Students work in teams. They write ten general knowledge questions on the topic of the unit. Teams take turns to ask their questions.

# Emergency lessons

The *Move Intermediate* Teacher's Book contains 24 photocopiable resource sheets (see pages 88–117). 12 of these are one page games and communicative activities and 12 are 45 minute discussion lessons requiring little or no preparation. Both types are linked to the topic of the units in the Coursebook and can be used as emergency lessons or activities.

Below is an idea for an emergency lesson, built around a single, simple activity. It requires no preparation and can be used at any point in the book, with any topic.

### Storytime
- Explain that students are going to write a story using ten words from their Coursebook.
- Students work in small groups. Each group chooses ten words from the previous two units: 3 nouns, 3 verbs, 3 adjectives and 1 adverb. They can do this using the wordlists for the correct module. Check the groups' lists to ensure that they have complied with the instructions.
- The groups discuss and write their story.
- Each group checks its story carefully. Encourage students to revise their work.
- The groups present their story to the class. Each group can nominate one person to read out the story or they can take it in turns to read a section. They can draw pictures, use realia or make sound effects to add interest.

| Topic | Language study | Vocabulary | Main skills |
|---|---|---|---|
| • A life in the day of ... (Lifestyle of a chess champion)<br>• A new start (Surviving life at a health farm) | • Routines and habits (present simple)<br>• Adverbs of frequency | • Daily activities and lifestyles | • **Reading:** understanding key information<br>• **Speaking:** responding to a lifestyle text; a lie-detector game<br>• **Listening:** identifying key information<br>• **Writing:** a leaflet |

## Learning aims

- Can discuss routines and habits
- Can use adverbs of frequency
- Can discuss daily activities

### Ideas for preparation

- A chess board (see Ex 1 p23)
- Pictures of interesting people cut out from magazines (see Optional activity p24)
- Cards with adverbs of frequency (see Optional activity p25)
- Leaflet(s) from a health farm (see Ex 1 p25)

### Warmer

- Ask students: *What do you do in your free time?*
- If students need prompting, tell them about your free time activities and ask: *What about you? Do you [go swimming]?*

## Lead-in

**1**

- Ask students to open their books on page 2. Students look at the photo. Ask: *What does Rachel do in her free time?* (goes shopping, phones her friends).
- Students look at the chart. Ask: *What activity does Rachel spend the most time on?* (sleeping).
- Students work in pairs. Explain the task and check that students understand the questions.
- Check the answers with the class. Ask students to give reasons for their answers where appropriate.

### Answers

1 Rachel is a student. She spends 25 hours a week studying.
2 In her free time she likes watching TV and videos most.
3 Rachel isn't a sporty person – she only does 3 hours of sport and exercise each week, but she watches 18 hours of TV. She is more of a couch potato.
4 She likes reading, listening to music and shopping. Other hobbies could be using the internet / playing computer games or gardening.
5 (individual answers)

**2**

- Brainstorm a list of hobbies and daily activities on the board with the class.
- Students work individually and make their own chart, using the list on the board to help them.

**3**

- Students work in pairs. Explain the task.
- Ask some students to tell the class about their partner.

## Reading and vocabulary

### Background information

Vladimir Kramnik was born on 25.06.1975 in Russia. He started to play chess when he was five years old and became the world junior champion when he was 16. In 2000, Vladimir Kramnik became the fourteenth world Chess Champion by defeating Gary Kasparov, who had been the champion for fifteen years. The match lasted from October 8 to November 2.

**1**

- Show students a chess board (or draw their attention to the board in the photo on page 3). Ask: *What do you know about chess? Does anybody play chess? What do you like about it?*
- Students look at the photo in the reading text on page 3. Ask: *Do you know the man in the photo? Who do you think he is?* (Vladimir Kramnik, world chess champion).
- Students work in pairs. Explain the task.
- Make a list of student predictions on the board.

**2**

- 🎧 **01** Students read the magazine article on page 3 and check their predictions. Students can also listen to the article on CD while they read.
- Students look at the class predictions on the board from Ex 1. Ask: *Which predictions were correct?*

**3**

- Students look at the paragraph headings. Check they understand them.
- Students match the headings to the correct paragraphs in the text.
- Check the answers with the class.

### Answers

a 3   b 4   c 5   d 2   e 1

**4**

- Students look at the statements. Check they understand them.
- Students work individually or in pairs and decide if the statements are true or false.
- Check the answers with the class. Ask students to correct the false statements.

**Answers**
1  False (He gets up late and doesn't have a proper breakfast)
2  True
3  False (He's got less time because everybody wants to speak to him)
4  False (He thinks the best way to improve is by analysing games and strategies)
5  True

## 5
- Explain the task.
- Check the answers with the class.
- Check any other problematic vocabulary with the class.

**Answers**

| | | |
|---|---|---|
| 1  no point | 3  in a row | 5  tournament |
| 2  delicate | 4  opponent | 6  to unwind |

# Speaking

## 1
- Tell students they are going to talk about the importance of things in Vladimir Kramnik's life. Ask two or three students: *What do you think is important in Vladimir's life?*
- Students work in pairs. They find the words and numbers in the text and underline them.
- Students discuss the importance of the words and numbers.
- Discuss the answers with the class.

**Answers**
The Internet: he uses it to study games and analyse them.
Caviar: it's his biggest luxury and he eats it every other day.
4 am: this is the time he goes to bed.
Noon: this is the time when he gets up.
10: this stands for the ten minutes in the morning when he lies in bed and thinks of nothing.
Mobile phones: he has four of these and they are very important because people are always calling him.

## 2
- Read out the question to the class. Ask individual students to give their opinion.
- Tell the class your opinion.

## 3
- Students work individually. Explain the task. Make a list of your own words and numbers on the board. Ask the class to guess their meaning.
- Students write down their own six words and numbers.

## 4
- Students work in pairs. Explain the task.
- Students exchange lists and guess the meaning of their partner's words and numbers.
- Ask one or two students to present their partner's list and say if they guessed correctly.

# Language study

## Routines and habits

> **Optional activity**
>
> **Routines**
> - Hold up a magazine picture of an interesting (but not famous) person.
> - Say: *Let's talk about this person's daily routine. What do you think his job is? When do you think he gets up? What does he have for breakfast? What does he do in the morning? Do you think he reads newspapers?* Elicit content about possible routines without overtly correcting grammar.
> - Do the same for another picture.

## 1
- Students look at the sentences from the text. Ask: *Which two sentences describe routines and habits?*

**Answers**
a, d

- Students underline the verbs in sentences a and d. Ask: *Which tense is used to describe routines and habits?*

**Answer**
present simple

- Revise the formation of the present simple: write the rules on the board after prompting students, or refer students to the table and the rules in the Grammar reference section on page 26.
- Refer students back to the example sentences. Ask: *What other habits does Vladimir Kramnik have?* (he eats caviar every other day, he talks on the phone a lot etc). Students write these sentences on the board, paying attention to the present simple tense.
- Ask some students: *Tell me a habit you have.*

## 2
- Remind students that adverbs of frequency describe how often we do something.
- Students underline the adverb of frequency in the example sentence.

**Answer**
sometimes

## 3
- Read the explanation and task with the class.
- Students do the task individually or in pairs.
- Check the answers with the class.

**Answers**
I **often** study games and analyse them. (paragraph 4)
I **usually** go to bed at 4 am. (paragraph 5)

## 4
- Read the explanation with the class. Look at the sentences together and ask students to underline the adverbs of frequency in the sentences first. Point out that 'occasionally' is usually pronounced /əˈkeɪʒn(ə)li/.

- Students complete the rules individually or in pairs.
- Check the answers with the class.

### Answers
1  often, usually, occasionally (in any order)
2  always
Note: This rule does not apply for imperatives.

## 5
- Students work in pairs. Explain the task. Tell them to use the adverbs in the text and in the examples in the Language study.
- Check the answers with the class. Draw a horizontal scale on the board from high frequency (100%) to low frequency (0%). Complete it with help from the class.

### Possible answers

high frequency                                                    low frequency
100% ◄──────────────────────────────────► 0%
always, usually, normally, frequently, often, sometimes, occasionally, seldom, rarely, never

---

### Optional activity

**Frequency line up**
- Prepare large cards with the ten adverbs of frequency in Ex 5. Alternatively, assign the individual adverbs to students and ask them to write their adverb on a sheet of paper.
- Students stick their adverbs on to their clothes or simply hold up their adverbs.
- Students line up from low to high frequency, grouping together where adverbs have similar meanings.
- The rest of the class checks that the line-up is correct.

---

## 6
- Explain the task. Look at the example with the class. Ask some students to complete the example sentence about themselves.
- Students work individually and complete the sentences so they are true for them.
- Ask individual students to read out a sentence each.

## Speaking

### 1
- Tell students: *I often go to the cinema. I go to the cinema at least once a month.* Refer students to the table in Ex 1. Ask: *How often do you go to the cinema?* Elicit replies from some students.
- Students work in pairs and say six sentences about themselves using the table.
- Ask individual students to say a sentence each.
- Practise the structure further by asking students questions: *How often do you send text messages? How often do you watch DVDs at home? How often do you buy clothes?*

### The lie-detector game

### 2
- Say: *You are going to play the lie-detector game. Do you know what a lie detector is? Do you think lie detectors work?*

- Students work individually. They write three sentences about their routines and habits. At least one sentence must be false. Go around the class giving help.

## 3
- Explain the task and look at the example with the class.
- Tell students, or write on the board, three unusual statements about your own routines and habits. Say: *Ask me questions.* Then ask: *Which statement was false?*
- Students work in small groups of three or four. They take it in turns to ask questions about each other's statements from Ex 2. They should note down which statements they think are true or false.

## 4
- In their groups, students guess for each person which statements are true and which are false.
- Ask: *Did you guess correctly? Did you find out anything interesting about the people in your group?*

# A new start

## Listening and writing

### 1
- Students look at the pictures in the health farm leaflet. If possible, show students other health farm leaflets.
- Say: *The title of the text is 'A new start'. In what way is a health farm a new start?* (it's a chance to change your lifestyle, become fitter and healthier and perhaps also change your appearance).
- Ask: *Would you like to go to a health farm?*

### 2
- 🔘 **02** Read out the questions and check that students understand them.
- Play the CD. Students listen and answer the questions.
- Students compare their answers with a partner.
- Play the CD again. Students check their answers.
- Check the answers with the class.
- Refer students to Listening script 02 on page 30 if necessary.
- Say: *Jenny thinks the health farm is awful. Do you think it sounds awful?*

### Answers
1  She thinks it's absolutely awful.
2  At six o'clock in the morning.
3  She goes for a run around the lake.
4  She goes to at least two exercise classes.
5  A bowl of soup and a glass of carrot juice.
6  She says she feels wonderful.

### Listening script 02
(S = Sarah; J = Jenny)
S: Hello?
J: Hello, Sarah, is that you? It's me – Jenny.
S: Oh hi Jenny! Why are you whispering? Where are you?
J: I'm phoning from the health farm and I don't want anyone to overhear.

S: Oh dear – how are you getting on?

J: Well, I've been here for seven days and it feels like 17. At first I thought it was going to be great but in fact it's absolutely awful.

S: Oh no, why?

J: Well, you won't believe this but we're forced to get up at six o'clock in the morning and go for a run around the lake before breakfast.

S: Oh, poor you! That sounds awful.

J: And if that wasn't bad enough, all we get for breakfast is grapefruit and water.

S: You're joking! You can't survive on that.

J: I don't think I am surviving. And then we're expected to go to at least two exercise classes before a really miserable lunch.

S: Really? What do you have for lunch then?

J: A bowl of soup and a glass of carrot juice.

S: Any bread?

J: Not a chance.

S: Well, do you get a decent meal in the evening?

J: I suppose dinner's slightly better. We usually get a baked potato and a green salad.

S: Oh well, never mind. Not much longer to go.

J: Yes, I'm leaving in a couple of days. Can't wait.

S: Anyway, how are you feeling?

J: Oh absolutely wonderful. I've lost three kilos.

S: Oh, it's all been worthwhile then …

## 3

- Students work in pairs. Explain the task.
- Students plan their leaflet. Go around the class giving help.

---

**Optional activity**

**Describing things**

- Tell students that when they write a leaflet, it is important to use lots of adjectives to make things sound attractive.
- Students work in groups. They brainstorm adjectives they can use to describe:
  - the health farm's location (quiet, peaceful, beautiful, picturesque)
  - food (delicious, tasty, healthy, nutritious, low-fat)
  - activities (healthy, enjoyable, relaxing, invigorating, beneficial)
  - feeling good (great, fantastic, healthy, energetic / full of energy, relaxed, fresh)
- Collect adjectives on the board. Remind students to use adjectives like these in their leaflet.

---

## 4

- Students write their leaflet using the information they discussed in Ex 3.
- Check the leaflets. Write on the board and discuss any recurring errors.

## 5

- In pairs, students present their course to the class.
- After the presentations, take a vote on the best course by asking for a show of hands.
- Ask: *Why did you think this course was the best?*

---

**Revision activity**

**A typical day**

- Ask the class to invent a character: name, age, appearance, personality. Make brief notes on the board or ask a talented student to draw a picture.
- Tell students they are going to describe a typical day for this character. Remind them to use the present simple and adverbs of frequency.
- Start the description (eg *Violet Green always wakes up at 5 o'clock*). Ask another student to say the next sentence. Go around the class, with each student saying a sentence in turn until the day finishes.
- Note any mistakes and correct them with the class.

# Extra practice

Students complete the Extra practice material on page 22 either in class, or for homework.

---

**Extra practice answers**

**1**  1  We never go out on Monday evenings. / On Monday evenings we never go out.

2  I usually go on holiday in July. / I go on holiday in July, usually. / Usually I go on holiday in July.

3  I always read a newspaper in bed on Sundays. / On Sundays I always read a newspaper in bed.

4  He often listens to music during his lessons. / He listens to music during his lessons often. / Often he listens to music during his lessons.

5  They sometimes go camping in spring. / In spring they sometimes go camping. / They go camping in spring sometimes. / Sometimes they go camping in spring.

**2**  In sentences 2, 4 and 5.

**3**  1  What time do you leave home?

2  How do you get to work?

3  About twice a week.

4  What does your boss think about it?

5  She wants me to arrive at 9.00 every day.

6  What do you do?

Jo is a teacher and she's sometimes late for work.

**4**  pilot

**5**  1  every day, twice a year, once a month, less than three or four times a year

2  usually, sometimes, almost always, occasionally

**6**  (individual answers)

---

# References

Grammar reference: Coursebook page 26
Wordlist: Coursebook page 28
Photocopiable resources: Teacher's Book pages 88–89
Test: Teacher's Book pages 121–122

# CD-ROM

Unit 1 My life
Language exercise: A typical day
Vocabulary activity: It's all in the mind
CEF-linked exercise: I can discuss daily activities
Game: The neighbourhood

| Topic | Language study | Vocabulary | Main skills |
|---|---|---|---|
| • From fame to despair (Charles Lindbergh's story)<br>• Advantages and disadvantages of being famous | • Sequencing events (*before, after, beforehand, afterwards, earlier, while, later*) | • Celebrity and privacy | • **Listening:** identifying key information<br>• **Pronunciation:** word stress<br>• **Reading:** identifying particular information<br>• **Speaking:** discussing celebrity and privacy |

## Learning aims

- Can sequence events
- Can discuss celebrity and privacy
- Can identify word stress

### Ideas for preparation

- Realia to help students focus on jobs (eg tennis ball, football, DVD, musical score, music CD, paintbrush) (see Lead-in p27)
- Stickers with the names of famous people (see Optional activity p27)
- Words divided up into 3 syllables and stuck on card (see Optional activity p29)
- Magazine pictures of celebrities caught unawares (see Ex 1 p31)

### Warmer

- Ask: *Who's your favourite celebrity? Why is he / she famous? Why do you like him / her?*

## Lead-in

**1**

- Ask students to open their books on page 6. If possible, show students a collection of realia relating to jobs. Ask: *What jobs do you think of when you see these things?* For example, a tennis ball (tennis player), a DVD (actor / director).
- Look at the names in the box with the class. Ask: *What did Beethoven do? Why was he famous?* (he was a composer / a musician).
- Write Beethoven's name and occupation on the board. Point out that we always use the indefinite article with occupations.
- Students work in pairs and make a list of occupations for the names. Encourage them to use dictionaries. Point out several occupations may be possible.
- Check the answers with the class. Write the names on the board and fill in the occupations.
- Ask additional questions about the people in the list (eg *Where did Beethoven come from? Who is Venus William's sister? What is Leonardo da Vinci most famous for?*).

### Answers

Beethoven: composer / musician
Venus Williams: tennis player
Leonardo da Vinci:
painter / sculptor / architect / engineer / inventor
Jackie Chan: actor / Kung-Fu expert
Quentin Tarantino: film director
Jennifer Lopez: singer / actress
Donatella Versace: fashion designer
Rudolf Nureyev: ballet dancer
Michael Schumacher: racing driver
Ronaldinho Gaucho: footballer

### Optional activity

**The name game (celebrity edition)**

- Three or four students come to the front of the class. Put stickers with the names of famous people on their foreheads.
- The students ask *yes / no* questions in turn to find out the identity of the person on their forehead (occupation, nationality, appearance, relationships etc). The class answers.
- The student who guesses their identity first is the winner!
- Repeat with different students and names.

## Listening and vocabulary

**1**

- Students work in pairs. Explain the task. Elicit an example of an advantage and disadvantage if necessary.
- Check the answers with the class. Make a list of advantages and disadvantages on the board. Discuss them with the class.

### Possible answers

Advantages: success, money, attention, exciting lifestyle
Disadvantages: no privacy, too much media attention, pressure to look good / behave well, too much travel, crazy fans, nothing else to achieve

**2**

- 🔘 **03** Explain the task.
- Students listen and make a list of the advantages and disadvantages mentioned. Do not check the answers at this stage.

## 3

- Students compare their lists from Ex 2 with a partner.
- Students listen again if necessary to check their answers.
- Check the answers with the class. Check students can pronounce *privacy* /'praɪvəsi/.
- Ask: *Did the journalist mention the same things you discussed with your partner?*
- Ask: *Would you like to be famous? Why | Why not?*

### Answers

Advantages
Sense of achievement
No financial worries
Free clothes, easy to get tables in restaurants, football tickets etc
Meet interesting people
Disadvantages
No privacy
Security (threat of being followed)
Constant pressure to live up to the expectations of the public
Difficult to have normal relationships

### Listening script 03

(I = Interviewer; S = Sue)

I: Sue, you've been writing articles about famous people for the last 20 years. What do you think the advantages of being famous are?

S: Well, I think the first is a sense of achievement, which is so important to them. They've done it. They've got to the **top of their tree** and so they feel good about themselves. Then, of course famous people usually, but not always, make a lot of money, so they have no financial worries, especially sports people, film stars, fashion designers, singers and others in the entertainment industry. Often famous people don't even have to spend money on clothes as fashion designers give their latest designs to them. When stars are seen wearing a designer's clothes, it's great free advertising. And of course you can always get a table at a restaurant or a ticket for a football match if you are famous.

I: Anything else?

S: The famous are always attracted to each other so I suppose you get to meet some interesting people.

I: What about the downsides?

S: I think there are several of these. Firstly, you have no privacy. Journalists and photographers follow you everywhere, taking pictures and writing stories about you. Then of course, there's the threat of being followed by crazy people or having your child kidnapped, so security is a big issue. John Lennon is perhaps the most famous example of a star whose security wasn't good enough. Then there's the constant pressure on you to **live up to the expectations of the public** – if you are a film star you're expected to appear glamorous and exciting all the time. Finally they often find it hard to make friends and have a normal relationship with someone. Famous people seem to be getting together and **breaking up** all the time.

I: So, would you like to be famous yourself?

S: Oh, let me see ... erm ... I think just for a month to see what it feels like – I'd probably hate it after that!

I: Why do you think some people are so desperate to become famous?

S: That's a very interesting question. I often get this feeling that most of the people I've interviewed for magazines are really trying to compensate for some problems they think they have with their character. They **suffer from low self-esteem**; maybe they feel they weren't really loved by their parents, or they were **bullied at school**. So then there's this big desire to prove themselves and they have this **terrific drive to succeed**.

## 4

- Students work in pairs. They explain the meanings of the phrases.
- Students check their answers in Listening script 03 on page 30.
- Check the answers with the class.

### Answers

1  the most successful position in their profession
2  be how fans expect you to be
3  finishing a relationship
4  think you are not important or a nice person
5  attacked by other pupils
6  strong feeling of wanting to be the best

## 5

- Read out the questions and discuss them with the class. Ask further questions to elicit as much information as possible. Ask, for example: *Why did they break up? What happened? Has he | she got a new girlfriend | boyfriend.* Alternatively, ask students to answer the questions in writing and then discuss with a partner.

### Optional activity

**Role-play**

- Students work in pairs. They role-play a discussion about famous people as follows:

Student A: Thinks fame is a great thing. Would love to be famous, rich and have an easy life.
Student B: Thinks fame is a terrible thing – no privacy, broken relationships etc.

# Pronunciation

## Word stress

### 1

- Write the word *pronunciation* on the board. Underline and say the first syllable.
- Ask: *How many syllables has this word got?* (five). Underline them.
- Write two headings on the board (*Two syllables; Three syllables*). Read out the words in the box in turn. Students tell you which list the words belong to.

### Answers

Two syllables: famous, pressure, public, worry,
Three syllables: advantage, article, exciting, journalist, magazine, privacy, terrific

### 2

- 04 Play the first word and look at the example with the class.

- Students listen to the rest of the words and underline the stressed syllables.
- Check the answers with the class. Play the CD again, or repeat the words if necessary.
- Students repeat the words in chorus. Alternatively, ask individual students to say a word each.

### Answers
article   exciting   famous   journalist   magazine   pressure
privacy   public   terrific   worry

## 3
- Students work in pairs. They complete the examples for the rules using the words in Ex 1.
- Check the answers with the class.

### Answers
1 journalist      2 terrific      3 famous / pressure

---

### Optional activity

**Jumbled syllables**
- Students work in pairs or small groups. They think of five 3-syllable words. (They can use the Wordlist on page 28 or a dictionary to do this.)
- Students divide the words into syllables.
- Students write the syllables for each word on a piece of paper and cut them out. They should put the syllables together with a paperclip and give them to another pair or group.
- Students put the words back together and decide on the stress.
- Ask: *What words did you have?* Students read out the words with the correct stress. Write them on the board with the stress marked.

(You can control the words used in this activity and save time in class by preparing cards yourself in advance.)

---

## Reading

### Background information
**Charles Lindbergh** /lɪnˌbɜːɡ/ (1902 – 1974) started to study engineering at college, but gave it up to become a stunt pilot at fairs. A short time later he trained as an army pilot and then worked as a commercial pilot, transporting mail. A prize of $25,000 to fly non-stop from New York to Paris was the incentive for Lindbergh's transatlantic flight. Lindbergh helped design the plane especially for the flight.
**Anne Morrow Lindbergh** (1906 – 2001) was her husband's co-pilot and accompanied him on flying trips all over the world. She was also a writer and published 13 books. She was married to Charles Lindbergh for 45 years (until his death from cancer) and they had six children together.

## 1
- Read out the words in the list and explain the task.
- Students work in pairs and match the words to the correct definitions. They should first try without a dictionary, looking carefully at the form of the word.
- Check the answers with the class.

### Answers
2 e   3 f   4 c   5 a   6 b

## 2
- Ask: *What can you see in the photos?*
- Say: *The man in the photo is Charles Lindbergh. Think about the photos and the magazine article vocabulary in Ex 1. What was Charles Lindbergh famous for?*
- Focus students' attention on the title *From fame to despair*. Explain the word *despair* and ask: *What do you think the article is about?* Elicit various predictions from students but do not comment on them.

## 3
- 05 Students read the article quickly and check their predictions. They can also listen to the article on CD.
- Check the answers with the class.

### Answers
In 1927 Charles Lindbergh became the first person to fly solo across the Atlantic. He became very famous, but his fame had an unhappy ending.

## 4
- Read out the questions and check that students understand them.
- Students read the article again and answer the questions.
- Check the answers with the class. Explain in 2, that a *ticker tape reception* is an occasion in New York when people throw pieces of paper to honour a famous person. In 5, check students have understood the expression 'ransom note'.
- Check any other problematic vocabulary such as: *parachute, engine, adoration, introspective, to arrest.*

### Answers
1 The brakes had been removed to avoid extra weight. The plane was very heavy because it was carrying so much fuel.
2 On 13th July Charles Lindbergh returned to America after his solo flight and a tour of Europe. He was given the biggest ticker tape reception ever seen in New York.
3 Anne was very shy and didn't like being the centre of attention. Anne and Charles couldn't go out in public without journalists following them.
4 Their servants gave journalists information about the Lindberghs in return for money.
5 He was kidnapped from his cot and later murdered, although the Lindberghs paid money for his return.
6 They left America to escape media attention and try and lead a normal life.

## Optional activity

### Famous trials

- Discuss other trials involving famous people with the class. Ask: *What was the person on trial for? Did you follow the trial? What happened at the trial? Did the court find him / her innocent or guilty? What was your opinion of the trial / verdict?*
- You can extend the activity by asking students to write a short newspaper article about one of the trials.

### 5

- Read out the questions and check that students understand them.
- Students work in pairs and discuss the questions.
- Discuss the questions with the class.

# Language study

## Sequencing events

### 1

- Read out the example sentences.
- Read the questions. Students answer them orally.

**Answers**
1  Similar meanings
2  Past simple: sentences b and c
   The *-ing* form: sentence a
   A noun: sentence d

### 2

- Students work individually. They read the sentence and complete the rule.
- Check the answer with the class.
- Check students have understood by asking them to link the following sentences in four different ways with *before* and *after*: *I had dinner. I watched TV.* (After I had dinner, I watched TV. / After having dinner, I watched TV. / After dinner, I watched TV. / Before I watched TV, I had dinner.)

**Answer**
They can be followed by the past simple, the *-ing* form or a noun.

### 3

- Explain the task.
- Students work individually or in pairs. They look at the pairs of sentences and answer the question.
- Check the answer with the class. Check that students can pronounce *afterwards* /ˈɑːftəwədz/.

**Answer**
*After* and *before* are followed by a verb or a noun; *afterwards* and *beforehand* replace a verb or a noun to avoid repeating it.

## Optional activity

### Sequencing events in the article

- Write the sentences below on the board.
- Students put the events from the story in the correct order. (The correct order is in brackets.)
- Students link sentences 1 and 2, 3 and 4, 6 and 7 together using *after, afterwards, before, beforehand, while, earlier* and *later*. Do this orally, prompting students for alternatives.

Charles Lindbergh married Anne Morrow. (3)
Charles Lindbergh flew solo across the Atlantic. (1)
The interest of the public in Anne and Charles increased. (4)
Their son was kidnapped. (6)
They moved to Britain. (7)
Charles and Anne had a son. (5)
Charles became famous. (2)

### 4

- Explain the task.
- Students work individually and complete the rule.
- Check the answer with the class.

**Answer**
We can use *while* to talk about two events that are happening at the same time.
We can use *later* and *earlier* to talk about the different times that two events happen.

### 5

- Read out the task.
- Ask students to look back at the examples in Ex 3 and 4 and replace *afterwards / beforehand* and *later / earlier* with the definitions in Ex 5.
- Check the answers with the class.

**Answers**
a  later / earlier
b  afterwards / beforehand

### 6

- Ask students to read the summary for sequencing events in the Grammar reference on page 26.
- Explain the task.
- Students work individually or in pairs and choose the correct alternatives.
- Check the answers with the class.

**Answers**

| | | |
|---|---|---|
| 1  After | 5  earlier |
| 2  while | 6  later |
| 3  before | 7  Afterwards |
| 4  after | |

### 7

- Read the questions with the class. Explain the words *admire, sympathise* and *condemn* if necessary.
- Students work in pairs and discuss their ideas.
- Discuss the questions with the class.

# What's your verdict?

## Speaking

**1**

- Ask: *Do you like looking at pictures of celebrities in magazines or on the Internet? Do you like reading stories and gossip about them?* If possible, show the class magazines with pictures of celebrities caught unawares and discuss them.
- Explain the task.
- Students work individually. They read the situations and decide on their answer to each question.
- Check that students had no problems understanding the situations.

**2**

- Students work in groups. They discuss their opinions about the situations and try to reach an agreement.
- Discuss the results with the class. Did all groups have the same answers?

**3**

- Read out the task.
- Brainstorm ideas with the class on the board.
- Ask pairs of students to formulate five rules.
- Ask individual pairs to read out their rules.

---

### Revision activities

**1) Wordlist activity**

- Revise vocabulary from this Unit by choosing a Wordlist activity from Teaching tips 'Reviewing and revising' on pages 21–22.

**2) An event in the life of …**

- Students choose a famous person – from history or a modern celebrity.
- Students write an article about their chosen person. They should first explain who the person is and why he or she is famous. Then they should describe an interesting incident in his or her life. Remind students to link events using the sequencing words from this unit. They can also add a photo.
- Ask some students to read out their articles to the class. Alternatively, put copies of all the articles together in a magazine and let students take it in turns to read it.

---

## Extra practice

Students complete the Extra practice material on page 23 either in class, or for homework.

### Extra practice answers

**1**
| | | | | |
|---|---|---|---|---|
| 1 | composer | | 4 | footballer |
| 2 | ballet dancer | | 5 | tennis player |
| 3 | actor | | 6 | director |

**2** Number of syllables

| 2 | 3 | 4 |
|---|---|---|
| <u>aw</u>ful | <u>del</u>icate | pho<u>tog</u>raphy |
| <u>bor</u>row | fan<u>tas</u>tic | psy<u>chol</u>ogist |
| com<u>plain</u> | <u>strat</u>egy | |
| <u>dec</u>ent | te<u>rrif</u>ic | |
| <u>whis</u>per | | |

**3** complain

**4**
| | | | | |
|---|---|---|---|---|
| 1 | kidnapped | | 4 | compensation |
| 2 | trial | | 5 | verdict |
| 3 | sue | | 6 | escape |

**5**
| | | | | |
|---|---|---|---|---|
| 1 | leaving | | 5 | parking |
| 2 | later | | 6 | earlier |
| 3 | while | | 7 | afterwards |
| 4 | earlier | | | |

**6** (individual answers)

---

## References

Grammar reference: Coursebook page 26
Wordlist: Coursebook page 28
Photocopiable resources: Teacher's Book pages 90–91
Test: Teacher's Book pages 123–124

## CD-ROM

Unit 2 Who needs fame?
Language exercise: Watching paint dry
Vocabulary activity: Being famous is good for you
CEF-linked exercise: I can use *before / after / while / later / earlier*
Game: The big squeeze

# UNIT 3
# A place to live

| Topic | Language study | Vocabulary | Main skills |
|---|---|---|---|
| • Somewhere completely different (Unusual homes) <br> • Flat to let (Renting accommodation) | • Modifying comparisons (*nearly, far, by far, a bit, much more, quite*) <br> • Comparing people, places and things | • Types of houses <br> • Renting property | • **Reading:** summarising and taking notes <br> • **Speaking:** discussing unusual and ideal homes; housing needs <br> • **Listening:** identifying key information |

## Learning aims

- Can modify comparisons
- Can describe houses
- Can use vocabulary for renting accommodation

### Ideas for preparation
- Pictures of properties for sale from your local paper or property magazine (see Optional activity p33)
- Realia to illustrate comparisons such as books, music CDs, DVDs etc (see Ex 2 p33)
- Photocopied sheets with correct and incorrect comparisons (see Optional activity p34)

### Warmer
- Tell students about the housing situation in Britain (see Background information below).
- Ask: *Do most people live in houses or in flats in your country? Are gardens important? Do most people own or rent the property they live in? Do people prefer to live in towns or in the country? Are house makeover programmes popular in your country?*

### Background information
In Britain people prefer to live in houses with a garden rather than in flats. In London more people live in flats (37%) than in the rest of the country (16%). 70% of people own the property they live in. Most people buy their property with a mortgage from the bank. Property is most expensive in south-east England. British people are very keen on DIY and home improvements. House and garden makeover TV programmes are very popular.

## Lead-in

**1**
- Ask students to open their books on page 10. Students look at the photos. Ask: *Do these houses look typically British to you? Do you have all these types of houses in your country?*
- Read out the words in the box. Students repeat them. Make sure they can pronounce the words correctly with the correct stress (<u>bun</u>galow, <u>cott</u>age, semi-de<u>tach</u>ed, <u>terr</u>aced).
- Students match the words to the correct pictures.

- Check the answers with the class. Ask: *Which type of houses are most typical of this area? What are the advantages and disadvantages of each type of house?*

### Answers
a  semi-detached
b  cottage
c  terraced house
d  bungalow
e  flat

**2**
- Read the questions with the class.
- Students ask you the questions. Tell the class about the property you live in.
- Students work in pairs and talk about their house or flat, using the questions to help them. <u>Alternatively,</u> they can ask each other the questions.
- Two or three students tell the class about the place their partner lives in.

## Reading

**1**
- Students look at the photos of the houses on page 10. They match them to the correct words in the box.

### Answers
a windmill    b narrow boat    c warehouse

**2**
- Read out the question. Elicit answers.
- Ask: *Why aren't places like this used for their original function?*

### Possible answers
Windmill: used to grind grain into flour (today it isn't profitable to make flour in small, wind-powered mills; flour is ground in large mills using modern machinery)
Narrow boat: used to transport goods along canals (today most goods are transported over land by train and lorry)
Warehouse: used to store goods transported by water (today fewer good are transported by water; modern warehouse buildings have replaced old ones)

**3**
- 🔊 **06** Look at the table with the class. Check students understand the line headings and the examples.

- Students work in groups of three and agree which home they are going to read about.
- Each student reads about one of the homes. They complete the part of the table about that home. They should use notes as in the examples.

**4**

- Students exchange information in their group about the homes they have read about. They complete the other columns in the table.
- Play the texts on CD. Students listen and check they have all the information.
- Check the answers with the class.

**Answers**

Warehouse
Location: by the River Thames in London
Age: built in the 19th century
Number of bedrooms: 1
Living room: light, spacious, white walls, wooden floor
Bathrooms: 1, luxurious
Main advantages: lots of character, wonderful location
Main disadvantage: very expensive

Windmill
Age: from the late 18th century
Number of bedrooms: 4
Living room: on the second floor, old photographs of the windmill on the walls
Kitchen: on the first floor, old-fashioned
Bathrooms: 3
Main advantages: round rooms – different from other houses, cosy, large garden
Main disadvantage: long way from town

Narrow boat
Location: just outside Leeds
Age: 25 years old
Number of bedrooms: 2
Kitchen: well-equipped
Living room: 1, cosy
Bathrooms: 1 shower room
Main disadvantage: high maintenance costs

**5**

- Students work in the same groups as Ex 3 and 4. They discuss which house they would prefer to live in and why.
- One person in each group briefly presents the results of their discussion to the class.

**6**

- Read out the questions. Check students understand what *décor* means (interior design or style).
- Students work in pairs and discuss the questions.
- Students report their ideas to the class.

**Optional activity**

**House for sale**

- Students cut out a picture of an interesting house from a property magazine. They write a description of it for a 'For Sale' advert, using the details given in the magazine and their imagination.
- Display the adverts in the classroom. Which house do students think looks the most interesting?

# Language study

## Modifying comparisons

**Optional activity**

**Class comparisons**

- Three students of varying heights line up in front of the class. Ask: *Who is the tallest? Who is the smallest?*
- Write the names of two of the students on the board and the word *tall*. Say: *Can you compare [Florence] and [Paolo]?*
- Ask the students their ages and write them on the board. Say: *Can you compare their ages?*
- Encourage students to make other (objective) comparisons about the three students: hair length, feet size etc. Avoid anything that might ridicule or embarrass students.
- Ask the class: *Who is the sportiest person in the class? Who is the cleverest? Who has the coolest clothes?* etc.

**1**

- Read out the statements.
- Students work in pairs and decide if the statements are true or false. Refer them back to the text on page 11 if necessary.
- Check the answers with the class.

**Answers**

1 True   2 False   3 False   4 True   5 True

**2**

- Read out the questions. Students answer orally. Write the words on the board for each type of comparison.
- Using the words on the board, revise the different type of comparisons and the formation of comparatives and superlatives. You can use realia to illustrate (eg three books: *thick, thicker, thickest / exciting, more exciting, most exciting; This book is thicker / more exciting than this book*). Alternatively, ask students to compare their mobile phones, bags, jackets etc.
- Refer students to the Grammar reference on page 27 if necessary.

**Answers**

1 larger than (sentence 1), more convenient than (sentence 3)
2 as modern as (sentence 2)
3 the least spacious (sentence 4), the fewest rooms (sentence 5)

**3**

- Draw students' attention to the words in bold. Say: *These words are modifiers. They make comparative or superlative adjectives stronger or weaker.*
- Do the first sentence as an example. Ask: *Does 'far cheaper' mean 'a lot cheaper' or 'a little cheaper'?* (a lot cheaper), *So does this modifier make the comparison weaker or stronger?* (stronger).
- Students work individually. They complete the rest of the table.
- Check the answers with the class.

**Answers**

| | Comparative | as ... as | Superlative |
|---|---|---|---|
| Strong | *far, much* | *nowhere near* | *by far* |
| Weak | *a bit* | *not quite, nearly* | – |

**4**

- Explain the task. Look at the examples with the class.
- Students work with a partner. They write true sentences using the phrases.
- Students swap their sentences with another pair. They read and check the sentences.
- Ask each pair to read out a sentence to the class.

**5**

- Look at the pairs of items with the class.
- Choose one pair (eg two different types of food). Elicit some examples from students and write them on the board (eg *Burgers are far cheaper than steak. Steak is much healthier than burgers. Burgers are a more convenient food. Burgers are far more popular among young people*).
- Students work in pairs. They choose one pair of items and compare them orally. Alternatively, they can write comparisons.
- Each pair says a sentence to the class. Alternatively, pairs swap their written sentences with another pair. They read and check the sentences.

**Optional activity**

**Grammar auction**

- Ask students if they know what an 'auction' is and if they have been to one. If necessary, teach them the verb 'to bid' and the phrase 'Going, going, gone!'.
- Write ten comparisons on the board or give students a photocopied sheet with the comparisons. Some of the comparisons should contain grammatical mistakes.
- Students work in pairs. Say: *Each pair has £1000. You must use the money to buy correct comparisons. You must bid at least £10. The winners are the students who have bought the most correct sentences for the least money.* Check students have understood the rules.
- Auction the comparisons in turn. Read out each sentence and start the bidding. Finish the bidding with 'Going, going, gone!'.
- Write the names of the buyer and the amount on the board.
- Tell the class if the comparison was correct. If the comparison was incorrect, say the correct version.
- After the auction, work out which pair is the winner.

# Flat to let

## Vocabulary and listening

**1**

- Students work in small groups and discuss the answers to the questions. Encourage them to use dictionaries to find the meaning of unknown words.

- Check the answers with the class. For question 3, ask different students to say their opinions and give reasons. Ask: *Has anybody ever shared a flat? What were the advantages and disadvantages?*

**Answers**

1. A tenant
2. A landlord / landlady
3. (individual answers)
4. No (furnished = furniture is provided)
5. Yes (immaculate = very clean)
6. Usually every month
7. For example: appliances such as fridge, freezer, washing machine and TV, crockery and cutlery (plates, knives etc), vacuum cleaner and other cleaning equipment
8. A good location (for example, in the centre of a city or in an expensive suburb) means the price is much higher
9. Because the flat isn't free then / the previous tenant might still be there
10. Nothing (inclusive means all the bills for gas, electricity and water are included in the price)

**Optional activity**

**Wanted: flatmate**

- Say: *Imagine you have found a great flat but you need a flatmate to share the bills.*
- Students write a description of the sort of person they would like to share a flat with. Write your description as an example on the board (eg *Wanted to share flat: Female aged 20–30. You should be sociable, enjoy going to clubs and pubs and like music. You should be tidy and a non-smoker. Vegetarian preferred*).
- Students walk round the class and read out their description to other students. Can they find somebody who fits the description?
- Students report back to the class. How many people found their perfect flatmate?

**Background information**

Edinburgh, the capital of Scotland, has a population of about 450,000. Since 1999 Scotland has had its own Parliament in Edinburgh.

There is an Old Town in the city centre, which includes Edinburgh Castle and the famous street the Royal Mile. The main shopping street is Princes Street in New Town. Edinburgh is famous for the Edinburgh International Festival, a huge arts festival with plays, concerts and comedy performances in August.

**2**

- Tell students they are going to listen to a student who has moved to Edinburgh. Ask: *What do you know about Edinburgh? Has anybody ever been there?*
- A student reads out the introduction about Maria to the class.
- Ask: *What kind of place do you think she is looking for? Why?* Prompt students with these words: *price, size, location*.

**Possible answers**

Cheap (she's a research student); small (she is alone); near the university (where she will be doing research); quiet (she needs to study); sharing (she probably doesn't know anybody in Edinburgh)

## 3

- 🔘 **07**  Read out and explain the task.
- Students listen to the first part of the conversation and tick the correct boxes.
- Check the answers with the class. Play the CD again if necessary.

**Answers**

1 (cost), 3 (location)

### Listening script 07

(F = Fiona; M = Maria)

F:  ... and I really don't mind if you want to stay a bit longer.

M: Well I've found some adverts on the Internet. Some of them look quite interesting.

F: Oh? Let's have a look.

M: I can't afford it if the rent's more than about four hundred pounds a month really.

F: £400 a month? Well, you should be able to find something for that. You might have to travel a bit.

M: Well that's the thing. I don't want to spend time travelling, waiting for buses in the cold. I want to be able to go into the university easily and be close to the centre.

F: Well yes, I can understand that. I mean Edinburgh's a great city and there's lots going on.

M: That's what I think. Anyway, have a look at these.

## 4

- 🔘 **08**  Read out and explain the task. (Off Princes Street = on a road leading off from Princes Street / next to Princes Street.)
- Students listen to the second part of the conversation and make notes about the disadvantages of each flat. They tick the one Maria chooses.
- Students compare their answers with a partner.
- Check the answers with the class.

**Answers**

1  Old Town: too expensive (£500; Maria only wants to pay £400)
2  New Town: no separate bedroom (one room with sofa bed)
3  Off Princes Street: room in a shared flat (Maria doesn't want to share)
4  Leith Walk: non-smoker wanted (Maria smokes)
She chooses to look at the shared flat off Princes Street

### Listening script 08

(F = Fiona; M = Maria)

F:  OK. How about this flat? Central location, one double bedroom, bathroom, hall, lounge, fully-equipped kitchen.

M: That sounds nice, Where is it?

F: It's in Old Town.

M: That's nice. And how much is it?

F: £500 per month I'm afraid.

M: Ooh. That's too much.

F: Yes, it sounds a bit expensive. How about this one in New Town? That's not as central as Old Town, but it's still a nice area, though. Listen. £400 per calendar month, a studio flat fully-furnished and equipped. Bright double-windowed room with sofa bed. Separate kitchen and shower room.

M: Hmm. So it has a sofa bed because there isn't a separate bedroom. Is that right?

F: Yes. What do you think?

M: I'd rather have a separate bedroom really.

F: Yes. OK. Let's have a look at this one. Room to let. Single fully-furnished bedroom to rent in spacious and immaculate city centre flat off Princes Street.

M: Does that mean it's to share?

F: Yeah. But it's in an excellent location. And listen to this: lounge, dining room, bathroom and kitchen. The building even has a swimming pool! Wow! And it's only £350 per month.

M: But, of course, it's sharing. It sounds nice and it's much cheaper than the others, but I really don't want to share.

F: Let's have another look. Leith Walk with stunning view. Bedroom, sitting room, oh but it says non-smoker. That's no good for you is it?

M: Unfortunately not.

F: Couldn't you give up?

M: No! I'm not going to give up smoking just to find a flat! ... Let's go back to that one to share with the swimming pool.

F: What was it? Ah yes! Single fully-furnished bedroom to rent in spacious flat ... off Princes Street ... Building has a swimming pool ...

M: Yes, that's the one.

F: Views of Edinburgh castle! Of course, it depends on who you're sharing with.

M: Absolutely.

F: But I think it's worth having a look at. It sounds fantastic. And it could be nice, having other people around. You don't have to be good friends with them.

M: That's true. It would be someone to talk to. OK I'll have a look!

F: Good idea. After all you like swimming don't you ...?

## 5

- Read out the task.
- Students listen again and decide on the flat they would choose.
- Discuss students' answers with the class.

# Speaking

## 1

- Explain that students are going to do a communication activity in pairs. Each student will have different information. Read the instructions with the class.
- Students work in pairs. They read their information carefully.
- Students role play the conversation with their partner.
- Discuss the results of the conversations with the class. Ask: *Did you find accommodation for all the language students? Which accommodation did you match with which person? Were there any problems?*

**Possible answers**

Kenjii: (2) country cottage (Potential problem: very expensive)

Francesca: (1) large room in shared house (Potential problem: walls are black)

Wen Ling: (3) room with host family (Potential problem: with a family)

Ahmed: (4) 3$^{rd}$ floor flat (Potential problem: needs decorating)

## Revision activity

**Housing quiz**

- Divide the class into two teams, A and B.
- In turns, ask different students in the teams the questions below. The team gets 2 points for each correct answer. (1 point if someone else in the team can answer the question.)
- The team with the most points wins. If the teams have the same number of points, ask this bonus question: *How many British towns or cities can you name?* The teams make a list on paper. Set a time limit of two minutes for this. The team with the most names wins.

Team A questions

What is the name for:

1 a house that is joined to other houses in a row? (terraced house)
2 a person who rents a house? (a tenant)
3 a building that was used to grind flour? (windmill)
4 a small country house? (cottage)
5 the money you pay for electricity, gas etc? (bills)
6 a house on one level? (bungalow)
7 a woman who lets you a flat? (landlady)
8 the part of a room that is above your head? (ceiling)
9 a building where things are stored? (warehouse)
10 a house that is attached to one other house? (semi-detached)

Team B questions

What word means:

1 warm and comfortable? (cosy)
2 the place where a house is? (location)
3 there is furniture provided? (furnished)
4 bills are included in the price of a flat? (inclusive)
5 the function of a building has been changed? (converted)
6 a flat is free? (available)
7 very clean? (immaculate)
8 very comfortable and expensive (luxurious)
9 near to a particular place? (convenient)
10 the style inside your home? (décor)

# Extra practice

Students complete the Extra practice material on page 24 either in class, or for homework.

**Extra practice answers**

**1** 1 f  2 g  3 e  4 b

| **2** | | |
|---|---|---|
| 1 f/f | 5 nr |
| 2 u/f | 6 n/s |
| 3 c/h | 7 inc |
| 4 pcm | |

**3**
1 far bigger / much bigger
2 much greater / far greater
3 much wetter / far wetter
4 a bit longer
5 not quite as rich as

**4** (individual answers)

# References

Grammar reference: Coursebook page 27
Wordlist: Coursebook page 28
Photocopiable resources: Teacher's Book pages 92–93
Test: Teacher's Book pages 125–126

# CD-ROM

Unit 3 A place to live
Language exercise: Family features
Vocabulary activity: To let
CEF-linked exercise: I can listen for details about a flat
Game: Crossword

# UNIT 4
# Life changes

| Topic | Language study | Vocabulary | Main skills |
|---|---|---|---|
| • Being 18 (Hopes and ambitions) <br> • How independent are you? | • Verbs for talking about the future (*hope, intend, be due, would like, expect, plan, aim*) | • Phrasal verbs: life changes <br> • Jobs and courses | • **Listening:** identifying life changes <br> • **Pronunciation:** word stress <br> • **Writing:** a letter <br> • **Speaking:** predicting life changes; conducting a questionnaire and presenting results |

## Learning aims

- Can use verbs for talking about the future
- Can conduct a class survey
- Can use phrasal verbs for life changes

### Ideas for preparation
- Interesting pictures from magazines for story telling (see Optional activity p39)
- A hat or container for putting pieces of paper in (see Revision activity p41)

### Warmer
- Say: *The title of this unit is 'Life changes'. What sort of personal things change during a person's life?*
- Brainstorm a list of ideas on the board with the class (eg relationships / friends, family, education / jobs, place you live in, likes and dislikes, attitudes towards things etc).

## Lead-in

**1**
- Ask students to open their books on page 14. Ask: *How old are you? What are the good things about being this age? What are the bad things?*
- Look at the table with the class. Go through the laws and check that students understand them. Ask: *What is parental consent?* (when your parents officially allow you to do something), *What is the difference between a moped and a motorbike?* (a motorbike is bigger and more powerful), *What does 'vote' mean?* (to officially choose a politician or political party in an election). Check students can pronounce *parental* /pəˈrentl/ and *tattoo* /tæˈtuː/ with the correct word stress.
- Ask: *How are these laws different from the laws in your country?* Or ask specific students: *Can you drive a car at 17 in your country? Can you be sent to prison at 17 in your country?* etc.
- Ask: *Do you agree with these laws? Should the age be lower for buying cigarettes or buying alcohol, for example?*

### Optional activity

**New laws for young people**
- Say: *Imagine you are writing laws for a newly independent country. You can create laws for young people. They can be about anything that affects young people. For example: All students should receive £100 support from the government every month / Anybody who smokes should pay extra money for healthcare.*
- Students work in small groups and think of new laws for young people. Encourage them to be realistic.
- Groups present their laws to the class. Decide which is the best law. Will it be easy to implement?

## Reading

**1**
- Read out the task.
- Brainstorm a list of ideas on the board with the class.

### Possible answers
education, career, relationships, friends, moving away from home

**2**
- 🎧 09 Read out the questions and check that students understand them.
- Students read the magazine texts and answer the questions. They can listen to the texts on CD while they read.
- Check the answers with the class.
- Draw students' attention to the ideas on the board from Ex 1 and ask: *Did they talk about the topics you predicted?*

### Answers
| | | | |
|---|---|---|---|
| 1 | Peter | 5 | Sophie |
| 2 | Maria | 6 | James |
| 3 | Sophie | 7 | Peter |
| 4 | Maria | 8 | James |

## 3

- Read out the questions and check that students understand them.
- Students work in pairs and discuss the questions.
- Check the answers with the class. Encourage students to give reasons for their answers.

### Answers

1 James – he's always wanted to be a doctor and is going to study medicine; Sophie – she is already training to be a dancer and wants to work for a well-known company and live in New York. (Peter and Maria want to go to university but they don't seem to know what they want to study there)
2 (individual answers)
3 (individual answers)

# Listening

## 1

- 🔘 **10** Look at the photos of the four people with the class. Say: *These are the four people from the reading text. They are ten years older now. Do they look happy?*
- Explain that students are going to listen and complete the table with the jobs they do now.
- Students listen and complete the first part of the table.
- Students compare their answers with a partner.
- Check the answers with the class. Ask: *Do you know what a solicitor is?* (a lawyer who advises clients and prepares legal documents, but does not work in court), *What does a fundraiser do?* (contacts donors, organises fundraising events), *What is a personal trainer?* (advises people on their physical fitness and develops programmes for them).

### Answers

Peter: works for a computer company.
Maria: solicitor for a big company.
James: fundraiser for medical charities.
Sophie: personal trainer.

## 2

- Say: *Now listen again and make notes about the four people's plans for the future.*
- Students listen again and complete the second part of the table.
- Check the answers with the class.
- Refer students to Listening script 10 on page 31 if necessary.

### Answers

Peter: going to set up his own business; hopes he'll be rich and successful.
Maria: hopes to start a company with her husband who's training to be a laywer.
James: intends to get married next year.
Sophie: intends to produce her own DVD and book.

## Listening script 10

(I = Interviewer, P = Peter, M = Maria, J = James, S = Sophie)
(Peter)
I: Well, Peter, does it feel strange to read about what you hoped for when you were 18 now that you're 28?
P: Yeah, I guess it does in a way. I'm not so confident about the future now as I was when I first started college.
I: Any particular reason?
P: When you're 18, you don't think anything is going to get in your way, but you learn there's a lot you can't control.
I: Such as?
P: Well, the way you work, for one thing. I work for a computer company and people are always telling me what to do. So I've decided I'm going to set up my own business. In the next five years I hope that I'll be rich and successful, but I know that's going to take a lot of hard work to achieve
(Maria)
I: So Maria, when we last spoke you were getting worried about getting a good job and going to university. What's happened to you since then?
M: Yeah, it was difficult at first. Sure, I had to work hard to get to university, and then I began to work as a solicitor for a big company. Five years ago I got married and now I've got two children. My husband and I are saving hard, and intend to send them both to college, to make things a bit easier for them.
I: And what do you do?
M: I still work as a solicitor. My husband is studying to be a lawyer, and so we're hoping to start our own company in the future.
I: Good luck to you both!
(James)
I: James, ten years ago you wanted to become a doctor ...
J: Yeah, but unfortunately I didn't get the grades I needed.
I: So what did you do then?
J: Well, I was very disappointed, but I just had to move on and do something else with my life. So I took a year off and worked as a volunteer on an aid programme. That made me realise how important fundraising is for medical charities. So that's what I do.
I: Can you explain a bit more about what you actually do?
J: I contact likely donors, put forward our case and organise big fundraising events.
I: So have you achieved any of your ambitions?
J: Well, I always said I wanted to help other people, so I guess so.
I: And what about the future?
J: My fiancée and I intend to get married next year.
I: Congratulations!
(Sophie)
I: Are you still a dancer, Sophie?
S: Well, I soon realised that I would never make it to the top of my profession as a dancer, so I looked around for something else.
I: And?
S: And I found I could make a lot of money as a personal trainer.
I: What do you mean?
S: I mean someone who advises people on their physical fitness, and develops programmes for them to follow. Dance exercises are a great way to keep fit, you know. Next year I intend to produce my own DVD and book, and I hope it'll be successful.
I: And did you ever get to New York?
S: Only for a holiday!

## 3

- Read the instructions and look at the example with the class.
- Students work in pairs and discuss how Peter, Maria, James and Sophie's lives have changed.
- Ask: *Do you think these stories are inspiring or depressing?*

**Possible answers**

Maria did what she wanted to do: she managed to go to university and now has a good job as a solicitor. She now has children too.

James didn't get the grades he wanted to become a doctor. But he achieved his ambition to help people by becoming a fundraiser for medical charities. He also said he'd probably get married and he is going to do that next year.

Sophie wasn't good enough to be a top dancer so she found a new career. Her ambition was to live in New York but she only managed to go there on holiday.

# Vocabulary

## Phrasal verbs: life changes

### 1

- Revise what phrasal verbs are. Note: point out that the meaning of a phrasal verb can sometimes be guessed from the meaning of the words that form it, but that sometimes it cannot: students have to learn their meaning. Write an example on the board: *put something down* = stop holding something, put it down onto a table, for example (easy to guess); *put somebody down* = make somebody look stupid in front of friends (cannot be guessed).
- Do the first sentence as an example.
- Students read the other sentences and match the words to the correct definitions.
- Check the answers with the class.

**Answers**

1 e   2 d   3 f   4 b   5 a   6 c   7 g

### 2

- Read out the questions and check that students understand them.
- Students work in pairs and discuss the questions.
- Discuss the questions with the class. Ask: *Do you think it's important to take time off? What advice will you give your children when they are growing up? Would you like to set up your own business? Do you have concrete plans for your future?*

**Optional activity**

**Phrasal verbs story**

- Students work in small groups. They write a short story using all the phrasal verbs in Ex 1. It can be a serious story or a funny or silly story.
- One student from each group reads their story to the class.

(You can make this activity more fun and give students more support by showing them a picture cut out from a magazine which sets the scene for the story.)

# Language study

## Verbs for talking about the future

### 1

- Ask: *Are you confident or not so confident about the future?*
- Briefly revise the ways of talking about the future that students already know: *going to* for plans and intentions, present continuous for future arrangements and *will* for predictions. Students give examples.
- Say: *Let's look at some verbs for talking about the future.* Read the example sentences and the questions with the class.
- Students work individually and answer the questions.
- Students read the Grammar reference on page 27 and check their answers.
- Check the answers with the class.

**Answers**

1  a (more sure): sentences b, c, e, h
   b (less sure): sentences a, d, f, g
2  b, c, d, e, f, g,
3  a, h

### 2

- Write the two headings on the board and complete the lists with the class.
- Say: *Give me an example about you for each verb.*

**Answers**

More sure: intend, be due, expect
Less sure: hope, would like, aim

### 3

- Explain the task. Say: *Decide whether the person is more sure or less sure. Use the lists on the board to help you.*
- Students work individually or in pairs. They choose the correct alternatives.
- Check the answers with the class.

**Answers**

1 intends   2 aim   3 would like   4 expect

### 4

- Read out the questions.
- Students work in pairs and discuss the questions.
- Ask students to tell the class about their partner's plans and expectations.

# Vocabulary and pronunciation

## Jobs and courses

---

**Optional activity**

**Alphabet jobs**
- Divide students into four teams.
- Read out the letters of the alphabet in turn. Students write a job beginning with that letter. Keep the pace quite fast so that students have to think quickly. Encourage students to be creative.
- Check the jobs. The team with a job for the most letters wins.

**Possible answers**
actor, bank clerk, cleaner, doctor, engineer, florist, gardener, hairdresser, interpreter, journalist, karate teacher, lawyer, manager, nurse, optician, politician, queen, receptionist, social worker, taxi driver, university lecturer, violinist, writer, xylophone player, yoga teacher, zoologist

---

**1**
- Look at the table and the completed example with the class. Ask: *What is number 2?* (accountancy).
- Students work individually and complete the table.
- Students compare their answers with a partner.
- Check the answers with the class.

**Answers**

| | | | |
|---|---|---|---|
| 2 | Accountancy | 7 | Physicist |
| 3 | History | 8 | Physiotherapist |
| 4 | Linguistics | 9 | Law |
| 5 | Pharmacist | 10 | Statistician |
| 6 | Psychologist | 11 | Teaching |

**2**
- 🔊 **11** Look at the stress pattern table with the class. Read out the words in the table. Students repeat each word with the correct stress pattern.
- Explain the task.
- Students listen and match the words to the correct stress pattern.
- Students listen again and check their answers.
- Check the answers with the class.

**Answers**

| 0 | Oo | | Ooo | oOo |
|---|---|---|---|---|
| Law | Doctor | Physics | Pharmacist | Accountant |
| | Medicine | Teacher | Pharmacy | Linguistics |
| | History | Teaching | Physicist | Statistics |
| | Linguist | | | |

| oOoo | ooOo | oooOo |
|---|---|---|
| Accountancy | Statistician | Physiotherapist |
| Historian | | Physiotherapy |
| Psychologist | | |
| Psychology | | |
| Solicitor | | |

**3**
- Students listen to the words and repeat them.
- Ask individual students to repeat words. Correct any errors.

---

**Optional activity**

**Say it quietly, loudly, quickly**
- Students practise the words in Ex 1 by repeating them in a particular way, for example quietly, loudly or quickly. They can do this in chorus or individually.

---

**Background information**
The most popular degree subject in the UK is business studies, followed by biology and social studies. The least popular subjects are veterinary sciences, agriculture and maths.

---

**4**
- Read out the questions and check that students understand them.
- Students work in pairs and discuss the questions.
- Discuss the questions with the class.

# Writing

## A letter to me

**1**
- Ask several students: *How old will you be in 30 years' time? Can you imagine what you'll be doing then?* Explain that students are going to write a letter to themselves which they will read in 30 years' time.
- Students read the example letter.
- Briefly check comprehension of the letter. Ask: *How old will the writer be in 30 years? What is she doing now? What does she intend to do in the holidays? What does she intend to do within five years of graduating? What would she like to do by the time she's 35?*
- Emphasise the structure of the letter: now, short-term future, long-term future. Ask how the writer starts and ends the letter (*When I read this letter …; After that who knows …*).
- Point out that the writer uses lots of verbs to talk about the future. Students underline them (*hope, intend, expect, aim, 'd like*).
- Students write their own letter, using the structure of the example letter to help them, and verbs to talk about the future.
- Students swap with a partner and read each other's letters.
- Check the letters. Write on the board and discuss any recurring errors.
- Tell students to keep their letter in a safe place and read it in 30 years!

## Optional activity

### Adjective noun collocations

- Write these collocations from the letter in Ex 1 on the board as two lists of jumbled adjectives and jumbled nouns.

| | |
|---|---|
| good | degree |
| competitive | profession |
| practical | experience |
| useful | contact |
| national | newspaper |
| local | event |

- Students match the adjectives to the nouns to form collocations.
- Check the answers. Students may have different solutions. Discuss which adjectives could potentially go with different nouns (eg *useful experience*, *good contact*).
- Brainstorm other adjectives which could go with each noun with the class.

# Speaking

### 1
- Ask: *What does independent mean?* (able to do things without other people; confident of your own abilities). Ask: *Are you an independent person? Is being independent a good thing? Or is it better to have help from friends and family sometimes?*
- Tell students they are going to complete a questionnaire about how independent they are. Quickly check comprehension of problematic vocabulary such as: *special occasion, argue, sort out.*
- Students work individually and complete the questionnaire. Alternatively, they can work in pairs: one student reads out the questions and notes their partner's answers. Then they swap roles.

### 2
- Students check their answers (or their partner's answers) on page 32.
- Students compare their answers with another student or with the partner they have worked with.
- Discuss the answers with the class. Ask: *Do you think the summary on page 32 was correct about you?*
- Do a quick class survey. Ask for a show of hands for mostly As, Bs and Cs. How independent is the class?

### 3
- Tell students that they are going to prepare their own questionnaire. Look at the topic examples with the class.
- Students work in pairs. They choose one of the titles or think of their own title.

### 4
- In their pairs, students prepare a questionnaire and answer key using the questionnaire in Ex 1 as an example. There should be five questions and the questions and answers should be short and simple.

### 5
- Students ask at least four other students in the class their questions. They note their names and answers. Set a time limit for this activity.

### 6
- Students work in pairs. They collate their results and summarise their findings in writing. They should start their summary as in the example.
- Students report their findings to the class.
- Discuss the findings with the class. Was anything particularly interesting or surprising?

## Revision activity

### Whose plans are they?
- Students write three sentences on a clean piece of paper about their plans for the future. They should use the verbs they have practised in this unit. They shouldn't write their name on the paper.
- Collect the pieces of paper in a hat or a container of some kind. Mix them up.
- Individual students pick out a piece of paper and read it out. The class guesses who has written it.

# Extra practice

Students complete the Extra practice material on page 25 either in class, or for homework.

## Extra Practice answers

**1**
| | | | | | |
|---|---|---|---|---|---|
| 1 | painter | 6 | historian | 11 | trainer |
| 2 | teacher | 7 | doctor | 12 | composer |
| 3 | physicist | 8 | psychologist | 13 | linguist |
| 4 | statistician | 9 | dancer | 14 | journalist |
| 5 | solicitor | 10 | pharmacist | 15 | accountant |

Extra job: physiotherapist

**2**
1 What do you intend to do after you finish this course?
2 When is your next class due to start?
3 What would you like to do in the future?
4 Do you expect to get married soon?
5 Where do you hope you'll spend your next holiday?

**3** (individual answers)

**4**
| | | | |
|---|---|---|---|
| 1 | grew up | 5 | looking around |
| 2 | end up | 6 | take off |
| 3 | set up | 7 | move on |
| 4 | get into | | |

# References

Grammar reference: Coursebook page 27
Wordlist: Coursebook page 28
Photocopiable resources: Teacher's Book pages 94–95
Test: Teacher's Book pages 127–128

# CD-ROM

Unit 4 Life changes
Language exercise: Cherry Tree College future
Vocabulary activity: Career advice
CEF style activity: I can discuss the main ideas in a text
Game: Swamp disaster

Before starting this unit, ask students to read the Grammar reference on pages 26–27 and study the Wordlist on page 28 in the Coursebook.

## Ideas for preparation

- Dice and counters for the *Wordbuster* game (see Vocabulary Ex 2 p43)
- Video or radio recording of a chat show (see Speaking Ex 1 p44)
- Small prizes for the winners of the best chat show (see Speaking Ex 1 p44)

## Warmer

- Ask: *How often do you watch TV? What sort of programmes do you usually watch? Do you listen to radio programmes?*

## Lead-in

**1**

- Ask students to open their books on page 18. Read out the questions. Check that students understand the word *chat show* (a talk show where a presenter / host interviews guests).
- Discuss the questions with the class.

## Language study

**1**

- Read the instructions with the class.
- Students work in pairs. They think of six questions for Megan Robinson and Johnny Wade and write them down.

**2**

- 🔘 **12** Explain the task.
- Students listen. They compare their questions from Ex 1 with Paul Logan's questions.
- Ask: *Were any of your questions the same as Paul Logan's?*

**3**

- Read out the questions and check that students understand them.
- Students listen again and answer the questions.
- Students compare their answers with a partner.
- Check the answers with the class.

## Answers

1 From conversations he overhears in pubs, bars and on the bus, and from people's mobile phone conversations.
2 Next week.
3 The singles tournament in Melbourne.
4 Very badly, he can't hit the ball.
5 Before lunch.
6 What she can and can't eat.
7 Take a short break and then get back into training for the grass court season.
8 Fed up.

**4**

- Explain the task.
- Students work individually and complete the sentences.
- Students check their answers in Listening script 12 on page 31.
- Check the answers with the class. Discuss any problems. Refer students to the Grammar reference pages on pages 26–27 if necessary.

## Answers

1 listening
2 by far the funniest
3 due to start
4 usually train, doing
5 a bit lighter
6 to have

## Listening script 12

(P = Paul Logan; M = Megan Robinson; J = Johnny Wade)

P: … So Johnny, where did you find the inspiration for your new TV series?

J: I create a lot of characters from conversations I overhear in pubs and bars and on the bus. I also love listening to people's conversations on mobile phones. After listening to them I always make a note of what they said.

P: Well, I guess we'll all have to be careful about what we say on the phone in case Johnny's around. The reviews say that your new series is by far the funniest new show this year, and we're all looking forward to seeing it. It's due to start next week. Ladies and gentlemen – Johnny Wade. Our next guest in the studio is Megan Robinson. For years we've gone without winning a major tennis title. Now we have someone who's tipped to win Wimbledon one day. She's just won her first singles tournament in Melbourne. It's the Maria Sharapova of British tennis, Megan Robinson. Is this the first time that you two have met?

M: Yes it is.

J: Yeah, but I watched your final in Melbourne on TV and thought you were fantastic. Your tennis was pretty good too.

M: Oh thanks Johnny.

P: Er, right Megan, many congratulations on your recent success. What was that like?

M: Well it was by far the biggest tournament I've ever been in. There are some strong players out there and there's always an

element of luck, really, so on the day, in the final I was just a
bit luckier than my opponent.

J: Not true, not true.

P: Yeah, well it's a fantastic achievement at the age of 18. Do
you play Johnny?

J: Well, I've tried occasionally but I can't hit the ball. Maybe I'd
better have some lessons. How about it Megan?

M: Mmm. Technique is the most important thing. I could give
you a few tips if you like …

P: But you must have a tough training schedule which keeps you
busy?

M: Yeah, I usually train for a couple of hours with my coach in
the mornings before doing an hour in the gym to build up my
strength. After that I try to have a light lunch and then have
a bit of a knock about with my doubles partner. Then finally I
go for a jog for about 30 minutes. It's tough but I enjoy it.

J: Wow, what a woman!

P: What about your lifestyle though, that must have a downside?

M: I suppose the worst thing is what I can and can't eat. I really
need to be a bit lighter than I am at the moment. It would
make me faster on court.

J: But you're gorgeous as you are!

P: All right. So, what happens next for you?

M: I intend to have a short break, maybe a week or so and then I
hope to get right back into training ready for the grass court
season which is coming up.

J: Say Megan, I've got an idea for a series about tennis players.
Maybe we could get together so you could fill me in on some
background.

M: I'm sure I could. I've got some spare time at the moment …

P: Well tonight I've been talking to …

J: Hang on I've got a pen somewhere. Yeah, here it is. What's
your phone number?

P: Megan Robinson

M: Its 0203 …

P: … and Johnny Wade

J: Do you like Italian food? There's this great little place I know
near …

P: Time for another record I think. Here's the latest release from
…

## 5

- Look at the pictures with the class. Ask: *What sort of
story is this?* (a love / romantic story), *Does it have a
happy ending?* (yes).
- Students work individually. They look at the pictures
and complete the story.
- Students compare their ideas with a partner.
- Check the answers with the class. Ask individual
students to read out their answers.

### Possible answers
1  While they were dancing, Paul asked Julie for her
   telephone number.
2  After Paul got home, he phoned Julie.
3  Earlier she had bought a new dress.
4  Afterwards, they talked for a long time.
5  He intends to ask her to marry him.

## 6

- Explain the task. Revise the words in the box by asking
students to provide a short example sentence for each
one.
- Students work individually. They write a short story,
including at least four of the words in the box. They
should underline these words.
- Students swap their story with a partner. They read
their partner's story and comment on it.
- Check students' stories. Make sure they have used the
words correctly. Discuss any recurring errors.

# Vocabulary

## 1

- Tell students they are going to play two vocabulary
games. The first game is a guessing game with a
partner, called the *Five minute challenge.*
- Students work in pairs. Student A looks at page 29 and
student B looks at page 32. They both read the rules for
the game. Check they understand that the letter next to
each clue is the first letter of the answer.
- Start the clock. Students begin writing the answers to
the clues.
- Call 'stop' after five minutes. Students check their
partner's answers and count up their points. (The
maximum number of points possible is 24.)
- Compare the results of the class. Ask: *Who got more than
ten points? More than 15? More than 20?* Students raise
their hands. Finally, ask: *How many did you get?*
- Present the winner.

## 2

- Tell students they are now going to play a board game
called *Wordbuster.*
- Look at the picture of a dice and counters with the
class. Ask: *What is this?* (a dice), *What are these?*
(counters).
- Students read the 'How to play' rules and look at the
categories. Check that students have understood
everything.
- Students work in groups of 2–4 players. They play the
game.
- Note who is the quickest winner. While students are
waiting for others to finish, they can make lists of words
in the categories.

# Song

## 1

- Look at the photos of the two men with the class. Say:
*These men are Burt Bacharach and Hal David. What are
the men holding? What is behind them? Who do you think
they are? Why are they famous?*
- Students read the factfile about Burt Bacharach and
Hal David and answer the questions.
- Check the answers with the class.

**Answers**

1   They write songs for famous singers.
2   In 1958.
3   Over fifty.
4   At least five.

**2**

- 🔘 **13** Tell students they are going to listen to the song *I say a little prayer for you*. Ask: *Do you know this song? Who is the singer in the photo?* (Aretha Franklin).
- Look at the words in the box with the class. Check that students understand them all.
- Students listen to the song and read the words. They choose the best words in the box to describe how the woman in the song feels. Tell students to pay attention to the music as well the words when they listen.
- Check the answers with the class. Encourage students to give reasons for their answers.

**Possible answers**

cheerful (because she loves the man she's singing about)
hopeful (that they will always be together)

**3**

- Read the statements with the class. Check that students understand them.
- Students read the words of the song and decide if the statements are true or false, underlining the words which support their answers.
- Check the answers with the class.

**Answers**

1   False (Before I put on my make up I say a little prayer for you)
2   True (wondering what dress to wear)
3   True (To live without you would only mean heartache for me)
4   True (I run for the bus)
5   False (At work I just take time)
6   False (For me there is no one but you)

**4**

- Read out the question.
- Students offer advice. Ask: *Why do you say that?*
- To finish, play the song again and invite the braver students to sing along.

**Possible answers**

Get a life! Stop thinking about a man all the time.
Stop wasting time at work or you'll lose your job.
Good luck! People don't find true love very often.

# Speaking: a chat show interview

**1**

- Look at the photo with the class. Ask: *Do you know this show? Do you like it?*
- Tell students they are going to create a chat show interview in groups of three.
- If you have a video or a radio recording of a chat show, play this to the students.
- Students read the instructions carefully.
- Check that students have understood the instructions. Go through the three steps quickly with the class.
- In groups of three, students complete the celebrity role cards for two guests and the question card for the host.
- Students practise their show once or twice. If you have other rooms available, it would be better for students to do this in separate rooms.
- Students act out their chat show to the class.
- Take a vote on the best show by asking for a show of hands and, if possible, award a small prize.

# References

Module 1 test: Teacher's Book pages 129–131

# UNIT 1
# Family ties

| Topic | Language study | Vocabulary | Main skills |
|---|---|---|---|
| • Can your birth order change your personality?<br>• Networks (Family and friends) | • Talking about the past and present (past simple and present perfect) | • Describing character | • **Reading:** summarising key information<br>• **Listening:** completing a network diagram<br>• **Speaking:** describing family and friend networks |

## Learning aims

- Can talk about the past and present
- Can describe character
- Can describe relationships with family and friends

### Ideas for preparation

- A photo of your family showing you and your brothers or sisters or you and your parents (see Ex 1 p45)
- Ask students to bring in pictures of their families (see Ex 1 p45)
- Pictures of people from magazines (see Optional activity p48)

### Warmer

- Tell students the next topic is about family and friends. Write on the board: *Blood is thicker than water*. Ask: *What do you think this saying means?* (family members are more important than friends).
- Discuss the saying with the class. Ask: *Do you agree or disagree with this? Why?*

## Lead-in

**1**

- Ask students to open their books on page 34. Students look at the picture. Ask: *How would you describe the family members? Would you like to be part of this family?*
- If possible, show students a photo of your family and tell them about your brothers or sisters. If students have bought in pictures of their family, ask them to show the class.
- Read the statements with the class. Check any problematic vocabulary such as *strict, left out*.
- Students work with a partner and discuss the statements.
- Ask some students to report their ideas to the class.

**2**

- Read out the question. Discuss it with the class. Make a list of the best and worst things on the board.

### Optional activity

**Family words web**

- Write the word *parents* in the middle of the board as the start of a word web. Draw lines to the words *brother* and *sister*.
- Ask: *If your parents end their marriage legally, what are they?* (divorced), *If one of your parents gets married again, what do you call your new parent?* (stepmother / stepfather), *If they have another child, what relationship is that child to you?* (half brother / half sister). Add the words to the web so that the relationship is clear.
- Continue to add words and extend the web with the class. Other possibilities: stepbrother / stepsister, brother-in-law / sister-in-law, parents-in-law.

## Reading

**1**

- 🔊 **14** Say: *Look at the title of the article on page 35*. Ask: *What do you think birth order is?*
- Read out the questions and check that students understand them.
- Students read the text and answer the questions.
- Check the answers with the class.

### Answers

1 Your place in the family: whether you're the oldest, middle, youngest, or an only child.
2 It has a significant influence on your personality, and how you relate to your family.
3 Because they are quite independent and often feel they don't have a role in the family.
4 Because they have the same desires and approach to life, and they often have the same problems.
5 It helps you to understand your relationships with your family and other people. In business, it can also help you to negotiate with clients more successfully.

**2**

- Read out the paragraph headings.
- Students match the headings to the correct paragraphs. Tell them to look for key words in the paragraphs to help them and underline them.
- Check the answers with the class. Ask students which words helped them to decide.

**Answers**

a 2   b 3   c 4   d 1

## 3

- Ask students to read the statements and check that they understand them.
- Students decide if the statements are true or false without reading the text again. They explain why the false ones aren't correct.
- Students compare their answers with a partner. They can check in the text if they have different answers.
- Check the answers with the class.

**Answers**

1 False (Birth order has a significant influence on your personality)
2 False (Oldest children are obedient, they obey rules)
3 True
4 False (They are sociable, they like being with other people)
5 True
6 True
7 True

## 4

- Students find words and phrases for the definitions. They should check that the word is the same word class as that in the definition, and that the definition fits the context.
- Check the answers with the class.

**Answers**

| 1 | claim | 3 | a rebel | 5 | approach |
| 2 | status conscious | 4 | conventional | 6 | negotiate |

## 5

- Ask individual students to read out the descriptions in the boxes.
- Students match the boxes to the correct child.
- Check the answers with the class.

**Answers**

Box 1: only child          Box 3: middle child
Box 2: oldest child        Box 4: youngest child

## 6

- Students read the summary descriptions in Ex 5 again and decide if the birth order theory fits them. Then they decide if their brothers or sisters fit these descriptions.
- Students work in pairs. They discuss their ideas.
- Do a quick survey in the class. Ask: *How many of you think that the birth order theory is true?*

---

**Optional activity**

**Famous people's birth order**

- Write a list of famous people on the board. You can use the ones below or do some research on the famous people from Module 1, Unit 2.
- Ask: *Do you think that these people are the oldest, middle or youngest child, or an only child?* Students discuss in groups according to the birth order theory.
- Students report their ideas back to the class. Do these examples prove or disprove the theory?

<u>Possible famous people</u>

Charles Darwin, scientist: middle child – fifth of 6 children (risk taker)
Robbie Williams, singer: only child (motivated)
George W. Bush, politician: first child (high achiever, parent-pleaser)
Princess Diana: middle child (insecure)
Jim Carrey, comedian and actor: youngest child (sociable, entertainer)

# Language study

## Talking about the past and present

## Past simple and present perfect

## 1

- Ask individual students: *Did you have a good day yesterday? What happened? What did you do?* Then ask: *Have you had a good day so far today? What have you just done?*
- Students read the example sentences and answer the questions.
- Check the answers with the class. Show the use of the present perfect on the board using a timeline (see Grammar reference p58).
- Ask: *Can you give me more examples of the simple past and the present perfect?* Write the examples on the board in two columns. Correct any wrong examples before you write them down and discuss errors with students.
- Briefly revise the formation of the present perfect.

**Answers**

1 b
2 a
3 b (has affected)
4 a (wanted)
5 a (when I was a child)

## Optional activity

### Perfect participle quiz

- Divide the class into two teams, A and B.
- Read out the list of infinitives below, one by one, to Team A. They have to say the correct participle before you read out the next infinitive.
  <u>Alternatively</u>, if you would like to focus on spelling, one student runs to the board and writes the participle. Say the verbs fairly quickly. Accept corrections if they come from the same student.
- Read out the Team B list.
- If the score is equal, read out a tiebreaker. The quickest team to say the participle is the winner!
- Alternative for large classes: Divide the class into several teams. Read out all the infinitives and ask the teams to write the answers. Then read out the answers: teams check each other's answers.

<u>Team A list</u>

1 go (gone)   2 be (been)   3 take (taken)   4 influence (influenced)   5 feel (felt)   6 escape (escaped) 7 become (became)   8 think (thought)   9 ride (ridden)   10 draw (drawn)

<u>Team B list</u>

1 fly (flown)   2 come (come)   3 see (seen)   4 make (made)   5 forget (forgotten)   6 help (helped) 7 learn (learnt / learned)   8 explain (explained) 9 speak (spoken)   10 write (written) Tiebreaker: choose (chosen)

## 2

- Read out the time words in the box.
- Students work in pairs. They decide if the time words or phrases go with the past simple, the present perfect or both.
- Check the answers with the class. Write lists on the board. Ask students to give examples for the time words which can be used with both tenses.
- Ask students to read the Grammar reference on page 58 if necessary.

### Answers

<u>Past simple</u>

always   for (two days)   last year   never two weeks ago   when I was a child

<u>Present perfect</u>

always   ever   just   never   since   for (two days)

<u>Both</u>

always   for (two days)   never

## Optional activity

### Write it down

- Say: *I'm going to read out a paragraph at normal speed. You have to write down as many words as you can – but you won't be able to write down everything. I'm only going to read the paragraph once, so listen carefully.* Check that students understand the task.
- Read out the text below at normal (but not fast) speed. Students write as much as they can.
- Students work in pairs. They compare their versions and complete them further, paying particular attention to time phrases and tenses.
- Each pair joins another pair. Again, they compare their versions and complete them further.
- Reconstruct the text on the board with the class.

<u>Text</u>

I've always had a good relationship with my family. When I was four, my parents got divorced and both my parents got married again soon afterwards. Until I was fifteen, I lived with my mother for one week and then my father for one week. I had two families and two rooms in different houses. It was difficult sometimes, but I've never regretted it. Four years ago my father moved to the USA, so since then I've lived with my mother. But a year ago I met a great guy and we've just found a flat together. I'm moving out next week.

## 3

- Explain the task.
- Students work individually. They complete the sentences with the correct form of the verbs.
- Students compare their answers with a partner.
- Check the answers with the class. Ask students why the tense is used.

### Answers

1   behaved, did, told
2   didn't play, haven't seen
3   've lived
4   've just come back, had
5   've never visited

## 4

- Explain the task.
- Students discuss whether the sentences in Ex 3 are true for them.
- Each student tells the class one thing about their partner.

# Vocabulary

## Describing character

### 1

- Ask: *Can you remember the descriptions for birth order? How were you described?* Write a few adjectives on the board. Ask students for definitions.

- Look at the words in the box with the class. Practise the correct pronunciation and word stress by reading in chorus and individually. Point out that in compound adjectives with -ed, the stress is usually on the second word (unless the first word is emphasised or contrasted): bad-<u>tempered</u>, narrow-<u>minded</u>.
- Students match the adjectives to the correct definitions.
- Check the answers with the class.

### Answers
| | | |
|---|---|---|
| 1 reliable | 4 arrogant | 7 generous |
| 2 affectionate | 5 sociable | 8 bad-tempered |
| 3 insensitive | 6 narrow-minded | |

## 2

- Ask: *Which words in Ex 1 are positive? Which are negative?* Write two headings on the board. Put the adjectives in two lists with the class. Encourage students to discuss the answers if they have different opinions.
- Ask: *What other character adjectives do you know?* Students suggest adjectives and assign them to the correct list.

### Answers
<u>Positive</u>
affectionate    generous    reliable    sociable
<u>Negative</u>
arrogant    bad-tempered    insensitive    narrow-minded

---

### Optional activity

**Prefix quiz**
- Remind students they can make opposites by adding a negative prefix to an adjective, for example: *reliable – unreliable.*
- Write prefixes -un, -in, -im, and -dis on the board.
- Say: *We're going to do a prefix quiz.* Divide the class into two teams. Ask students to make cards with the prefixes on the board.
- Say: *I am going to read out a list of adjectives. Each student has to hold up the correct prefix to make a word with the opposite meaning. Your team will get a point for each correct card. The team with the most points is the winner.*
<u>Adjectives</u>
sociable (unsociable), sensitive (insensitive), helpful (unhelpful), obedient (disobedient), sincere (insincere), patient (impatient), fair (unfair), loyal (disloyal), kind (unkind), honest (dishonest), mature (immature), tolerant (intolerant)

---

## 3

- Explain the task. Refer students back to the list of adjectives in Ex 1.
- Read through the situations with the class. Ask: *Which behaviour is positive and which is negative?* (Positive: 4, 5, 6 Negative: 1, 2, 3)

---

- Students work in pairs and describe the behaviour of the people in the situations, using the adjectives in Ex 1.
- Check the answers with the class. Students may have more than one adjective for each situation.

### Answers
| | | |
|---|---|---|
| 1 insensitive | 3 arrogant | 5 reliable |
| 2 bad-tempered | 4 generous | 6 sociable |

---

### Optional activity

**First impressions**
- Show students pictures of people cut out from magazines. Ask: *What do you think they are like?* Encourage students to describe them using adjectives from this section. They should give reasons for their answers.
- Ask: *Do you think first impressions are always correct? Is appearance a good indicator of personality?* Discuss with the class.

---

# Listening and speaking

## Networks

### 1
- Ask: *Do you have lots of friends or just one or two special friends? What do you do with your friends?*
- Look at Dave's network with the class. Explain that the nearer the name in the network, the closer the relationship with that person.
- Point out the pronunciation of *close* (with voiceless 's' /kləʊs/).
- Read out the questions and check the answers with the class.

### Answers
Closest friend: Katy
Furthest family member: Liz

### 2
- 🔘 **15** Read out the task instructions and the names in the box.
- Students listen and complete Amanda's network.
- Students listen again and check their answers.
- Check the answers with the class.

### Answers
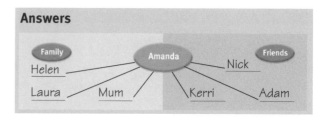

### Listening script 15
(Amanda)
People closest to me? Well the two people that I'm closest to are my mum, and my boyfriend, Nick. Mum and I have been through some difficult times, especially when I was about 14 to 15, but now that I don't live at home any more we get on much better.

I always talk things through with her. I met Nick about a year ago. He's a very affectionate and generous person, but he's also really good fun to be with. The only thing is that I don't see him as often as I want to because he lives about an hour away from me. I spend a lot of time with my friend, Kerri. We see each other at least twice a week. We've known each other since we were 10 and totally share the same sense of humour. She's one of those people that are always cheerful and look on the bright side of life. I used to be quite close to a boy called Adam, who I met at university, but about six months ago he met his girlfriend and now he ignores his old friends and spends all his time with her. When we go out together he tries to phone his girlfriend every five minutes, which is really irritating.

My family? Well I've got two sisters, but the age gap between us is so big that I'm not really close to either of them. I see Helen about once every six months, but Laura's very selfish. She only cares about herself and her career. She didn't even call me when I broke my leg and was in hospital for a week! How insensitive is that?

## 3
- Students work individually. They draw their own family and friends network with at least six people, using the networks in Ex 1 and Ex 2 as models.

## 4
- Explain the task.
- Students work in pairs. They show their partner their network from Ex 3 and explain it.
- Ask students to tell the class who their partner's closest friends and family members are.

---

### Revision activity

**Consequences**
- Explain that students are going to write a short story in five stages. If possible, ask students to work in groups of five.
- Do an example together with the class. On a piece of large paper write:

A girl's name and a short description. (eg *Anna, a sociable, affectionate student)*
*MET*
A boy's name and a short description (eg *Fred, a stupid football player)*
*AT*
A place (eg *the local pizza restaurant)*
*WHAT SHE SAID*
A sentence with the present perfect. (*She said, 'I've just had breakfast')*
*WHAT HE SAID*
A sentence with the present perfect. (*He said, 'I've never been to America')*
*AND SO*
Something they did together (*They went swimming*)

- Students start their own consequences by writing the name of a girl at the top, folding their paper and passing it to the person next to them.
- When all the stories are complete, students unfold the papers and read out their stories to their group.
- Groups read out their favourite story to the class.
- The class votes for the best story.

---

## Extra practice

Students complete the Extra practice material on page 54 either in class, or for homework.

### Extra practice answers

**1**
| | | | |
|---|---|---|---|
| 1 | affectionate | 6 | arrogant |
| 2 | selfish | 7 | generous |
| 3 | bad-tempered | 8 | sociable |
| 4 | cautious | 9 | insensitive |
| 5 | narrow-minded | 10 | reliable |

**2** (individual answers)

**3**
| Verb | Past simple | Present perfect |
|---|---|---|
| affect | affected | have / has affected |
| arrive | arrived | have / has arrived |
| behave | behaved | have / has behaved |
| go | went | have / has gone |
| hear | heard | have / has heard |
| know | knew | have / has known |
| live | lived | have / has lived |
| make | made | have / has made |
| play | played | have / has played |
| see | saw | have / has seen |
| tell | told | have / has told |
| visit | visited | have / has visited |

**4**
| | | | |
|---|---|---|---|
| 1 | met | 7 | told |
| 2 | have been | 8 | was |
| 3 | was | 9 | never thought |
| 4 | complained | 10 | have just heard |
| 5 | hated | 11 | has always wanted |
| 6 | has never liked | | |

## References

Grammar reference: Coursebook page 58
Wordlist: Coursebook page 60
Photocopiable resources: Teacher's Book pages 96–97
Test: Teacher's Book pages 132–133

## CD-ROM

Unit 1 Family ties
Language exercise: Family history
Vocabulary activity: Drama series characters
CEF-linked exercise: I can describe family and friendship networks
Game: Witch's pot

# UNIT 2
# Neighbours

| Topic | Language study | Vocabulary | Main skills |
|---|---|---|---|
| • Neighbours from hell<br>• My housemates are slobs! | • Degrees of politeness and formality | • Describing antisocial behaviour | • **Listening:** checking predictions<br>• **Reading:** listing particular information<br>• **Pronunciation:** sentence stress<br>• **Speaking:** resolving disputes<br>• **Writing:** a note |

## Learning aims

- Can understand degrees of politeness and formality
- Can describe antisocial behaviour
- Can resolve disputes

### Ideas for preparation
- A blank tape and tape recorder (see Optional activity p51)
- Objects to prompt ideas about problem housemates (eg cleaning products, CDs, telephone, an electricity bill) (see Ex 1 p53)
- Slips of paper with requests and replies (see Revision activity p54)

### Warmer
- Write these verbs and nouns on the board in two lists.

| Verbs | Nouns |
|---|---|
| 1 water | a the weather |
| 2 have | b the hedge |
| 3 chat about | c noise |
| 4 feed | d coffee |
| 5 empty | e the flowers |
| 6 cut | f the post box |
| 7 complain about | g an argument |
| 8 drink | h the cat |

- Students match the nouns to the verbs.
- Check the answers with the class.

**Answers**
1e   2g   3a   4h   5f   6b   7c   8d

- Ask: *Look at these verb–noun phrases. What do you think the topic of the next unit is?* (neighbours), *How do all these things relate to neighbours?*

## Lead-in

**1**
- Ask students to open their books on page 38. Say: *We're going to talk about neighbours. What are good neighbours like? How do they behave?* Elicit ideas and make notes on the board. Ask: *What do bad neighbours do?* Elicit further ideas and make notes.
- Read out the task and the information students should include. Check that students understand *get on with* (have a good relationship with).

- Students work in pairs and describe their neighbours, including the information in the list.
- Ask: *Who has got really good neighbours? Who has got terrible neighbours?*

# Neighbours from hell

## Listening and vocabulary

**1**
- 🔘 **16** Say: *You are going to listen to a news item about neighbours. Look at the title of this section. Is the news item going to be about good or bad neighbours?*
- Explain the task. Encourage students to use dictionaries to find the meaning of unknown words.
- Students work individually or in pairs. They match the words to the correct definitions, paying attention to the word class of the words.
- Check the answers with the class.

**Answers**
1e   2g   3d   4f   5c   6b   7a

### Optional activity

**Word grammar**
- Write these sentences on the board.
1 to sue somebody _____ something
2 to be obsessed _____ something
3 to have a conviction _____ something
4 to be convicted _____ something
5 to suffer harassment / to be harassed _____ somebody
6 to be _____ probation
7 to swear _____ somebody
- Students find the missing prepositions using their dictionary.
- Check the answers with the class.

**Answers**
1 for   2 by   3 for   4 of   5 by   6 on   7 at

- Tell students that when looking up a word in a dictionary or noting down vocabulary, they should always check how the word is used (eg with a particular verb or preposition). They should learn the word as a phrase with these parts.

## 2

- Explain the task.
- Students work in pairs. They look at the photo and the words in Ex 1 and predict what the story will be about.
- Discuss students' ideas with the class and write them on the board.

## 3

- Explain the task.
- Students listen to the news story and check their predictions.
- Ask: *What is the news story about?*
- Look at students' predictions on the board from Ex 2 and check if they were correct.

## 4

- Read out the list of behaviour points and check that students understand them.
- Students listen to the news story again and tick the correct points.
- Students check their answers with a partner.
- Check the answers with the class.

### Answers
1, 2 and 5 are correct

### Listening script 16

(NR = Newsreader; Mrs T = Mrs Thomas)

NR:   ... the hospital which cost £100 million was opened two months ahead of schedule. A Brighton couple are considering suing their neighbour for reducing the value of their home by £50,000. Robert and Annabel Thomas are unable to sell their £200,000, three-bedroom house as a result of a five-year campaign of hate by their neighbour, Dennis Rogers.

Mrs T: One day, Mr Rogers suddenly became obsessed with making our lives a living nightmare. From then on it hasn't stopped. Every day there is something. He throws bits of old rubbish into our garden and shouts and swears at us and our visitors – it's so embarrassing ... and frightening.

NR:   The problem began when Mr Rogers became annoyed with the Thomases over a party they held five years ago. Apparently Mr Rogers became angry because guests parked cars in front of his house and he claimed that loud music went on until 3 o'clock in the morning. The Thomases say that they had informed all their neighbours in advance of their party and that no-one complained at the time. They say that since then Mr Rogers has shouted insults over the fence and thrown old beds, chairs, bicycles, and bits of wood into their garden. They also claim that every summer he has continuously sung the song 'Happy Hippo' whenever he sees Mrs Thomas sunbathing in the garden.  In December, the Thomases took Mr Rogers to court and he was convicted of harassment. Mr Rogers had to pay compensation of £1,000 and was given 18 months probation. The Thomases have now decided they want to move away from their neighbour from hell. However, there is a problem. Legally house sellers have to inform potential buyers of any disputes with neighbours and the Thomases have been warned by their estate agent that the conflict has decreased the value of their house by £50,000. According to Mr and Mrs Thomas several potential buyers have lost interest after being told about Mr Rogers.

Mrs T: Who would want to live next to someone like Mr Rogers? I don't think he's normal. He needs treatment. You never know what he's going to do next. If we lose money on the

sale of our house we will definitely sue Mr Rogers. We have suffered enough. Why should we have to pay for his unreasonable behaviour?

NR:   And now the weather: After a chilly start, there will be sunny intervals ...

## 5

- Read out the questions and check that students understand them.
- Students work in pairs and answer the questions.
- Students listen again and check their answers.
- Check the answers with the class. Refer students to Listening script 16 on page 62 if necessary.

### Answers
1   The Thomases had a party: their guests parked in front of Mr Rogers house and the Thomases played loud music until 3 o'clock in the morning.
2   In December the Thomases took Mr Rogers to court and he was convicted of harassment.
3   The Thomases have to inform potential buyers about disputes with their neigbours.
4   They're planning to sue Mr Rogers.

## 6

- Read out the questions and check that students understand them.
- Students work in groups and discuss the questions.
- Discuss the questions with the class.

### Optional activity

#### A news report

- Students work in groups of three. Each group decides if there was a happy ending or not to the Rogers–Thomas case. They then write a short news report reporting the final outcome of the case. The story should include quotes from Mr Rogers and Mrs Thomas, as in the listening.
- Each group presents their report with the students taking the parts of the reporter, Mr Thomas and Mrs Thomas. Record each group on tape.
- Play back the tapes to the class. Students vote for the best news report.

# Language study

## Degrees of politeness and formality

### 1

- Ask: *Have you ever had an argument with anybody in English? What was the problem?*
- Explain that conflict can often be avoided by using polite requests and apologies. Look at the examples of requests. Ask: *Which is the most polite and formal? Which is the most informal?*

### Answers
Most polite and formal: I was wondering if you could move your car.
Most informal: Can you move your car?

## 2

- Read out the question to the class.
- Students look at the examples and underline the verbs.
- Check the answer with the class.

### Answer
Past tense verb forms

## 3

- Read out the question to the class. Check that students understand *introductory phrase* (a phrase that starts a sentence and introduces the main idea).
- Check the answer with the class and write it on the board. Say: *This is now an indirect question, so the word order is not inverted as in direct questions.*

### Answer
I was wondering if …

## 4

- Read out the question and the example sentences.
- Check the answer with the class. They should give a reason for their answer.
- Read the note with students. Emphasise that good friends will feel insulted by too much politeness.
- Students read the Grammar reference on page 59 if necessary.

### Answer
The first sentence (The speaker uses 'I'm very sorry, but …' as an introductory phrase of apology)

## 5

- Explain the task and check students understand it.
- Students work in pairs. They decide which questions or statements in each group are the most and least polite.
- Check the answers with the class.

### Answers
Order of politeness from most to least polite:

| | | |
|---|---|---|
| 1  a – c – b | 3  a – b – c | 5  b – c – a |
| 2  c – b – a | 4  a – b – c | |

### Optional activity

**What was the situation?**

- Look at the sentences in Ex 5 again with students. Ask: *Who do you think the speaker is? Who is the speaker speaking to? And in what situation?* Discuss sentence 1a as an example (eg an older person speaking to a neighbour he doesn't know very well, but who is having a loud party).
- Divide the class into five groups. Each group discusses one set of questions and statements in Ex 5. They decide who the speaker is, who he / she is speaking to and what the situation is. Encourage them to develop a story behind the situation.
- Students present their ideas to the class.

## 6

- Read the situations with the class and check that students understand them.
- Students work in pairs. They discuss what they would say in each situation and make a note of their ideas.
- Discuss each situation with the class. Ask students for their ideas and write all the suggestions on the board. Check that the level of formality is right and correct sentences with the class if necessary.

### Possible answers
1  Could you open the window, please?
2  Can you stop swearing!
3  I'm very sorry, but I've got a terrible headache. Could you play your guitar a bit more quietly?
4  I'm very sorry, but I'd like to read my book.

### Optional activity

**Mini role-play**

- Students work in pairs. They choose one of the situations in Ex 6 and expand it into a mini role-play by adding dialogue before and after the sentences discussed.
- Students act out their role-play to the class.

## 7

- Look at the phrases in the box with the class. Explain that *I apologise for* … is usually used to apologise after an event and is fairly formal. *I'm afraid that* … has the same meaning as *I'm sorry but* …, but *I'm afraid that* … is more formal. *Well, actually* … is used to correct wrong information (eg *Are you 18 yet? Well, actually I'm 25!*)
- Students complete the sentences with the correct phrases. They should check that the phrase fits the meaning and grammatical pattern of the sentence. Point out that some sentences can have different answers, depending on the meaning and the person spoken to.
- Check the answers with the class. Discuss why different phrases are possible.

### Answers
1  I'm afraid that / I'm sorry but / Well, actually
2  I apologise for (+ -*ing*)
3  I'm afraid that / I'm sorry that / Well actually
4  I apologise for (+ -*ing*)
5  I'm afraid that / I'm sorry, but / Well, actually
6  I'm afraid that / I'm sorry, but / Well, actually

# We don't get on

## Reading

**Background information**

**Student accommodation**

In Britain, universities and colleges provide accommodation in 'halls of residence' (university rooms on campus) for first (and sometimes final) year students. Students in other years usually have to find private accommodation – a room in a private house or a rented flat. Flat sharing with other students is very common.

In the USA, most students live on campus in 'dormitories' or 'residence halls'. Students usually have to share a room. Some small colleges or some colleges in large cities do not have any on-campus accommodation and so these students usually live together in shared flats.

In Australia, students can choose between living on campus in self-catering halls of residence or apartments or in residence colleges where meals are provided. A popular option for foreign students is 'homestay' and 'farmstay', where students live with an Australian family in their home or on their farm.

**1**

- 🔊 **17** Say: *You're going to read an article about housemates who don't get on. What problems do you think there could be between flatmates?* Discuss a few ideas, using the photo of the washing up as a first prompt. If possible, show students objects to prompt them such as cleaning products, CDs, telephone, an electricity bill.
- Ask a student to read the introduction to the article. Students look at the photos and write the names of the housemates underneath the photos.
- Read out the questions with the class and check that students understand them.
- Students work individually. They read the article and write the answers to the questions.
- Students check their answers with a partner.
- Check the answers with the class.

> **Answers**
> 1 Matt.
> 2 Somebody who is very untidy.
> 3 Jenny, because she often has loud friends round and never buys bread, tea or coffee.
> 4 Carl.
> 5 Carl and Jenny.

**2**

- Read out the task and the example with the class. Ask students to find *untidy* in the article. Students find another adjective for Carl as a further example.
- Students underline adjectives of character in the text and make lists for each person.
- Check the answers with the class. Write the names as headings on the board and ask individual students to read out their list for one person.

- Ask students to find adjectives for other personality traits in the article not described with an adjective (eg Carl: *great sense of humour* = amusing; Jenny: *doesn't buy bread* = mean; Matt: *takes life too seriously* = serious, *complains the whole time* = dissatisfied).

> **Answers**
> Carl: untidy, generous, unreliable, forgetful
> Jenny: untidy, selfish, cheerful
> Matt: bad-tempered, bossy, mature

**3**

- Ask: *What jobs around the house does each of the students do?* Make lists on the board under the correct names with the class.
- Ask: *Do you think this is a fair division of work? What do you think of rotas / timetables for housework in a shared house?*

> **Answers**
> Matt: tidies up, does the shopping
> Jenny: defrosts the fridge, does the hoovering
> Carl: takes the rubbish out

**4**

- Read out the questions and check that students understand them.
- Students work in pairs and discuss the questions.
- Students report back to the class.

## Pronunciation and speaking

**1**

- 🔊 **18** Explain that in a sentence some words are stressed and some unstressed. Ask: *Which word is stressed in the sentence 'I'm a teacher'?* (teacher). Check that all students heard this correctly.
- Explain the task.
- Students listen to the example.
- Students listen to the two sentences and underline the stressed words.
- Students listen again and check their answers.
- Check the answers with the class. Ask: *Are content words or grammatical words stressed in these sentences?* Point out that it's content words that are usually stressed, but grammatical words can also be stressed in certain sentences if their meaning is being emphasised or contrasted (eg I always do <u>your</u> share of the housework).

> **Answers**
> 1 I do your share housework
> 2 take rubbish tonight
>
> In these sentences the content words are stressed.
> In sentence 1, 'your' is also stressed for emphasis.

**2**

- 🔘 **19** Look at the sentences with the class and check that they understand them.
- Students listen and repeat the sentences.
- Ask individual students to say the sentences without the CD.

**3**

- Explain that students are going to do a role-play about sharing a house. Students read the task. Check that they understand it.
- Students work in pairs. They choose a complaint and plan their role-play using the information given.

**4**

- In their pairs from Ex 3, students role-play their conversation and discuss their complaint.

**5**

- Students work in pairs. Explain that they are going to do a communication activity, where student A and student B have different information. Students decide if they are A or B and read the instructions.
- Students A and B in each pair read their information on the correct page. Explain that some sentences may seem quite strange! Students should check any new words in their dictionary. Give individual help as necessary.
- Students hold their conversation in pairs.
- Ask: *Did you manage to use all the sentences? Did you enjoy the conversation?*
- Invite one or two pairs of students who used all the phrases to act out their conversation to the rest of the class.

## Writing

**1**

- Read out and explain the task.
- Students write their note including the information given and not exceeding 150 words.
- Students read their partner's note. Are both partners happy with the result? If not, why?
- Discuss any recurring errors with the class.

## Extra practice

Students complete the Extra practice material on page 55 either in class, or for homework.

**Extra practice answers**

**1**  1  sue, harassment
   2  obsessed
   3  swear / scream
   4  conviction, probation

**2**  1  untidy         3  polite      5  forgetful
   2  bad-tempered    4  bossy       6  mature

**3**  1  I was wondering if you could turn off that radio, please?
   2  I'm afraid that you can't park your car here.
   3  I'd be very grateful if you could give me your telephone number.
   4  Would you mind lending me a pen?
   5  I'm sorry but you're too late for the film.
   6  I apologise for forgetting to post your letter.
   7  Could you explain why you're so bad-tempered today?
   8  Is it alright if I leave early today?

**4**  1  round     4  out     7  on
   2  with      5  up      8  out
   3  up        6  out     9  round

## References

Grammar reference: Coursebook page 59
Wordlist: Coursebook page 60
Photocopiable resources: Teacher's Book pages 98–99
Test: Teacher's Book pages 134–135

## CD-ROM

Unit 2 Neighbours
Language exercise: Show me respect!
Vocabulary activity: The worst boss I ever had
CEF-linked exercise: I can describe antisocial behaviour
Game: The neighbourhood

---

**Revision activity**

**Requests and replies**
- Prepare slips of paper with enough polite requests and replies for your class.

Examples

| | |
|---|---|
| Would you help me take my boots off? | No chance! Your feet smell! |
| I apologise for being late. | Don't worry, we haven't started yet. |
| Would you mind telling your dog to go away? | He's just being friendly. |
| Will you stop making that noise! | I'm only practising for the school concert. |
| I'm sorry, but would you stop blowing smoke in my face? | You can't have a cigarette in peace anywhere! |
| Can you explain the homework to me? | Sorry, I don't understand it either. |

- Mix up the pieces of paper. Students take one each.
- Students mingle around the classroom, making their requests and giving replies until they have found their partner.
- Each pair reads out their requests and replies. They say if the request is polite and formal or informal.

# Partners

| Topic | Language study | Vocabulary | Main skills |
|---|---|---|---|
| • Is it worth it? (Relationship issues) <br> • A radio programme (Phone-in) | • Giving advice (*should, might think about, If I were you*) | • Phrasal verbs: relationships | • **Reading:** identifying key information <br> • **Listening:** identifying details of a problem <br> • **Speaking:** discussing and agreeing advice <br> • **Writing:** an advice email |

## Learning aims

- Can give advice
- Can use phrasal verbs for relationships
- Can discuss relationship problems

### Ideas for preparation

- Magazine pictures of people with a good mix of ages and 'types' (see Optional activity p55)
- Props such as a headphones and mike for a radio programme role-play (see Optional activity p57)

### Warmer

- Write the phrase *Love is …* on the board. Ask students if they know the *Love is …* cartoons. Write an example: *Love is … missing a big football game on TV to spend a romantic evening with your partner.* Students work in groups and write down five more phrases to complete the sentence.
- Ask groups to read out their phrases. Which one does the class like the best?
- Ask: *What is love? How does love change when people become older?*

## Lead-in

**1**

- Ask students to open their books on page 42. Students look at the picture of the penguins. Ask: *Can animals and birds have a 'relationship' with a partner? How are relationships between human partners different?*
- Read out the statements and check that students understand them.
- Students work in small groups and discuss the statements.
- Discuss the questions with the class. Encourage students to agree and disagree with each other.

**2**

- Read out the task. Discuss the questions of time, money and space with the class. Ask: *What do you think is most likely to cause problems in a relationship when the couple are in their late teens, early twenties? What do you think is most likely to be a problem among older couples with children and busy jobs?*

### Optional activity

**Whose partner?**

- Put up various pictures of people (from magazines) on the board. Number them. If you wish, you can write information such as jobs, personality etc next to each picture.
- Students work in pairs. They discuss which people they think would make the best partners and why.
- One pair of students puts the pictures on the board together to make couples. Ask if other students agree or disagree and why. Discuss if age is important in a relationship, whether it is a good idea to have the same job and if students think it is true that 'opposites attract'.

## Is it worth it?

### Reading

**1**

- 🎧 **20** Look at the photo of the couple with the class. Say: *Rob and Sara are partners. What do you think their relationship is like? What does this title tell us about Rob and Sara's relationship?*
- Read out the task. Check that students understand the verb *to get on.*
- Students read the interviews and answer the questions. Students can also listen to the interviews on CD while they read. Alternatively, divide the class into pairs. Each student reads one of the interviews and then exchanges information with their partner.
- Check the answers with the class.

### Answers

Rob and Sara get on really well most of the time. They have the same sense of humour. They also have some common hobbies like reading books and listening to music.
Problems: Sara doesn't think Rob is serious about her because he is going away with friends instead of coming to her birthday party. He also wants her to go on holiday with his friends and she wants to go alone with him. Rob thinks Sara doesn't give him enough space – he wants to spend time with his friends and doesn't like Sara's friends at their flat. Rob also thinks Sara is terrible with money and is worried about having a joint bank account with her.

**2**

- Read out the questions and check that students understand them.
- Students work in pairs. They discuss the questions.
- Discuss the questions with the class.

---

**Optional activity**

**My ideal partner**

- Students work in pairs. They describe their ideal partner to the other student: appearance, personality, hobbies and interests. The other student draws a picture.
- Students swap roles.
- Pairs of students show each other their pictures and comment on them.

---

# Vocabulary

## Phrasal verbs: relationships

**1**

- Explain the task.
- Students work individually or in pairs. They match the phrasal verbs to the correct definitions. Encourage students to use dictionaries to find the meaning of unknown words.
- Check the answers with the class.

---

**Answers**

1 e    2 c    3 a    4 b    5 i    6 h    7 d    8 f    9 g

---

**2**

- Read out the task. Find the second sentence with the class.
- Students work in pairs. They put the statements in the correct order.
- Check the answers with the class.

---

**Answers**

2 d    3 j    4 f    5 c    6 e    7 h    8 a    9 g    10 i

---

**Optional activity**

**Phrasal verb memory**

- Students work in pairs. They take a piece of paper and cut or tear it into 18 pieces.
- One student writes the verbs in Ex 1 on the pieces of paper, the other student writes the particles in Ex 1.
- Students mix up the pieces of paper. They put them face down on the desk. Set a time limit for the activity.
- Students take turns to turn over two pieces of paper. If the pieces of paper make a phrasal verb, students keep them. If not, they should try and remember where the words are. The winner is the student with the most phrasal verbs when there are no more left on the table.

---

**3**

- Read the instructions with the class and check that students understand them.
- Students work in pairs. Each student writes down the words in the list.
- Students swap lists with their partner and prepare a short story. Encourage them to use the phrasal verbs in Ex 1.
- Students tell their stories to the class.
- The class votes for the best story.

---

# Listening

## A radio programme

**1**

- 🔘 **21** Look at the photo. Ask: *What is Arabella Doyle's job?* (radio presenter), *Would you like to work in radio or TV? Have you ever phoned in to a radio programme?*
- Read the statements with the class and check that they understand them.
- Students listen to the programme and decide if the statements are true or false.
- Students compare their answers with a partner.
- Check the answers with the class. If the class seems to find the task fairly easy, ask them to explain the false questions.

---

**Answers**

1 False (It's a problem / advice show)
2 True
3 False (She has called to ask for advice because her husband feels awkward about it)
4 True
5 False (They have a full-time nanny)
6 True
7 False (Arabella advises Jane to give her husband money before they go out)
8 True

---

**Listening script 21**

(AD = Arabella Doyle; J = Jane)

AD:   Welcome to today's Dr Arabella Doyle Show. I'm Arabella Doyle and I'm here to help ordinary people with everyday problems. Our first caller is Jane on line 1. Hello, Jane.

J:   Hello Dr Doyle. I'd just like to say that I'm a great fan of your show. I think it's wonderful how you help people.

AD:   Thanks for that Jane. Now, what's your problem?

J:   Well, my problem is this. My husband feels less of a man because I earn more than him and pay for everything.

AD:   I see and do you resent having to pay for everything?

J:   Oh no, I'm not complaining about him. That's not the case at all – I'm perfectly happy to do it. I don't mind that he doesn't contribute, but he feels awkward about it.

AD:   How do you deal with this situation?

J:   Well, if we're having a meal in a restaurant with friends, I sometimes pass him money under the table so that he can be seen to pay in public. Other times I pretend to win cash prizes so that we can go on holiday without him feeling guilty.

AD:   Do you have children?

J:   Yes, we've two children under five.

AD:   So, does your husband stay at home to look after them?

J:   No, he works. But his salary is very low.

AD:   So, he isn't a house husband.

J:   No we have a full-time nanny. I've often wondered if he'd feel better being a house husband, but I'm not at all sure that it's the right thing to suggest.

AD:   Hmm, Jane, if your husband wanted to be at home all day with the kids, he'd offer. You shouldn't push him into being a house husband.

J:   I see. What would you do, if you were me?

AD:   Well Jane, the truth is that if I were you I'd probably do what you're doing. You know, although most men have accepted aspects of equality with women, many still make an exception when it comes to money matters. The rule seems to be that your salary is a wonderful thing to be celebrated and enjoyed, as long as you don't earn more than he does.

J:   That doesn't make dealing with my problems any easier, though!

AD:   True, but you might think about giving your husband money before you go out rather than in the restaurant. That would make it easier. Or you could open a joint bank account for his salary and either all or part of yours. What do you think about that?

J:   Well it's certainly something to consider. Thank you so much for your advice.

AD:   Thank you Jane and good luck. Now for our next caller …

## 2
- Read out the questions and discuss them with the class.

### Optional activity

**Phrases for giving advice**
- This activity is preparation for the Language study on page 44. Say: *You are going to listen to the radio programme again for the phrases Arabella uses to give advice.*
- Students listen to the radio programme again and read Listening script 21 on page 62. They underline the phrases used to give advice.
- Check the answers with the class and write the phrases on the board. Do not discuss the grammar of the phrases at this point.

**Answers**

You shouldn't push …        You might think about …
If I were you, I'd …          You could …

# Language study

## Giving advice

### 1
- Read out the questions.
- Check the answers with the class.

**Answers**

Sentence a. *Could* is used to give advice

## 2
- Look at the phrases in the example sentences with the class. Students say which phrases are followed by the -ing form and which phrases are followed by the infinitive.
- Ask students if they can think of advice for Jane's husband using these structures (eg *You shouldn't be embarrassed about your wife's salary*).
- Read the note with the students.

**Answers**

*You should / shouldn't* and *If I were you, I'd* are followed by the infinitive
*You might think about* is followed by the -ing form

## 3
- Explain the task.
- Students work in pairs and think of advice for the three friends. They make notes of their ideas.
- Write three headings on the board: *lose weight, give up smoking, save money.* Ask students for their ideas and write them on the board. Encourage them to comment on each other's ideas.

### Optional activity

**Role-play**
- Students work in pairs. They role-play one of the situations in Ex 3. One student explains their problem and the other student gives advice.
- The student with the problem should refuse all the advice for various (flimsy) reasons (eg: *You should stop eating chocolate. – I can't live without chocolate, it makes me happy! You should eat more fruit. – I can't, I'm allergic to fruit!*).
- One pair of students for each situation (weight, smoking, money) acts out their role-play to the class.

# Speaking

### 1
- Read out the problems in speech bubbles and check that students understand them.
- Students work in groups. They discuss the advice they would give to each problem.

### 2
- A student sits at the front of the class and reads out problem 1. Each group (from Ex 1) offers him / her a piece of advice. The student decides which piece of advice is best.
- Do the same for the other situations with different students.

# Writing

### 1
- Look at the picture with the class. Ask. *How do you usually communicate with your friends? Do you prefer to send emails, write letters or talk on the phone? Who do you usually send emails to?*

- Look at the address and subject of the email. Ask: *Who is it from?* (Dave Blackwell) *What is it about?* (a problem – he is replying to a request for advice).
- Read the questions and check that students understand them.
- Students read the email and answer the questions.
- Check the answers with the class.

**Answers**
1 They are friends.
2 He's a student.
3 Dave doesn't know whether to visit his parents in Sweden without his girlfriend or to stay with his girlfriend.
4 She's going to be 20.

**2**
- Look at the structure of the email with the class. Read out the questions and check the answers.

**Answers**
a second paragraph  b first paragraph  c third paragraph

**Optional activity**

**Informal letter phrases**
- Write the definitions below on the board.
- Students find informal phrases in the email which match the definitions.
- Check the answers with the class. Revise other ways of starting and ending informal letters and emails.
1 I really enjoyed seeing you
2 To tell the truth
3 Another thing I wanted to mention is …
4 Look after yourself
5 Hope we'll meet again shortly
6 With good wishes

**Answers**
1 It was great to meet up       4 Take care
2 To be honest …                5 See you soon
3 By the way …                  6 All the best

**3**
- Read the task with the class and check that students understand it.
- Students write their emails giving advice about an imaginary problem. Remind them to use Simon's email as a model and the phrases for giving advice on page 44.

**4**
- Students work in pairs. They show their partner their email. Their partner guesses what the problem is by asking questions.
- Students say what they think of their partner's advice.

**Revision activities**

**1) Wordlist activity**
- Revise vocabulary from this unit by choosing a Wordlist activity from Teaching tips 'Reviewing and revising' on pages 21–22.

**2) Radio advice programme**
- Tell the class that they are going to present their own radio advice programme.
- Pick two students as the presenters. Ask them to sit behind a table at the front of the class with a mike and headphones as props if available. They should revise phrases for giving advice. They should also look at Listening script 21 on page 62 and note down ways of starting the programme and talking to callers. The other students are callers. They should think of an interesting / silly / complicated problem to call in about. The can use their own mobile phones as props.
- Students act out their programme. Make notes of any major errors for discussion and correction later.
- Briefly discuss the programme. Ask: *What was the most interesting problem? Were the presenters helpful?*
- Write on the board and discuss any recurring errors with the class.

# Extra practice

Students complete the Extra practice material on page 56 either in class, or for homework.

**Extra practice answers**
1  1  hit it off            4  going out
   2  got together          5  let down
   3  break up              6  get on

2  1  broke up with         5  let down
   2  got together          6  gets on with
   3  hit it off            7  has taken over
   4  fell out              8  go out with

3  (individual answers)

# References

Grammar reference: Coursebook page 59
Wordlist: Coursebook page 60
Photocopiable resources: Teacher's Book pages 100–101
Test: Teacher's Book pages 136–137

# CD-ROM

Unit 3 Partners
Language exercise: Take my advice
Vocabulary activity: Soap opera update
CEF-linked exercise: I can use phrasal verbs for relationships
Game: Swamp disaster

# Troubles

| Topic | Language study | Vocabulary | Main skills |
|---|---|---|---|
| • The twelfth day of July (Conflict in Northern Ireland)<br>• How do you deal with conflict? | • Verb + preposition | • Describing conflict<br>• Ways of dealing with conflict | • **Reading:** understanding a timeline; identifying key information<br>• **Speaking:** discussing the results of a questionnaire<br>• **Listening:** completing lists |

## Learning aims

- Can recognise verb + preposition patterns
- Can discuss ways of dealing with conflict
- Can understand vocabulary to describe conflict

### Ideas for preparation
- Map or large atlas showing Ireland (see Warmer p59)
- Pictures of Ireland showing beautiful countryside, coast, Dublin, Derry, pubs, musicians etc (see Warmer p59)
- Cards with verbs and prepositions (see Optional activity p62)
- Photocopied questionnaires (see Revision activity p63)

### Background information
The island of Ireland is divided into the Republic of Ireland (*Eire* in Irish) and Northern Island which is a part of the United Kingdom.
<u>Republic of Ireland</u>
– area: 69, 895 km$^2$; 80% of the island
– population: about 4 million
– capital: Dublin
– religion: 92% Roman Catholic, 2.5% Protestant (+ other religions / no religion)
– official languages: Irish (Gaelic) and English
– currency: euro
– economy: booming; mainly industry and services
<u>Northern Ireland</u>
–14,150km$^2$, 20 % of the island
– population: about 1.5 million
– capital: Belfast
– religion: 40% Catholic, 36% Protestant (+ other religions / no religion)
– language: English
– currency: pound sterling
<u>Island</u> (known as the 'Emerald Isle' because it is so green)
– cool, damp climate
– flat farmland, hilly coasts, little forest
– culture: music (traditional music, U2, Enya, the Cranberries, the Pogues), pubs, literature (Oscar Wilde, James Joyce, George Bernard Shaw, WB Yeats, Samuel Beckett), Guiness, whiskey …

### Warmer
- Tell students the next topic is Ireland. Ask: *What do you know about Ireland?* Write any correct information students give you on the board. Elaborate as necessary (see Background information), but don't go into detail about the conflict between the Unionists and Nationalists as this is the topic of the unit. If possible, show students the location of Ireland on a map, and pictures from magazines and brochures showing Ireland and aspects of Irish culture.

Ideas for prompts:
| | |
|---|---|
| – nationality | – economy |
| – language | – landscape |
| – currency | – weather |
| – capital cities | – culture |

## Lead-in

### Background information
The south of Ireland declared its independence from the UK in 1916, provoking the Anglo-Irish War from 1919 to mid 1921. In 1921 the Anglo-Irish Treaty gave independence to 21 counties, while six chose not to join. The south of Ireland finally became a republic in 1948.

The 'Troubles' started in Northern Ireland in the late sixties with rioting and street fighting between Catholics and Protestants. Britain sent troops to Belfast and Derry in 1969. The nationalists (mainly Catholics in favour of a united independent Ireland), including the Irish Republican Army (IRA) and the unionists (mainly protestants loyal to the United Kingdom) began a campaign of violence, and terrorism also spread to Britain. In 1994 a ceasefire was negotiated, but terrorist acts have continued.

In 1998 there was an agreement (The Good Friday Agreement) which shared power between Protestants and Catholics in Northern Ireland and also gave the Republic of Ireland the chance to be involved in political affairs in Northern Ireland. The agreement devolved some political power from London to a Northern Ireland Assembly. The agreement was approved in two referendums by 71% in Northern Ireland and 94% in the Republic. The Unionists David Trimble, former First minister of the Assembly, and John Hume received the 1998 Nobel Peace Prize for their part in the agreement. However, one condition of the agreement was that all organisations stop criminal activity and give up their weapons and unfortunately, this did not happen. In 2002, therefore, the assembly was suspended and Northern Ireland came under direct rule from London again. In July 2005, the IRA implemented the agreement to lay down their weapons in favour of a political solution, as did one of the nationalist groups.

**1**

- Ask students to open their books on page 46. Students look at the map. Ask: *Which number is the Republic of Ireland?* (4), *Which is Northern Ireland?* (5).
- Read out the task and the places in the box.
- Students work in pairs. They match the places to the numbers on the map.
- Check the answers with the class. Check students have understood the difference between Great Britain, the United Kingdom and the British Isles. Ask: *Which countries make up Great Britain?* (England, Scotland, Wales), *What is the United Kingdom?* (Great Britain + Northern Ireland), *What are the British Isles?* (the United Kingdom + the Republic of Ireland).

**Answers**

| | |
|---|---|
| British Isles: 7 | Republic of Ireland: 4 |
| England: 1 | Scotland: 2 |
| Great Britain: 8 | Wales: 3 |
| Northern Ireland: 5 | United Kingdom: 6 |

**Optional activity**

**British Isles quiz**

- Test your students' knowledge! Students work in pairs or small groups. Read out the questions below.
- Students write the answers.
- Check the answers with the class.
1 Which country has the biggest population: England, Scotland or Wales? (England)
2 What is the capital of Scotland? (Edinburgh)
3 Which language is spoken in Wales in addition to English? (Welsh)
4 What is the name of the sea between Wales and Ireland? (Irish Sea)
5 In what part of England is London? (south-east)
6 What currency do people use in Scotland? (pound sterling)
7 Are people in Great Britain mostly Protestants or Catholics? (Protestants)
8 Which sport are Welsh people famous for? (rugby)
9 What is the name of Ireland's saint? (St. Patrick)
10 What is the name of the British flag? (the Union Jack)

**2**

- Look at the timeline of Ireland with students, section by section. Ask individual students to read out sections. Check comprehension of each section by asking brief content questions or asking students to explain the photos. (Note: the photo in section 5 shows Britain's Prime Minister Tony Blair and the Republic of Ireland's head of government Bertie Ahern.)
- Ask: *What are the two cultural and political communities in Northern Ireland? Why have there been political differences and violence between them?*

**Answers**

The two main communities are the Protestants (often unionists) and the Catholics (usually nationalists). There has been conflict between them about political rights and jobs in Northern Ireland.

# Reading and vocabulary

**1**

- 🎧 **22** Tell students they are going to read an extract from a book called the *The twelfth day of July*. Ask: *What does the title of this book refer to?* (the day in 1690 when King William of England defeated the Irish army – see section two in the timeline).
- Students read the introduction to the extract. Explain that the author Joan Lingard is Scottish but lived in Belfast from age 2 to 18.
- Read out the questions to the class.
- Students work individually. They read the extract, using the glossary to help them, and answer the questions.
- Check the answers with the class. Ask students to give reasons for their answer in 2.

**Answers**

1 They painted graffiti on a wall with a picture of King William of England on it.
2 Catholic (nationalist).

**2**

- Ask students to read the statements and check they understand them.
- Students read the text and decide if the statements are true or false.
- Check the answers with the class.

**Answers**

1 False (There was grudging admiration in his voice)
2 True
3 True
4 False (She tells him to stick with his own)
5 True
6 True

**3**

- Read out the questions with the class and check that students understand them.
- Students work in pairs and discuss the questions.
- Discuss the questions with the class.

## Possible answers

1  His mother thinks that it's stupid to fight and that there has been enough fighting in Northern Ireland already. His father seems to agree, although he admires his son for protesting.
2  His father. His mother is more forceful but he doesn't seem to respect her – he thinks women don't understand the situation.
3  Neither particularly happy nor unhappy. Kevin argues with Brede. Mrs McCoy doesn't really try to understand her children and dominates her husband. But there are no strong arguments.

### Optional activity

**What next for Kevin?**

- Ask: *What do you think happens to Kevin later in the story?* As a class, students speculate how Kevin's life continues.
- Explain that Kevin and his friends get to know a Protestant girl called Sadie and her friends. Initially they hate each other because of their political opinions, but at the end of the story, after a fight in which Brede is seriously hurt, they become friends. *The twelfth day of July* is the first part of a trilogy; in the next two books (*Across the Barricades* and *Into Exile*) Kevin and Sadie fall in love, leave Belfast for London and get married.

## 4

- Explain the task. Check that students understand it.
- Students work individually or in pairs. They find words and phrases in the lines given that match the definitions. Encourage them to use dictionaries to find the meaning of unknown words.
- Check the answers with the class.

### Answers

| | | |
|---|---|---|
| 1  grudging | 3  attacked | 5  startled |
| 2  daft | 4  slap on | 6  stick with your own |

## 5

- Look at the incomplete sentences with the class.
- Students complete the sentences so that they are true for them.
- Ask individual students to read out a sentence each. Correct any errors.

# Language study

## Verb + preposition

### 1

- Read the first explanation out to the class.
- Students look at the example sentences and explain the difference in meaning (*He talked to his son* = he had a conversation with him; *He talked about his son* = his conversation concerned his son).
- Read the explanations in the three categories with the class.

- Students work individually. They match the pairs of example sentences with the correct categories.
- Students compare their answers with a partner.
- Check the answers with the class. Discuss the differences in meaning in 2 and 3 (*dream of* = have a dream about; *never dream of doing something* = never even consider doing something).

### Answers

1 b     2 c     3 a

### 2

- Explain the task. Make sure students understand it.
- Students find the verbs in 1–5 in the text on page 47. They note down the preposition.
- Check the answers with the class.

### Answers

1 about     2 on     3 for     4 about     5 to

### 3

- Explain the task.
- Students work individually or in pairs. They make sentences using the correct preposition for the verb and the correct object. Tell them to refer back to the prepositions in Ex 2 if they have difficulties.
- Check the answers with the class. Write the sentences on the board.

### Answers

I think everyone should read about the political history of their country.
I would fight for my country if necessary.
I never pass my homework answers to my classmates.
I never speak to strangers.
I sometimes waste money on clothes that I don't need.
I believe people should protest about things they think are wrong.

### 4

- Read the instructions with the class. Refer to the correct sentences on the board from Ex 3. Number them.
- Do an example with the class. Ask a student: *Do you think everybody should read about the political history of your country? Which statements are true for you?*
- Students work in pairs. They discuss which of the statements are true for them.
- Students report back to the class.

### 5

- Explain the task.
- Students complete the sentences with the correct preposition or prepositions.
- Check the answers with the class.

### Answers

| | | |
|---|---|---|
| 1  to | 3  about | 5  to |
| 2  with, for | 4  about | 6  on |

## Optional activity

**Verb and preposition snap**

- Students work in small groups. Give each group a set of verbs and prepositions (those used in the exercises on page 48 and other common ones) on pieces of card.
- Students put the verbs and prepositions in two piles. Set a time limit. They take it in turns to turn over the cards. If the verb and preposition can be used together, the student shouts snap. If they can make a sentence with the verb and preposition, they can keep the cards.
- Students continue, mixing up the cards again as necessary. Call time. The winner is the student with the most cards.

# Speaking and listening

## Optional activity

**It makes me so angry!**

- Students write down five things that make them angry.
- Students work in pairs. They swap lists and discuss them, asking questions as necessary.
- Students report back to the class about their partner. Is there anything that makes several people in the class angry?

**1**

- Look at the questionnaire. Say: *You are going to complete a magazine questionnaire. Do you think this type of questionnaire is accurate?*
- Students work with a partner. They read out the questions to their partner and note down their answers. Encourage them to check the meaning of unknown words in the dictionary.

**2**

- Students count up their answers and decide if they are mostly a, b or c.

**3**

- Students work with a partner and discuss the potential meaning of their answers.

**4**

- 🔘 **23** Explain the task. Check that students understand the word *response* (reaction).
- Students listen and make notes.
- Students compare their answers with a partner.
- Check the answers with the class.

**Answers**

1 passive   2 aggressive   3 assertive

## Listening script 23

(Specialist)

Obviously conflict is an important part of human relations, it's something we can't avoid when we have dealings with other people. Other people inevitably do things that upset us, or say things that we disagree with. So it's not a question of avoiding conflict; it's how we deal with it that's important for our long term mental health.

There are basically three reactions. Firstly you can do nothing. This is what I call the 'passive' response. This may sometimes be a good idea, for example if you're faced with a difficult or violent person. Doing nothing may help him or her to calm down. But there are lots of disadvantages if you always avoid conflict, too. You are saying 'my opinion is not worth anything' and some people will take advantage of what they see as your weakness.

The second reaction to conflict is the complete opposite. This is what I call the aggressive response. It's what happens when you can't control your emotions, and you begin to shout at people or dominate them in other ways. It's useful in emergencies, or when you need to give orders, but most of the time it's just unkind or selfish. Most people don't like being bullied, and you will end up losing your friends if you are not careful.

The third reaction to conflict is to face up to it and put forward your own views. It's called the assertive response. If you have a viewpoint, and you feel strongly about what someone has done, you have the right to let the other person know how you feel, and so has the other person. If you and the other person can both walk away from the discussion feeling that you have put forward your points of view and listened to the other person's views, then you will both feel good about it, and there won't be bad feelings between you. I can't think of any disadvantages to the assertive response.

**5**

-  **23** Read out the task.
- Students listen again and write down the advantages and disadvantages of each method.
- Check the answers with the class. Refer students to Listening script 23 on pages 62–63 if necessary.

**Answers**

| | Advantages | Disadvantages |
|---|---|---|
| 1 | calms down violent or difficult people | says your opinion is not worth anything; people may take advantage of your weakness |
| 2 | useful in emergencies | people don't like being bullied: you'll lose your friends |
| 3 | both people feel they have been listened to: no bad feelings | none |

**6**

- Read out the task. Tell students to look back at the questionnaire.
- Students match responses 1, 2 and 3 with a, b and c in the questionnaire.
- Check the answers with the class.
- Ask: *According to your questionnaire answers, which type are you? Do you think the description fits?*

**Answers**

1 b (passive)   2 a (aggressive)   3c (assertive)

---

### Optional activity

**Another question**

- Students work in pairs. They write another question for the conflict questionnaire. The three answers should reflect the three types of response they discussed in Ex 6.
- Students swap their questions with another pair. They answer the question. Do their answers fit the pattern of their other answers (a, b or c)?

## 7

- Discuss the specialist's views with the class. Ask: *Do you agree with what the specialist said? Are there any other advantages and disadvantages?*

---

### Revision activity

**Find someone who ...**

- Write the sentences below on the board.
- Divide the class into three groups: sentences 1–3, 4–6 and 7–9.
- Students walk around the class and ask other students their three questions, noting down the names of people who answer positively. Encourage them to ask further questions if they are interested.
- Groups collate their results.
- Each group reports back to the class. Students discuss the results.

Find someone who ...

1   ... has been on a demonstration to protest about something.
2   ... has dreamt of living in a different country.
3   ... has never had an argument with their best friend.
4   ... got into trouble at school.
5   ... has been to Ireland.
6   ... has recently persuaded someone to change their viewpoint.
7   ... often argued with their parents as a child.
8   ... has spoken to somebody with an Irish accent.
9   ... has apologised to someone in the last week.

## Extra practice

Students complete the Extra practice material on page 57 either in class, or for homework.

**Extra practice answers**

| 1 | 1a | about | 3a | to | 5a | with |
|---|----|-------|----|-----|-----|------|
| | 1b | to | 3b | for | 5b | to |
| | 2a | about | 4a | on | 6a | of / about |
| | 2b | of | 4b | at | 6b | of / about |

2   Nouns: emotion, health, hostility, influence
    Adjectives: assertive, grudging, sensible, suitable, unwilling

3   assertive, healthy, influential, sensible, suitable

| 4 | 1 | tension | 5 | hostility |
|---|---|---------|---|-----------|
| | 2 | face up to | 6 | avoid |
| | 3 | weakness | 7 | bully |
| | 4 | react | 8 | power |

| 5 | 1 | daft | 4 | grudging |
|---|---|------|---|----------|
| | 2 | stick with | 5 | influenced |
| | 3 | delighted / startled | 6 | placed |

## References

Grammar reference: Coursebook page 59
Wordlist: Coursebook page 60
Photocopiable resources: Teacher's Book pages 102–103
Test: Teacher's Book pages 138–139

## CD-ROM

Unit 4 Troubles
Language exercise: Road opposed
Vocabulary activity: The US Civil Rights Movement
CEF-linked exercise: I can read and complete a personality questionnaire
Game: Cats in hats

Before starting this unit, ask students to read the Grammar reference on pages 58–59 and study the Wordlist on page 60 in the Coursebook.

### Ideas for preparation
- Dice and counters for the *On the right track* game (see Language study Ex 1 p65)
- A small prize for the winner of the board game (see Language study Ex 1 p65)
- CDs of hit bands (see Ex 6 p66)

### Warmer
- Tell students they are going to revise the relationships module. Write the word *relationship* on the board.
- Students work in small groups and brainstorm all the things they associate with the word *relationship* (eg relationship collocations, types of relationships).
- With the class, make a mind map on the board around *relationship*. Discuss students' ideas.

## Lead-in

**1**
- Ask students to open their books on page 50. Read out the questions and check that students understand them.
- Students work in pairs or small groups and discuss the questions.
- Discuss the questions with the class.

## Vocabulary

**1**
- 🔘 **24** Ask students: *Are you good at remembering events in the past?*
- Explain the task. Read out the questions and check that students understand them.
- Students listen and answer the questions in note form.
- Students listen again and check their answers.
- Check the answers with the class. Write them on the board in two columns. Refer students to Listening script 24 on page 63 if necessary.

### Answers

| | Tony | Jacquie |
|---|---|---|
| 1 | 1981 | autumn 1982 |
| 2 | local conservation society meeting | historical society meeting |
| 3 | he gave a speech, she interrupted him | he gave a speech, she asked questions |
| 4 | can't remember, it might have been blue | jeans, denim jacket, horrible shiny orange shirt |
| 5 | thought she was wonderful, fell for her immediately | thought he was fun and lively, but too full of himself, a bit arrogant |
| 6 | took her and her friend home and got her number | he went home with her and her friend and he kissed her good night |
| 7 | can't remember | went out to dinner |

### Listening script 24
(I = Interviewer; T = Tony; J = Jackie)
I: Tony, can you remember when you first met Jacquie?
T: 1981.
I: 1981. Oh! You remember!
T: Yes.
I: And, where were you?
T: In north London.
I: What was going on?
T: It was a meeting of the local Conservation Society.
I: And were you both at the meeting?
T: Actually, it was more of a party than a meeting. But, yes, we were both there.
I: I see. And were you introduced to Jacquie?
T: Not quite. Erm ... I was one of the guest speakers. And I did my little speech, but she, she kept interrupting me, shouting out from the back of the room!
I: Can you remember what she was wearing?
T: No.
I: You can't?
T: Not at all.
I: Okay.
T: Though it might have been blue.
I: Oh it might have been blue? So, anyway, what were your first impressions?
T: Oh! I was over the moon. I thought she was wonderful!
I: So immediately, you fell for her.
T: Oh yes! Absolutely. Immediately.
I: And did you ask her out?
T: No, I think I asked if I could take her home.
I: Yes?
T: To which she replied 'Yes, but I've got my friend with me.' So I ended up taking her and her friend home.
I: Okay. And then you got her phone number, and ...
T: Yes, I can't remember quite how it happened after that. I must have got her phone number.
I: So after that you got in touch with her and then you went on a date?
T: Yes, but I can't remember where we went.

I: Alright. Well, I think I'm going to ask Jacquie what she remembers.

T: That could be interesting!

I: Jacquie I've been talking to Tony about how you met. Can you remember when that was?

J: It was autumn 1982.

I: And where were you?

J: I'd gone with a friend to a little gathering of the Historical Society. It was near where we lived.

I: And Tony was there too?

J: Yes.  It was supposed to be a party but then this man, Tony, started to give a speech.

I: About architecture?

J: Oh something like that. Anyway it just went on and on and he had to be stopped, so I started to ask him some questions.

I: And what happened then?

J: Well I think erm … when he eventually finished the speech he came up to me and erm … we were chatting.

I: Can you remember what he was wearing?

J: Oh good heavens! Erm … I'm pretty sure it was jeans and a denim jacket. I can remember the shirt, too. It was a horrible shiny orange thing.

I: And what did you think?

J: Well, he was fun and lively, but maybe a bit too full of himself, you know, a bit arrogant.

I: What happened after the party?

J: Well I do remember I was with my friend Stella and Tony came home with us. I think he kissed me good night. That was nice!

I: Did you go out on date after that?

J: Well, yes, the next evening in fact. We went out to dinner.

I: And that was that!

J: That was that!

**2**

- Read out the question. Students answer orally, comparing the information on the board.
- Ask: *Who do you think was giving the correct information? Do you think women are more observant than men? Are women better at remembering details of events?*

> **Answers**
> The time is different, the event is different and they had different views on Tony's speech. Tony can't remember some information.

**3**

- Read out the list of adjectives with the class. Ask individual students to read out an adjective each and say if it is positive or negative.
- Students work in small groups. They discuss the three characteristics which they would most like and dislike for their partner.
- One student from each group presents the results of their discussion to the class.

**4**

- Explain the task.
- Students complete the text with the correct form of the verbs in the box, paying attention to the particles that follow them.
- Check the answers with the class. Discuss any problems with meaning.

> **Answers**
> 1 hit
> 2 go
> 3 get
> 4 get
> 5 fell
> 6 broke
> 7 went
> 8 made
> 9 lets

# Language study

**1**

- Read the instructions for the game *On the right track* with the class. Point to the various things mentioned such as *counter, track, station* and show students where the words for the sentences are. Explain that one person in the group should note down the points (passengers) for each player on a piece of paper.
- Check that students understand the game before they begin. Repeat the instructions if necessary.
- Students work in small groups and play the game.
- Ask each group to present their winner to the class and say how many points they got. Find out who had the most points overall and, if possible, award a small prize to the winner/s.
- Ask students if they had any problems with the sentences. Answer any queries about the structures.

# Song

**1**

- Ask students: *What sort of music do you like? Do you like love songs? What's your favourite love song? Why?*
- Read out the task and the questions.
- Students work in pairs and discuss the questions.
- Discuss the questions with the class.

**2**

- Tell students they are going to work with a song called *When a man loves a woman* by Percy Sledge. Ask: *Do you know this song? Have you heard it before?*
- Explain the task. Look at the example with the class and check that students understand it.
- Students work individually or in pairs. They read the statements and find lines in the song that mean the same. Encourage them to use dictionaries to find the meaning of unknown words.
- Check the answers with the class. Students say the line number and read out the line of the song. Check any problematic vocabulary.

**Answers**
1  line 10–12
2  line 8
3  line 2
4  line 4
5  line 20–21
6  line 25
7  line 3
8  line 24

## 3

- Read out the task to the class. Point out that missing letters are usually indicated by an apostrophe in the word.
- Students work in pairs and find four words containing missing letters.
- Check the answers with the class. Ask: *What are the missing letters?* Point out that it is very common to shorten *-ing* to *-in* in everyday speech and in songs. *'Cause* is also a very common shortened form.

**Answers**
1
nothin' (line 2) = nothin**g**
tryin' (lines 9 + 15) = tryin**g**
lovin' (line 22) = lovin**g**
'cause (line 28) = **be**cause

- Students work in pairs to find missing words at the start of three sentences.
- Check the answers with the class. Ask: *What are the missing words?*

**Answers**
2
[He] can't keep his mind on nothin' else (line 2)
[He'll] turn his back on his best friend (line 6)
[He'll] spend his very last dime (line 8)

## 4

- Read out the questions and check that students understand them.
- 🔘 **25** Students listen to the song.
- Discuss the questions with the class. Encourage students to give reasons and examples to support their answers.

## 5

- Read out the questions and check that students understand them (eg the word *string* and the phrase *one hit wonder*).
- Students read the factfile and answer the questions.
- Check the answers with the class.

**Answers**
1  He was a nurse.
2  Some people call him 'the golden voice of soul'.
3  In the 1970s his popularity decreased but he still tours the world and makes records.
4  No, he thinks this isn't a fair description because he had other hits too.

## 6

- Read out the task.
- Students work in pairs. They make a list of pop stars who have produced a string of recent hits and a list of one hit wonders.
- Make two lists on the board with the class. For stars whose names you don't recognise, ask students to tell you something about their music or their hit songs. If you are a music fan, you could bring in CDs of famous songs, play them and ask students if they recognise or know anything about the singers (a pop compilation CD would be ideal).

# Speaking: preparing a dialogue

## 1

- Tell students they are going to write a dialogue, step by step. Go through each step with the students as follows.
- Students read about the characters (step 1). Check that they understand the descriptions.
- Students read about the situation (step 2). Check that they understand it.
- Students read the instructions for step 3. Check that they have understood that they will be writing several dialogues at once. Set a time limit for the writing.
- Students work in groups of four or five and write their dialogues. Give help with vocabulary and structures as necessary.
- Stop the writing phase. Students read the instructions for step 4.
- Students choose, check and practise their dialogue.
- Each group acts out its dialogue to the class. Encourage students to clap and cheer at the end of each dialogue.
- Briefly discuss the performances. What was good? What could have been better? Write on the board and discuss any recurring errors with the class.

# References

Module 2 test: Teacher's Book pages 140–142

# UNIT 1
# Crossing the line

| Topic | Language study | Vocabulary | Main skills |
|---|---|---|---|
| • Beckham 1, Ferguson 1 (Managing anger)<br>• Famous Olympic moments | • Describing past events (past simple, past continuous, past perfect) | • Discussing sport<br>• Sports events | • **Reading:** ordering events<br>• **Speaking:** responding to text; presenting an argument<br>• **Listening:** identifying key information<br>• **Writing:** an opinion letter |

Note: Use CD2 for listening material in this module.

## Learning aims

- Can describe past events
- Can use sports vocabulary and discuss sport
- Can present an argument

### Ideas for preparation
- Pictures of sporting stars from different sports (see Optional activity p67)
- Pictures of David Beckham and his wife (see Reading Ex 1 p67)

### Warmer
- Revise the names of sports. Individual students come to the front and mime sports. Encourage them to use their dictionaries and choose more unusual sports. The class guess the sport. Help them with vocabulary and write the names of the sports on the board.
- Look at the list on the board. Ask students if they can add more sports.
- Students sort the sports on the board into categories. Ask, for example: *Which sports use a ball? Which don't use any equipment? Which sports use a vehicle? Which are water sports? Which belong to athletics?*

## Lead-in

### 1
- Ask students to open their books on page 66. Read out the task and the questions. Check that students understand the word *professional* (playing sport for money). Ask: *What's the opposite of 'professional'?* (amateur /ˈæmətʃuə/).
- Students work in pairs and discuss the questions.
- Discuss questions 2 and 3 with the class.

### Optional activity

**Sports stars**
- Show students pictures of famous sports stars. Ask: *Who are they? What sport do they do?*
- Ask: *Which sports stars do you admire? Why?* Students talk about their favourite stars, explaining what sport they do, what they have achieved in that sport and why students admire them.
- Ask: *Do you think famous sports people deserve to earn so much money?*

## Reading

### Background information
Manchester United (also known as Man United or Man U) is one of the biggest and most famous English football clubs. Its stadium is at Old Trafford in Manchester.
(Sir) Alex Ferguson, a former Scottish football player and manager of Scottish football clubs, became manager of Manchester United in 1986. Under his successful management, Manchester United have won many major English and European championships.
David Beckham (born 1975 in London) is the captain of the English football team and currently plays for Real Madrid. David Beckham started his career with Manchester United in 1991 as a junior player. He stayed with the club until 2003 (just after the incident described in the reading text) when he left because of conflict with Alex Ferguson. David Beckham is married to Victoria Beckham, a former member of the successful 90s pop girl group *The Spice Girls*, and has three sons. The Beckhams are well known for their celebrity lifestyle and their interest in fashion. David Beckham is particularly famous for his changing hairstyles.

### 1
- Look at the photos on page 67 with the class. Ask: *Who are they?* (David Beckham and Alex Ferguson), *How does Alex Ferguson look in this photo?* (unhappy, dissatisfied), *What is the connection between them?* (David Beckham used to play for Manchester United), *Who does Beckham play for now?* (Real Madrid at January 2006), *What do you know about David Beckham? Why do you think he has become a superstar?* If possible, prompt students with pictures of David Beckham and his wife and children.

### 2
- 01 Tell students they are going to read an extract from David Beckham's autobiography *My Side*. Explain the task. Look at the events and check students understand them. Ask: *Who are Arsenal?* (a very successful North London football club).
- Students read the extract on page 67 and put the events in the correct order. They can listen to the article on CD.
- Check the answers with the class.

**Answers**
1 b   2 a   3 c   4 e   5 f   6 d

## 3

- Read the task with the class. Point out that the words to be explained are in bold in the text.
- Students work individually or in pairs. They match the words from the text to the definitions.
- Check the answers with the class.

**Answers**

1 c   2 e   3 f   4 b   5 a   6 d

## 4

- Students read the discussion questions. Check that they understand *circumstances, lose your temper, accused, cruel*.
- Students work in pairs and discuss the questions.
- Students report back to the class. Discuss if students generally lose their temper in the same circumstances.

---

**Optional activity**

**Angry incidents**

- Write these questions on the board: *Who was involved? What happened? What was the cause of the conflict? How was the incident resolved?*
- Students work in small groups. They take it in turn to describe angry incidents which involved themselves or which they witnessed, using the questions on the board. <u>Alternatively</u>, one student can ask the questions.
- Students in the group comment on the incidents, saying whether they would have reacted in the same way.

---

# Language study

## Describing past events

## 1

- Explain that you are going to look at the past simple, past perfect and past continuous tenses. Look at the examples with the class. Read out the first example and the description of use. Ask: *Which past tense form are the words in bold in?* (past continuous).
- Briefly revise the formation of the past continuous. Point out that the past continuous is often used for background events. Say: *Can you give me other examples of the past continuous?* Write them on the board.
- Do the same for the other two examples.

**Answers**

1 past continuous   2 past simple   3 past perfect

## 2

- Read out the task.
- Students think about the differences in meaning.
- Discuss the sentences with the class. To prompt students, ask: *Which event happened first? Was the event finished?* Draw time diagrams on the board to show the order and duration of events in each sentence.
- Students read the Grammar reference on page 90.

**Answers**

1 First event: David takes off his boots. Second event: Alex gets to the dressing room. The first event is not completed and still in progress when the second event starts.
2 First event: Alex gets to the dressing room. Second event: David takes off his boots. Both completed events.
3 First event: David takes off his boots. Second event: Alex gets to the dressing room. Both completed events.

---

**Optional activity**

**Headlines to sentences**

- Write these headlines on the board.
1 Jones scores while goalkeeper ties boot
2 Wright hits referee after red card
3 Crowd cheer naked man on pitch
4 Stadium closed due to police bomb discovery
5 Beckham scores, England win
- Students work in small groups and expand the headlines into full sentences reinserting articles, verbs and using the correct past tense.
- Check the answers with the class. Different answers are possible.

**Possible answers**

1 Jones scored while the goalkeeper was tying his boot.
2 Wright hit the referee after the referee had given him a red card.
3 The crowd cheered when a naked man came onto the pitch.
4 The stadium was closed because police had discovered a bomb.
5 Beckham scored and England won.

---

## 3

- Explain the task.
- Students complete the story using the correct tense.
- Check the answers with the class.

**Answers**

| | | | | | |
|---|---|---|---|---|---|
| 1 | played | 6 | had become | 11 | shouted |
| 2 | were walking | 7 | started | 12 | was happening |
| 3 | saw | 8 | hit | 13 | didn't come |
| 4 | were wearing | 9 | kicked | 14 | ran away |
| 5 | came | 10 | saw | | |

## 4

- Read out the questions and check that students understand them.
- Students work in pairs and discuss the questions.
- Ask some students to report back to the class.

# Great Olympic moments

## Vocabulary and listening

## 1

- Ask: *Do you enjoy watching the Olympic Games? Have the Olympic Games ever been held in your country? Do you think all the money spent on the Olympic Games is well spent – or is it a waste of money?*

- Look at the Olympic symbols with the class. Ask: *What sports do they represent?* Tell students to use the first letter as a clue. Complete the gaps with the class, writing the names of the sports on the board.

### Answers

| | | | | | |
|---|---|---|---|---|---|
| 1 | long jump | 4 | rowing | 6 | gymnastics |
| 2 | basketball | 5 | sailing | 7 | relay |
| 3 | javelin | | | | |

## 2

- 🔘 **02** Read out the task and the names of the athletes. Ask: *Do you recognise any of the names? Can you match the three top pictures to the correct names?* Encourage students to say or predict the Olympic events the sports people were famous in.
- Students listen and write the names of the events.
- Students compare their answers with a partner.
- Check the answers with the class.

### Answers

| | | | | | |
|---|---|---|---|---|---|
| 1 | rowing | 3 | marathon | 5 | 100 metres |
| 2 | gymnastics | 4 | 100 metres | | |

### Listening script 02

(S = Sarah; J = Jenny; B = Ben)

S: Oh look they're doing one of those ten most memorable sporting moments on the TV – this time with the Olympic Games.

J: The ten most memorable moments, crikey that's difficult, there are so many!

S: Yeah, you're supposed to phone in with your top three and then they select the top ten entries.

J: Shall we do it?

B: Yeah, I'm up for it. Who shall we start with?

J: Well, there's Steven Redgrave's fifth gold medal for rowing in five games; that was a pretty fantastic moment especially when you think he had been suffering from diabetes at the time up to his last one in Sydney.

B: Yes I remember staying up at night to watch that. Did you know he had to inject himself six times a day, every day … and still does I suppose.

S: Nadia Comaneci was one of my favourites; she was only 14 when she won three gold medals for gymnastics

J: I don't think 14 year olds should be allowed to take part in the Olympics. Think of the pressure. What sort of life is it for a child? I mean think of the training she must have had to do!

B: Anyway it wasn't really a great moment was it? I remember reading about this Italian marathon runner way back in 1908. Dorando Pietri was his name. Apparently he was inside the stadium some way in front of everyone else when he collapsed four times and got up each time. The last time he was helped across the line by two officials. He was disqualified, poor bloke, even though he hadn't asked for help.

J: Yes, I read that story recently. Apparently one of the officials who helped him was probably Arthur Conan Doyle, you know, the guy who wrote Sherlock Holmes.

B: Really? I didn't know that. But you are forgetting the best of all.

S: What's that?

B: The 100 metres in Seoul; it's such a dramatic story. It was really about the rivalry between two very different people. There was Carl Lewis, a great Olympian, rather arrogant, someone who never stopped talking, and Ben Johnson a dark, brooding figure who found it extremely difficult to face the media. They came head to head in the final and most people thought Lewis would win again. However, after an amazing start, Johnson won in 9.79 seconds, a world record which has never been beaten – and Canada went crazy with joy. And then news later that night that he'd been taking drugs. I'll never forget that … it was greatness and tragedy all in one event.

J: And Lewis got the gold didn't he?

B: Yep, Lewis got the gold and Johnson fled back to Canada in disgrace.

S: The Olympics can be quite political. Do you remember those two black Americans, Tommie Smith and John Carlos, who, when they were collecting their medals, raised a black glove in the air to protest about the treatment of black people. They were sent home the next day by the American Olympic committee …

## 3

- Ask students to read the questions and check that they understand them.
- Students listen again and answer the questions.
- Check the answers with the class.
- Ask: *What do you think? Was it right that Dorando Pietri was disqualified? Was it right that Smith and Carlos were sent home?*

### Answers

1 Sydney.
2 He was helped across the finishing line by officials, so he was disqualified.
3 She was only 14 at the time. Jenny thinks children shouldn't be allowed to take part because of the pressure and training.
4 He'd been taking drugs.
5 Tommie Smith and John Carlos. They raised a black glove in the air when they got their medals to protest about the treatment of black people.

---

### Optional activity

**Memorable Olympic moments**

- Students imagine they are taking part in the phone-in for memorable Olympic moments. As a class they discuss their best moments.
- Write all the suggestions on the board. Stop when you have a reasonable number.
- The class decide on their top three, giving reasons.

---

# Speaking

## 1

- Divide the class into four groups by numbering students (see Teaching tips 'Pairwork and groupwork' on page 19) and assign one task to each group.
- Say: *You are going to prepare a five-minute presentation to the class on your topic.* Groups read their tasks.
- Students prepare their presentation. Set a time limit.

**2**

- Read the out the task.
- The four groups do their presentations. Students listening should make brief notes about the arguments (as preparation for the writing task).
- After each presentation the class asks questions and discusses the arguments. The class then votes to decide if the committee accepts the arguments or not.

# Writing

**1**

- Explain the task.
- Look at the phrases given with the class. Explain that these phrases are used to introduce a topic.
- Students write letters to the Olympic Advisory Committee using their notes from Ex 2. Remind them to give reasons for their opinions.
- Students read each other's letters.
- Check the letters.

### Optional activity

**Error check**

- Note down errors in the students' letters. Make an error sheet by writing the students' incorrect sentences (without names) on a sheet of paper. Make enough copies for one between two students.
- Students work in pairs. They correct the errors on the sheet.
- Check the answers with the class.

### Revision activity

**Call my bluff**

- Divide the class into two teams. Say: *We're going to play a game about unusual sports. Each team will get three unusual sports with a correct definition. You have to think of two false definitions for each sport. Then three speakers from each team present the correct and incorrect definitions of each sport. The other teams have to guess which is the correct definition.*
- Give the sports and definitions below to the teams.
- Teams play the game. Remind them to sound convincing!

Team A sports and definitions

URBAN GYMNASTICS: is a street sport which is also called 'free running'. Runners cross any barriers in their way: they jump over benches, climb walls and stairs – a bit like Spiderman!
SHOVEL RACING: a shovel is a large spade that you use to clear snow. In the 70s the people who operated the ski lifts started to slide down the mountains on their shovels. It was the quickest way to get home when the lifts closed. This developed into a sport.
CASTING: 'to cast' means 'to throw' and in this sport, people throw lines from fishing rods – but without any water nearby! Players have to hit targets with their lines or compete to throw their lines over the longest distance.

Team B sports and definitions

BLADE RUNNING: this is a mixture of slalom skiing and ski diving. Skydivers jump out a helicopter, open their parachute and move their body through ten slalom poles called 'blades', without touching the ground.
EXTREME IRONING: this is a sport for risk takers who like to look smart! It involves ironing clothes (with an iron and an ironing board) in extreme places, such as on the side of a dangerous mountain.
DRAGON BOAT RACING: this sport comes from the Far East and uses a boat with a dragon's head. 20 people make the boat move by paddling with oars. They paddle in time to the sound of a drummer.

# Extra practice

Students complete the Extra practice material on page 86 either in class, or for homework.

### Extra practice answers

**1**
| 1 | blamed | 5 | calm down | 9 | tie |
|---|---|---|---|---|---|
| 2 | disqualified | 6 | sprint | 10 | row |
| 3 | criticise | 7 | temper | 11 | swear |
| 4 | violent | 8 | memorable | | |

**2**
| 1 | score | 4 | beat |
|---|---|---|---|
| 2 | take | 5 | be disqualified from |
| 3 | win | 6 | take part in |

**3**
1 had
2 had already started
3 was standing
4 had bought
5 were beating
6 played / were playing, criticised / was criticising, scored, became

**4**
| 1 | had competed | 7 | hit |
|---|---|---|---|
| 2 | had won / won | 8 | fell over |
| 3 | became | 9 | was |
| 4 | wanted | 10 | lost |
| 5 | ran / was running | 11 | accused |
| 6 | approached / was approaching | 12 | upset / had upset |

# References

Grammar reference: Coursebook page 90
Wordlist: Coursebook page 92
Photocopiable resources: Teacher's Book pages 104–105
Test: Teacher's Book pages 143–144

# CD-ROM

Unit 1 Crossing the line
Language exercise: The modern Olympics
Vocabulary activity: Football letter
CEF-linked exercise: I can write a formal letter giving my views and reasons
Game: Crossword

# UNIT 2
# Is it art?

| Topic | Language study | Vocabulary | Main skills |
|---|---|---|---|
| • Basher (Modern art) <br> • Describing art | • Qualifying adjectives (*very, absolutely* and *quite*) | • Colours and shades | • **Listening:** checking information <br> • **Reading:** understanding opinions <br> • **Speaking:** expressing opinions about art <br> • **Pronunciation:** giving opinions using intonation |

## Learning aims

- Can qualify adjectives
- Can express opinions about art
- Can give opinions using intonation

### Ideas for preparation

- An abstract self-drawn picture (see Warmer p71)
- Pictures of controversial artwork (Lead-in p71)
- Brochures or catalogues from exhibitions (see Optional activity p71)
- Prints, postcards or magazine pictures of paintings and artwork (see Optional activities p73+p74)

### Warmer

- Draw a few squiggles and abstract designs on a piece of paper before the lesson. Don't spend too much time on it!
- Show your 'artwork' to the class. Ask: *Do you like this picture? What do you think it represents?* Students give ideas and suggestions.
- Ask: *Is this art?*

## Lead-in

**1**
- Ask students to open their books on page 70. Say: *Here are some examples of art. Which one is a painting? Which one is a sketch? A sculpture? Graffiti? Pottery?* Ask: *Do you like these artworks?*
- Ask: *What other examples of art can you think of?* If possible, prompt students by showing them postcards or pictures of controversial artworks and asking: *Is this art?*

### Answers
1 pottery  2 graffiti  3 sketch  4 painting  5 sculpture

**2**
- Read out the task.
- Students work in pairs and talk about art in their house.
- Ask some students to report back to the class.

### Optional activity

**Current exhibitions**
- Ask: *Has anybody been to an art exhibition recently? What was it about? / Who was the artist? Where was it? Would you recommend it?*
- If possible, show the class brochures or catalogues from exhibitions you have been to and briefly describe them.

<u>Alternatively</u>, set this task as homework: Students find out about interesting exhibitions on in the area and present them to the class in the next lesson.

## Basher

### Listening

**1**
- Tell students they are going to listen to an interview with an artist called Basher and the adjectives in the box are from the interview.
- Students match the words to the definitions.
- Check the answers with the class. Ask: *Can you give me an example using each word?*

### Answers
| 1 distinctive | 4 flexible |
|---|---|
| 2 contemporary | 5 emotional |
| 3 commercial | |

**2**
- 🔘 03  Look at the two examples of Basher's work with the class. Ask: *What do you think of these pictures?*
- Read out the task and the events. Check that students understand the word *illustrator* and can pronounce it /ˈɪləˌstreɪtə/.
- Students listen to the first part of the interview and put the events in the correct order.
- Students compare their answers with a partner.
- Check the answers with the class.

### Answers
1 d   2 c   3 a   4 e   5 b

## 3

- ● 04 Explain the task.
- Students listen to the whole interview and choose the correct alternatives.
- Check the answers with the class. Refer students to Listening script 04 on page 94 if necessary.

**Answers**

| | | | |
|---|---|---|---|
| 1 | one year | 4 | has been influenced by |
| 2 | didn't enjoy | 5 | uses |
| 3 | was | 6 | is |

### Listening script 03 and 04

(I = Interviewer; B = Basher)

I: Simon, could I ask you about how you started as an artist? You trained as a graphic designer. When you left university, did you work immediately as a graphic designer?

B: I started work as an illustrator first of all. I did about a year or so but then I went into the music industry.

I: And what did you do? Were you a musician?

B: Yes. At first I was in a band. We had a small record deal and we toured. Then I became a session musician, and later on I went into management, basically looking after a collection of pop bands and record producers.

I: Has that influenced your work as an artist or in the way you sell your art?

B: When I worked in the music industry I wasn't sure how to network with other people or how to conduct myself. Through the mistakes I made, I learnt how to push myself forward and be more adaptable when meeting new people.

I: So how did you become an independent artist?

B: Well, I was still working as a manager, not really enjoying it very much, when a friend told me about a place called Spitalfields market, where artists selling contemporary stuff can rent a cheap stall. I drew the first thing that came into my head, some Japanese characters, photocopied and enlarged them, stuck them on some wood and put them on the wall at the market. And that was it. In the first week I had some really excellent sales and so I decided to carry on.

• • •

I: OK. Now the images you produce are very distinctive. Tell us about them.

B: Stylistically they're graphic images, influences from graffiti and comics. I'm really interested in drawing people's characters, particularly their expressions. I try to make my images as simple as possible but with lots of emotional content.

I: I suppose your prints could be used for virtually anything?

B: Yes, all the images are basically created on a computer, so that they can be transferred to any medium; for example, clothing such as T-shirts. Or you can use them for computer games – for anything really.

I: Why do you think you are successful?

B: I think it's being flexible. A lot of artists are a bit set in their ways, not very open to other people's ideas or usages for their work because they're worried about being too commercial. I don't mind selling my work in different mediums, not just paintings, and I don't feel this is devaluing it. It's important to get the balance right. I'm an artist but I'm also a businessman.

I: What advice would you give somebody who wants to become an artist?

B: I think you have to be honest with yourself and do what you enjoy because it's difficult to make a living from art. If you hit on something which is working then follow it up and stay focused on that.

I: Finally, your real name is Simon. Where does the name Basher come from?

B: Basher is an old fashioned name for a school bully, and I thought these characters were so unlike that. So it was a bit of a joke really and it just stuck.

## 4

- Read out the questions.
- Students work in pairs and discuss the questions.
- Discuss the questions with the class.

---

**Optional activity**

**Basher: a magazine article**

- Tell students they are going to write a short article about Basher for a college magazine. They should write a brief biography, a description of his work and give their opinion of his work.
- Tell students to revise and correct their article.
- Check the articles. Read the best one to the class.

---

# Language study

## Qualifying adjectives

### *very, absolutely* and *quite*

### 1

- Read the examples. Ask: *Why can't we use 'very' with the word 'enormous'?* Prompt them if necessary: *What does 'enormous' mean?* (very big; so we can't use *very* with an adjective that already means 'very something').
- Read out the words in the box. Students say whether *very* or *absolutely* is used to qualify each one. If students answer incorrectly, ask: *What does the word mean?*

**Answers**

| | | | |
|---|---|---|---|
| 1 | very bad | 6 | very nice |
| 2 | very big | 7 | very small |
| 3 | absolutely fantastic | 8 | absolutely terrible |
| 4 | very good | 9 | absolutely tiny |
| 5 | absolutely huge | 10 | absolutely wonderful |

### 2

- Read out the task.
- Ask: *Which adjectives in Ex 1 are normal, gradable adjectives?* (bad, big, good, nice, small), *Which are extreme or ungradable adjectives that mean 'very something'?* (fantastic, huge, terrible, tiny, wonderful). Write them on the board in two lists.
- With students, formulate a rule about which adjectives use *very* and which adjectives use *absolutely*.

**Answers**

Gradable adjectives use *very*

Extreme or 'ungradable' adjectives use *absolutely*

## 3

- Read out the task. Tell students to use a mix of gradable and ungradable / extreme adjectives.
- Students work in pairs and make a list of ten adjectives.
- Students test another pair by asking whether each adjective takes *very* or *absolutely*.
- Students report back to the class about which adjectives they used. Make a list of other extreme adjectives that use *absolutely*. Ask students to explain their meaning.

## 4

- Ask students what the word *quite* usually means (a bit, fairly, rather).
- Read out the two sentences, using your voice to show the meaning of each.
- Ask: *What does 'quite' mean in sentence 1? And in sentence 2?*
- Ask: *What sort of adjective is extraordinary?* (ungradable / extreme). *What does it mean?* (very unusual). Point out that we couldn't say *quite extraordinary* with the usual meaning of *quite* as this would mean *quite very unusual*. Here it means the same as *absolutely extraordinary*.

### Answers

Sentence 1: a bit    Sentence 2: absolutely

## 5

- Read out the task.
- Go through the list of adjectives in Ex 1 with the class. Read out the adjective and ask students to say whether the use of *quite* would mean 'a bit' or 'absolutely'.

### Answers

a bit: bad, big, good, nice, small
absolutely: fantastic, huge, terrible, tiny, wonderful

## 6

- Read out the task. Emphasise that there is more than one answer so they should try all three adjectives in the sentence to see if they fit.
- Students work individually or in pairs and complete the sentences.
- Check the answers with the class.

### Answers

1  quite / very, quite / very     4  quite / very
2  absolutely / quite              5  quite / absolutely
3  absolutely / quite

## 7

- Explain the task. Tell students to look carefully at the meaning of the sentences and which qualifiers are used.
- Students complete the sentences with suitable adjectives.
- Check students' answers individually. Alternatively, ask individual students to read out a sentence to the class. Ask: *Has anybody got anything different?*

### Possible answers

1  extraordinary / amazing / fantastic / interesting / boring / good / bad / meaningful
2  terrible / awful / terrifying / disgusting / scary / frightening
3  beautiful / complicated / contemporary
4  terrible / horrible / awful

# Describing art

## Vocabulary

### 1

- Read out the colours in the box . Check pronunciation of *beige* /beɪʒ/, *khaki* /ˈkɑːki/ with a long 'a' and *turquoise* /ˈtɜːkwɔɪz/.
- Ask students if they know any of the colours and can describe them using colours they know (eg *beige* = a sort of brown, *khaki* = a sort of green).
- Students label the painting with the correct colours.
- Check the answers with the class.
- Ask: *Is anybody wearing these colours?*

### Answers

1  navy        3  beige        5  turquoise
2  purple      4  scarlet      6  khaki

### 2

- Read out the task and look at the shades of colour.
- Ask: *Can you find these shades in the painting? Can you see these colours in this room? Where?*
- Students describe each other's clothing using the shades vocabulary (eg *Maria is wearing a bright pink T-shirt*).

**3**

- Explain the task.
- Students match the descriptions to the artworks.
- Check the answers with the class.
- Ask: *Do you agree with these descriptions? What's your opinion of these artworks?*

**Answers**

a 2   b 1   c 4   d 3

**4**

- Explain the task and read out the phrases in the box.
- Students complete the table with the phrases.
- Check the answers with the class.

**Answers**

| Positive | Neutral | Negative |
| --- | --- | --- |
| I adore this | It makes me want to … | It's just a joke |
| This is a very interesting picture | It's completely abstract | For me this is quite boring |
| | | It does nothing for me |
| | | It's absolutely awful |

**Optional activity**

**An artwork description**

- Set this task for homework. Give students a picture of a work of art or ask them to find one. Students write a description of it. They should include a description of what is represented, the colours and their opinion of it.
- Take in the pictures and lay them on the floor of the classroom. Students swap their descriptions with a partner.
- Students read the description. Then they find the picture it matches. They tell their partner if they agree with their description.

**5**

- Explain the task.
- Students work in pairs, choose an artwork and role-play the situation. Allow them four minutes to do this.
- Ask the art dealers: *Who managed to sell a work of art? What did you sell? How much did you sell it for?* Ask the customers: *Was the art dealer good at persuading you to buy? What were his / her tactics?*

## Pronunciation

### Giving opinions using intonation

**1**

- 🔘 **05** Explain the task.
- Students look at the conversation and listen, paying particular attention to the intonation of the parts marked with arrows. They answer the questions.

- Check the answers with the class. Ask: *How are the speakers' feelings reflected in their intonation?* (certainty and strong feelings are indicated by steep rise-fall intonation. Lack of strong feelings is indicated with only slight intonation).

**Answers**

A feels strongly about the artwork. B doesn't have strong opinions about it.

**2**

- Students listen and repeat using the correct intonation.
- Pairs of students read the conversation to the class. Correct their intonation if necessary.

## Reading and listening

**1**

- 🔘 **06** Look at the painting with the class. Ask: *What do you think of it?*
- Tell students they are going to listen to an extract from a play where Marc and Serge are talking about this painting. Explain the task.
- Students listen and read the extract. They mark examples of the intonation pattern in Ex 1 using the arrows shown.
- Check the answers with the class. Ask students for examples.
- Students listen again, paying attention to the intonation patterns.

**Possible answers**

Marc:  Serge, you haven't bought this painting for two hundred thousand francs?

Serge:  You don't understand. That's what it costs. It's an Antrios.

Marc:  You haven't bought this painting for two hundred thousand francs?

Serge:  I might have known you'd miss the point.

Marc:  You paid two hundred thousand francs for this rubbish?

Serge:  What do you mean, 'this rubbish'?

Marc:  Serge, where's your sense of humour? Why aren't you laughing? … It's fantastic, you buying this painting.

Serge:  I don't care how fantastic you think it is, I don't mind if you laugh, but I would like to know what you mean by 'this rubbish'.

Marc:  This is a joke isn't it?

Serge: No, it isn't. By whose standards is it rubbish? If you
call something rubbish, you need to have some
criterion to judge it by.

Marc: Who are you talking to? Who do you think you're
talking to? Hello!

Serge: You have no interest whatsoever in contemporary
painting. You never have had. This is a field, about
which you know absolutely nothing, so how can you
assert that any given object, which conforms to laws
you don't understand, is rubbish?

Marc: Because it is. It's rubbish. I'm sorry.

**2**
- Ask: *What do Marc and Serge think about modern art?*

**Answers**
Marc isn't interested in modern art. He thinks it's rubbish and
a waste of money. Serge is a collector of modern art.

**3**
- Read out the questions to the class.
- Students work in pairs and discuss the questions.
- Ask: *Did you have the same opinions?* Ask some students
to report back to the class.

## Speaking

**1**
- Ask students to read the task instructions and check
that they understand them.
- Students work in pairs and decide on the artwork they
will use. This could be a picture they have drawn, such
as the one used by the teacher in the Warmer activity.
- Students prepare their sales presentations.

**2**
- Students give their sales presentations.
- After each presentation, students vote whether to buy
the artwork or not.

**Revision activity**

**Wordlist challenge**
- Students work in small groups. They look at the
Wordlist for Unit 2 on page 92. Write these
instructions on the board or dictate them to the
class.
Find:
– 5 gradable adjectives
– 5 ungradable / extreme adjectives
– 5 types of artwork
– 5 colours
– 5 verbs

- The first group to find all the words shouts *Finished!*
Wait until two other groups have shouted *Finished!*
- The first group to finish reads out their lists. Check
them. Ask other groups to read out their words if
they have something different.

## Extra practice

Students complete the Extra practice material on page 87
either in class, or for homework.

**Extra practice answers**
1  1  very, absolutely      4  absolutely, absolutely
   2  absolutely            5  absolutely
   3  very                  6  very

2  1  absolutely            3  absolutely
   2  a bit                 4  a bit

3  1  nothing for me
   2  absolutely fabulous
   3  quite nice
   4  prefer something more subtle
   5  really interesting
   6  quite boring
   7  want to

4  1  navy blue             2  purple
      dark blue                turquoise
      bright blue              khaki
      light blue               beige
                               scarlet

5  distinctive, unimpressive, grey, contemporary, huge, dull
   brown, large, secure, delicate

6  General appearance and reputation: distinctive,
   unimpressive, contemporary, secure, delicate
   Size and colour: huge, large, grey, dull brown

7  (individual answers)

## References

Grammar reference: Coursebook page 91
Wordlist: Coursebook page 92
Photocopiable resources: Teacher's Book pages 106–107
Test: Teacher's Book pages 145–146

## CD-ROM

Unit 2 Is it art?
Language exercise: Hotel Art opens its doors
Vocabulary activity: The modern art debate
CEF-linked exercise: I can give opinions using intonation
Game: Cats in hats

# UNIT 3
# Fashion victims

| Topic | Language study | Vocabulary | Main skills |
|-------|----------------|------------|-------------|
| • Hey, she's wearing my clothes! (Interview with a designer)<br>• Confessions of a shopaholic | • Linking ideas<br>• The order of adjectives | • Clothes (pattern, material, style) | • **Reading:** understanding main information in a text<br>• **Speaking:** discussing clothes and fashion; comparing responses to a survey<br>• **Listening:** extracting details from an interview |

## Learning aims

- Can link ideas
- Can use adjectives in the correct order
- Can discuss clothes and fashion

### Ideas for preparation
- Items of jewellery and fashion accessories such as sunglasses, a belt, a hat (see Warmer p76)

### Warmer
- Tell students the topic of the next unit is fashion. If possible, put several pieces of jewellery and fashion accessories on the table. Ask students to name them.
- Write objects on the board under two lists: *jewellery* and *accessories*. Ask students to add to the lists.
- Say: *Some fashion experts say accessories are more important than the clothes you wear. Do you think accessories are important? Do you wear jewellery?*

## Lead-in

### 1
- Ask students to open their books on page 74. Say: *The title of the unit is 'Fashion victims'. What is a victim? What is a fashion victim?*
- Look at the pictures with the class. Ask individual students to describe each picture in turn, revising the colours and opinions vocabulary from Unit 2.
- For each picture ask: *Do you agree? What do you think of these clothes? Would you wear them?*

### 2
- Read out the statements and check that students understand them.
- Students work in pairs and discuss the statements.
- Discuss the statements with the class.

## Reading and vocabulary

### 1
- 🎧 **07** Look at the picture of Romero Bryan and the title of the article with the class. Ask: *What's Romero Bryan's job?* (fashion designer), *What sort of clothes do you think he designs?* (cool clothes for young people).
- Read out the questions and check that students understand them. Point out the use of 'an item of clothing' as the singular for 'clothes'.
- Students read the article and answer the questions. They can listen to the article on CD while they read.

- Students compare their answers with a partner.
- Check the answers with the class.

### Answers
1. Trendy pop stars.
2. A dress inspired by the way his sister wore a bath towel. Pop star Samantha Mumba wore it to the Brit awards.
3. Fashion design.
4. Natural talent and qualifications in the technical side of fashion.
5. A shirt.
6. Pop duo Daphne and Celeste and Sabrina Washington from Mis-Teeq.
7. No fashion house wants to give him work experience because they already see him as a business.

### 2
- Read out the adjectives. Check that students can pronounce them with the correct word stress: out<u>ra</u>geous, <u>eye</u>-catching, over<u>whel</u>ming, unex<u>pec</u>ted.
- Check that the meaning of each word is clear by asking students to suggest definitions.
- Ask: *Can you say what each word refers to in the article, without looking back at the article?* Elicit ideas and write them on the board with the adjective.
- Students check their ideas by looking back at the article.
- Check the answers with the class.

### Answers
1. Romero's designs.
2. The dress Samantha Mumba wore to the Brit Awards.
3. Talent (for fashion design).
4. Romero's mobile phone voicemail message.
5. His success as a fashion designer.
6. His success as a fashion designer.

### Optional activity

**A letter of application**
- Students imagine they are Romero. They are going to apply to a fashion house for work experience.
- Students (as Romero) choose a fashion house and write a letter of application, saying what he has achieved so far, what he is doing now and why he wants to work there.
- Students swap letters and write a reply.
- Students read the replies.

**3**

- Look at the table with the class. Check that students understand the words for patterns by asking: *Who's wearing a stripy T-shirt? / a plain shirt?* etc.
- Check comprehension of *silk* and *scruffy* by asking students to give definitions.
- Students work in groups, adding words to the lists.
- Check the answers with the class.

**Possible answers**
Material: cotton, woollen, leather, nylon, polyester, plastic
Style: smart, elegant, casual, trendy, cool, outrageous

**Optional activity**

**Clothes brainstorm**
- Draw circles on the board. Write *clothes* in the centre and then categories such as: *casual wear, formal wear, outerwear, footwear, sleepwear, underwear, swimwear.*
- Brainstorm clothes words for the categories with the class and complete the word web on the board. Some words may fit into several categories.

**4**

- Explain the task.
- Students make lists of clothes they like and dislike, using the words in Ex 3.

**5**

- Explain the task. Look at the example with the class. Students underline phrases for talking about likes and dislikes (*I'm not keen on, I prefer, I can't stand*). Point out that we can say *I suit green* or *Green suits me*. Students also often confuse *suit* (look good on somebody) and *fit* (be the right size for somebody).
- Students work in pairs. They discuss what types of clothes they like or dislike using their lists from Ex 4.
- Students report back to the class. Ask: *Who has the same style as their partner? Who has a very different style?*

# Language study

## Linking ideas

**1**

- Ask: *What words do you know to link two ideas?* Make a list of all the linking words on the board.
- Look at the example sentences with the class. Ask: *Does 'but' add a new point or contrast two points?*

**Answer**
The word *but* contrasts two points

**2**

- Look at the categories of linking words and examples. Check that the categories are clear. Say: *Can you give me an example of use for 'however', 'unless', 'so' and 'and'?* Elicit sentences and write them on the board.
- Explain the task and read out the words in the box.
- Students work individually and add words to the lists.
- Check the answers with the class.

**Answers**
1  Contrast: although, though
2  Condition: if
3  Cause and effect: as a result, because
4  Addition: also, in addition, too

**3**

- Read out the questions. Students answer orally and give examples for questions 1 and 2.

**Answers**
1  too
2  though
3  but, unless, so, and, also, although, because, if

**4**

- Explain the task.
- Students join the sentences.
- Check the answers with the class.

**Answers**
1  Two famous pop stars liked his shirt, so they asked him to make clothes for them.
2  He is studying at the London School of Fashion because he wants to learn about the technical side of designing.
3  Unless he gets his degree, he won't be able to prove that he's a qualified designer.

**5**

- Explain the task.
- Students rewrite the sentences.
- Check the answers with the class. Point out that we use a comma after *however, in addition* and *as a result* at the beginning of sentences.

**Answers**
1  He was working hard to pass his 'A' level exams. He was also making clothes in his free time.
2  He is famous. However, he wants to be treated like the other students.
3  He listened to his mum's advice. As a result, he wore his shirt and became famous.

## The order of adjectives

**6**

- Point to somebody's bag. Say: *X's bag is [colour]. It's [size]. And it's made of [material].* Write the three adjectives on the board under each other. Ask: *How can we describe X's bag? Is it a [black leather big] bag? A [black big leather] bag? What order do we say these adjectives in? What sounds right?* Elicit suggestions and write them on the board.
- Look at the table in Ex 6 and check the correct order: *[big black leather] bag* (size, colour, material).
- Look at the adjective order in the table. Read out the order: *Opinion before size before colour before …* Check that students understand.
- Read the note with the class.
- Look at the examples in the table. Students say the order of adjectives.

**Answers**
1  opinion, colour, origin      3  opinion, colour, material
2  opinion, size

**Answers**
1  shopaholic      3  fashionable      5  versatile
2  designer        4  outfit           6  flatter

## 7
- Explain the task.
- Students work individually or in pairs. They put the adjectives in the correct order using the table in Ex 6.
- Check the answers with the class.

**Answers**
1  A short, floral Chinese dress.
2  An expensive, Italian, silk scarf.
3  A red and blue, nylon football top.
4  A long, blue and grey, plastic raincoat.
5  A trendy, multicoloured sports bag.

---

**Optional activity**

**Describe it!**
- Students look at the categories in the table in Ex 6. They say three adjectives (any adjectives) in any order (eg *white, soft, big*). Write them on the board.
- Ask: *What nouns can go with all three adjectives?* Elicit suggestions and write them on the board (eg *a cloud, a pillow, a pullover*). Ask students to describe the nouns using the correct order of the adjectives (eg *a big soft white cloud*).
- Repeat two more times with the class saying three adjectives at random, or students writing three adjectives on the board.

---

## 8
- Explain the task.
- Students work in pairs and sit back to back. Each student in turn describes their partner's clothes, using the correct order of adjectives. Students point out mistakes or correct their partner if necessary.
- Ask: *Did you remember correctly?*

## 9
- Read out the task.
- Students divide into pairs. They decide if they are A or B and read the information on page 93 or 96.
- Students do the activity in pairs.
- Listen to the conversations and discuss any recurring errors with the class.

# Confessions of a shopaholic
## Listening and speaking

## 1
- Look at the heading of this section with the class. Ask: *What is a shopaholic?* (someone who is addicted to shopping / can't stop shopping), *What is a confession?* (when you admit to doing something wrong).
- Explain the task and read out the words in the box.
- Students work individually and complete the sentences.
- Check the answers with the class.

## 2
- Read out the task.
- Students work in pairs and decide if the sentences are true for them.
- Discuss the questions with the class.

## 3
- 🔊 **o8** Explain the task to the class. Students read through the statements. Check that they understand what *heels* are.
- Students listen and decide if the statements are true or false.
- Students compare their answers with a partner.
- Check the answers with the class.

**Answers**
1  True
2  False (She buys clothes she likes, it doesn't matter if they are designer clothes or second-hand)
3  False (She likes to be comfortable and rarely wears high heels)
4  True
5  False (She doesn't read fashion magazines, she only gets fashion ideas from shopping or on the street)
6  False (She never wears short skirts because she hates her legs)
7  True
8  False (She doesn't like them because she thinks all men wear them and just look the same)

**Listening script o8**
(I = Interviewer; C = Claire)
I: So Claire, how often do you buy clothes?
C: Well as often as possible, actually. I'm a bit of a shopaholic. I don't spend nearly as much time or money on my hair. And I rarely wear make-up. But, to me, clothes are a really important part of my appearance. For that reason I do buy a lot of clothes, yeah.
I: If you had more money would you rather buy lots of new clothes or a few expensive ones?
C: Well, I'm not sure really, erm the cost of clothes is not really important to me. I like something, I buy it. I mean I've bought second-hand clothes, I've bought designer clothes. So I'm not sure about that.
I: How would you describe the way you dress – your style?
C: I wouldn't say I follow fashion. Erm, I think I'm quite individual. I like to find clothes that no one else will have. However, I also like to be comfortable. I rarely wear high heels and I hate being hot, so this affects what I wear.
I: Do you have a favourite outfit?
C: Well I mean it changes from time to time. At the moment I've got a favourite pair of trousers that I seem to be wearing all the time, to everywhere, with everything. Erm, they're very versatile so I can wear them with trainers or high heels, erm different belts and tops. They can be smart or casual.

I:  How aware are you of current fashion trends?

C:  Not particularly. I mean, I don't watch fashion shows on TV and I don't read fashion magazines. So really my only exposure to fashion is when … when I'm shopping or in the street when I see someone else wearing something. I think that fashion is quite hard to avoid. You're often not aware that you are aware.

I:  Is there anything that you wouldn't wear?

C:  Erm, I try not to wear anything that doesn't flatter me. I very rarely wear short skirts because I hate my legs. I also never wear anything too revealing as that's just not my style.

I:  Whose sense of fashion or style do you most admire?

C:  I really admire Cameron Diaz. I think everybody does. She's always very confident in the way she dresses and I think that's the most important thing. That's what fashion's about – having your own self-confidence.

I:  And what about for a man? What clothes do you like for a man?

C:  Well, I think it comes down to what I don't like men wearing. So it's things like white socks, sandals and trousers that are too short. I don't like short-sleeved shirts with jeans as all the guys wear them and they just all look the same. I like a man to look good, but not as if he has tried really hard. That's not too much to ask for, is it?

## 4
- Explain the task.
- Students listen again and complete the questions.
- Students look at Listening script 08 on pages 94–95 and check their answers.
- Check the answers with the class.

> **Answers**
> 1  How **often do you** buy clothes?
> 2  If you had more money, would you rather buy lots of new clothes or **a few expensive ones**?
> 3  How would you **describe the way** you dress?
> 4  Do you have **a favourite outfit**?
> 5  How **aware are you of current** fashion trends?
> 6  Is there anything that **you wouldn't wear**?
> 7  Whose **sense of fashion or style** do you most admire?
> 8  What clothes **do you like for a man**?

## 5
- Explain and read out the task.
- Students work in pairs. They ask and answer the questions in Ex 4.
- Students report back to the class.

## 6
- Tell the class if you think you are vain or not. Ask one or two students: *Are you vain?*
- Tell students they are going to do a questionnaire called *How vain are you?* Explain the task: the questionnaire is in two parts; students are going to work in pairs and each student will have different questions.
- Students work in pairs. They decide if they are A or B and read the information for their task on page 93 or 96.
- Students ask each other their questions and note down their partner's answers.
- Students compare their answers with the key.
- Students report their results to the class.

> **Revision activity**
>
> **Who is it?**
> - Students walk around the class, taking note of each other's clothes and shoes, particularly small details.
> - One person comes to the front and describes a student's clothes, sentence by sentence (eg *This person is wearing black, leather shoes*). After each sentence, the class can guess one name. Students can't say their own name.
> - If the student can say three correct sentences without the person being guessed, the student wins that match. Encourage students to describe less obvious things such as socks or accessories.
> - Continue with two or three more students.

## Extra practice

Students complete the Extra practice material on page 88 either in class, or for homework.

> **Extra practice answers**
>
> | 1 | Opinion / style | Colour / pattern | Material |
> |---|---|---|---|
> | | casual | black | silk |
> | | scruffy | plain | nylon |
> | | | stripy | woollen |
>
> 2  1  a scruffy, plain, leather jacket
>    2  a baggy, stripy, woollen jumper
>    3  smart, tight, black trousers
>    4  a baggy, patterned, cotton dress
>    5  a casual, nylon, checked bag
>
> 3  (individual answers)
>
> | 4 | 1 | because | 4 | and | 7 | So |
> |---|---|---|---|---|---|---|
> | | 2 | However | 5 | unless | | |
> | | 3 | though | 6 | As a result | | |

## References

Grammar reference: Coursebook page 91
Wordlist: Coursebook page 92
Photocopiable resources: Teacher's Book pages 108–109
Test: Teacher's Book pages 147–148

## CD-ROM

Unit 3 Fashion victims
Language exercise: Jeans past and present
Vocabulary activity: Celebrity fashion report
CEF-linked exercise: I can use adjectives in the correct order
Game: Witch's pot

# UNIT 4
# Globetrotting

| Topic | Language study | Vocabulary | Main skills |
|---|---|---|---|
| • Off the beaten track with David Abram<br>• (Travel writing) Nightmare journeys | • Verb + infinitive or *-ing* | • Phrasal verbs: travel<br>• Means of transport | • **Reading:** identifying particular information<br>• **Listening:** understanding key references<br>• **Speaking:** telling a story about a nightmare journey<br>• **Writing:** a review about a place |

## Learning aims

- Can recognise verb + infinitive or *-ing* patterns
- Can use phrasal verbs for travel
- Can write a review

### Ideas for preparation
- Pictures of the Taj Mahal and the Rio carnival (see Lead-in Ex 1 p80)
- Pictures of famous monuments cut out of magazines or printed from the Internet. (see Optional activity p80)
- Guidebooks (see Reading Ex 1 p81)
- A hat or basket (see Revision activity p84)

### Warmer
- Ask: *Do you know what the Seven Wonders of the Ancient World are?* (The Great Pyramid of Giza, The Hanging Gardens of Babylon, The Statue of Zeus at Olympia, The Temple of Artemis at Ephesus, the Mausoleum at Halicarnassus, the Colossus of Rhodes, the Lighthouse of Alexandria), *Which one still exists today?* (The Great Pyramid of Giza).
- Students work in small groups. Say: *You are going to make a list of your own Seven Wonders. First brainstorm ideas in your group and write them all down. Then agree on seven.*
- Groups present their Seven Wonders to the class.

## Lead-in

### Background information
The Rio de Janeiro Carnival takes place every year before Lent. Lent is the period leading up to Easter (March / April). There are street parades all over the city with music, dance and beautiful costumes. The Samba Parade is the most famous event: 14 samba schools, each with huge floats and thousands of dancers, compete to give the best performance.
The Taj Mahal in Agra, India was built by Emperor Shah Jahan as a monument to his dead wife Mumtaz Mahal. Mumtaz, a Persian princess, was his second wife and gave him 14 children. The Taj is built of white marble. Construction of the building began in 1631 and was completed 22 years later. The building contains the tombs of both the emperor and his wife.

### 1
- Ask students to open their books on page 78. Look at the picture of New York with the class. Ask: *Has anybody been to New York? What did you do there? Did you enjoy it? What did you like most about it?* (If nobody has been there: *What do you know about New York? Would you like to go there?*)
- Explain the task and read out the list of places. Check that everybody knows what happens at the Rio de Janeiro Carnival and what the Taj Mahal is. If possible, show the class pictures.
- Students work in pairs. They discuss which trip they would most like to go on.
- Do a survey in the class. Ask students to raise their hands to show which trip they would prefer.

### Optional activity

**Where is it?**
- For this activity you need pictures of famous monuments such as the White House, the Colosseum, the Sydney Opera House etc.
- Divide the class into two teams. Show the teams a picture in turn. The teams say the country the monument is in. They get a point for each correct answer. If a team is unable to answer, show the same picture to the other team who get a chance to answer for half a point.
<u>Alternatively</u>, to make this harder, ask the teams to name the monument as well as the country (one point for each).

### 2
- Read out the task.
- Students say which other countries they would like to visit and why.

## Optional activity

### Countries, nationalities and languages

- Revise countries, nationalities and languages with the class. Concentrate on pronunciation (particularly word stress).
- Write headings on the board. Complete the lists with the countries from Ex 1.
- Elicit more holiday countries from students.

**Possible answers**

| Country | Nationality | Language |
|---|---|---|
| Kenya | Kenyan | Swahili, English |
| Brazil | Brazilian | Portuguese |
| India | Indian | Hindi, Urdu, English etc |
| Thailand | Thai | Thai |
| China | Chinese | Chinese |
| Hungary | Hungarian | Hungarian |
| Morocco | Moroccan | Arabic |
| Iceland | Icelandic | Icelandic |
| Norway | Norwegian | Norwegian |

# Reading

## Background information

The *Rough Guides* are a series of guidebooks to places all over the world for independent travellers. Originally, the guidebooks were for young backpackers on a budget, but they now contain cultural and practical information for all sorts of independent travellers. *Rough Guides* also include guides on aspects of popular culture such as music, sport, TV and the Internet.

### 1

- 🎧 09 If possible, hold up a few guidebooks. Ask: *Do you use guidebooks when you travel? What sort of information do you look for in them? Do you have a favourite series?*
- Look at the picture of the *Rough Guide to India* with the class. Ask: *Do you know the Rough Guides? What sort of guides are they? Who are they for?* (See Background information above.)
- Read out the task and the questions.
- Students read the interview and answer the questions. They can listen to the interview on CD while they read.
- Check the answers with the class.

**Answers**
1  He spends three or four months travelling and then eight or nine months writing.
2  He always feels that he never wants to do another similar trip again.
3  He thinks it's a shame.

### 2

- Explain the task.
- Students read the text again and choose the correct alternatives.
- Check the answers with the class. If students have incorrect answers, look at the part of the text containing the answer with the class.

**Answers**
1 c   2 b   3 c   4 a   5 c   6 b

### 3

- Read out the task and the words and phrases. Point out that the words and phrases are in bold in the interview and that the text around the word usually gives a clue to its meaning.
- Students work individually or in pairs. They find the words and phrases in the interview and write a definition using the context to help them.
- Check the answers with the class.

**Possible answers**
1  be in the end
2  in places far away from other tourists
3  talking informally to
4  going through a place quickly or without stopping
5  not harmful to the environment
6  an author's share of the money from the sale of his / her book

### 4

- Read out the task and the questions.
- Students work in pairs and discuss the questions.
- Students report back to the class.

## Optional activity

### Tourism and the environment

- Ask: *How does tourism damage the environment?* Make a list of students' suggestions on the board (eg damage to monuments and erosion of paths and landscape due to too many visitors; litter problems; scaring away of wildlife; waste problems and water pollution in coastal holiday resorts; air pollution and traffic problems from too many cars, overdevelopment of unspoilt areas through hotels, restaurants, shopping malls etc).
- Look at the ideas on the board. Ask: *Can we do anything to stop this? How can we encourage the 'sustainable development' that David Abram talks about in his interview?*

# Language study

## Verb + infinitive or -*ing*

### 1

- Read out the explanation and the various verb patterns.
- Read out each example sentence slowly in turn. Ask: *Which verb pattern is this?* Students look at the verb patterns and answer orally.
- Ask students: *Can you give me another example for each pattern?* Prompt students with verbs if necessary (eg verb + -*ing* form: *avoid*, verb + object + -*ing*: *see*, verb + infinitive: *try*, verb + object + infinitive: *let / allow*).

**Answers**
1 d   2 c   3 b   4 a

## 2

- Explain the task.
- Students work individually and match the two parts of the sentences.
- Check the answers with the class.

**Answers**
2 d   3 e   4 c   5 b   6 a

## 3

- Read out the task.
- Students work individually or in pairs and match the sentences in Ex 2 to the patterns in Ex 1.
- Check the answers with the class. Write the sentences on the board and underline and label the verbs and objects if necessary.

**Answers**
1  verb + object + *-ing* form
2  verb + infinitive
3  verb + *-ing* form
4  verb + infinitive
5  verb + object + infinitive
6  verb + object + *-ing* form

## 4

- Read out the explanations and the examples.
- Students work individually. They complete the rule boxes with the correct pattern, referring back to the sentences in Ex 2 for help.
- Check the answers with the class.

**Answers**
Box 1: Verb + infinitive
Box 2: Verb + *-ing* form

### Optional activity

**Infinitive and *-ing* form tennis**
- Students work in pairs. One student looks at the verb list on page 91, the other closes their book.
- The student with the list reads out a verb (eg finish); the other student says either 'to travel' or 'travelling' (or 'to write / 'writing' etc), depending on the verb pattern it takes. The students continue 'batting' back and forth for three minutes.
- Students swap roles and do the same again.

## 5

- Say: *Some verbs can be followed by both the '-ing' form and by the infinitive with no change in meaning.* Write one or two examples on the board (eg *He hates travelling – He hates to travel, He started learning Italian – He started to learn Italian*).
- Read the explanation in Ex 5 to the class.
- Students look at the example sentences and answer the questions orally.
- Write examples of the different meanings of *try* and *remember* on the board. Students explain the meaning. For example: *I didn't remember to set my alarm clock and slept in* (I forgot to set the alarm clock); *I remember*

setting my alarm clock for seven o'clock but it didn't ring (I set it); *I tried finding a Russian class and learning Russian but it was too difficult* (I found a class); *I tried to find a Russian class, but there weren't any classes in my area* (I didn't find a class).
- Students read the Grammar reference on page 91 as a summary.

**Answers**
Kerri's friends got postcards. Danni's friends didn't get any because she decided not to continue sending postcards to her friends.
Kerri was doing something else and then stopped this activity and sent some postcards to her friends.

## 6

- Explain the task. Tell students to refer to the lists of verbs in the Grammar reference on page 91 if they are uncertain about the verb patterns.
- Students work individually and complete the sentences about them.
- Students swap sentences with a partner. They read and (if necessary) correct each other's sentences.
- Ask students read out a sentence each. Correct any errors with the class.

# Nightmare journeys

## Vocabulary and listening

### Phrasal verbs: travel

**1**
- Look at the heading of this section with the class. Ask: *Is this section about wonderful or terrible journeys?* (terrible). Students look at the picture. Ask: *Where are the people in the picture?*
- Explain the task and read out the phrasal verbs in the box.
- Students match the numbers in the picture to the phrasal verbs in the box.
- Check the answers with the class. Check students understand the meanings. Explain for example, that *get in* and *get out* are usually used for cars, and *get on / get off* are usually used for public transport.

**Answers**
drop off: 3   flag down: 9   get in: 1   get off: 6   get on: 7
get out: 2   pick up: 5   queue up for: 8   take off: 4

**2**
- Read out and explain the task.
- Students work in pairs. They make lists for each type of transport using the phrasal verbs in Ex 1.
- Check the answers with the class. If the class doesn't agree, ask the student for an example sentence or context.

## Answers

1 Bus: get on, get off, pick up, queue up for (also possible: drop off, flag down = in rural areas)
2 Car: drop off, get in, get out, pick up (also possible: flag down = for help / police check)
3 Ferry: get on, get off, queue up for (also possible: pick up = small island ferry picks up passengers on different islands, for example)
4 Taxi: drop off, flag down, get in, get out, pick up, queue up for
5 Train: get on, get off, queue up for
6 Tram: get on, get off, queue up for

## Optional activity

### Phrasal verb exercise

- Students write a gap fill exercise for their partner. They write five sentences using five of the phrasal verbs in Ex 1, but leaving gaps for the verbs.
- Students swap their exercise with a partner. They do each other's exercises.
- Students give the completed exercise back to their partner. Their partner checks it.
- Ask: *Did you get all the sentences right?*

## 3

- 🔘 10  Read out and explain the task.
- Students listen and note down what the numbers refer to.
- Students compare their answers with a partner.
- Check the answers with the class.

## Answers

a 3: the number of days the speaker and her boyfriend spent in Prague.
b 130: the kilometres an hour the first taxi driver was doing.
c 5: the number of minutes after which the taxi driver crashed into the back of a lorry.
d 4: the age of the grandson of the tourists who were already in the second taxi.

## 4

- Read out the question.
- Students answer orally.

## Answers

Their first taxi had no seatbelts and the driver drove very fast. This taxi crashed and they had to get another one. The second taxi was already full and they had to share it with two tourists and their grandson. Then the taxi dropped them off at the wrong hotel.

## 5

- Explain the task.
- Students look at the phrasal verbs in Ex 1. They listen again and tick all the phrasal verbs that they hear.
- Students check their answers (in bold) in Listening script 10 on page 95.

## Answers

take off, flag down, get out, pick up, drop off

## Listening script 10

My boyfriend and I had decided to spend a nice romantic three-day weekend in Prague. We managed to get to the airport on time. The plane **took off** and landed on time, and our baggage didn't get lost. The nightmare began when we **flagged down** a taxi from the airport. After haggling to agree a reasonable fare, we set off towards the city centre. The first thing we noticed was that there were no seatbelts, which was very unfortunate as the guy was doing 130 kilometres an hour while singing along to Kylie Minogue. It was no surprise that five minutes later he crashed into the back of a lorry at some traffic lights. Luckily we were OK. Unluckily he said that we had to **get out** and that he couldn't take us any further. But he said that he'd radioed his friend, who was also on his way into the city, and that he would **pick** us **up**. We noticed that his friend had a full taxi already. This, however, didn't seem to be a problem and we were asked to squeeze in anyway. We ended up sat on top of a couple of elderly German tourists and their four-year-old grandson. They were just as shocked as us. We finally made it into the city centre, and, not surprisingly, got **dropped off** at the wrong hotel.

# Speaking

## 1

- Ask: *What can go wrong on a journey?*
- Students work individually and make a list.
- Students compare their list with a partner.
- Students report their ideas to the class. Make notes on the board.

## Possible answers

- you can miss your plane / train / bus
- you can get on the wrong train / bus
- your car / taxi can break down
- there can be traffic jams / roadworks / diversions
- you can have an accident
- somebody can steal your luggage or your money / passport / tickets
- the airline can lose your luggage

## 2

- Read out the task.
- Students decide which journey they are going to describe.

## 3

- Explain the task. Read out the list of points to be included.
- Students plan a description of their journey by thinking about or making notes of the points given.

## 4

- Students work in pairs. They describe their journey to their partner.
- Ask some students to describe their journey to the class.

# Writing

**1**

- Explain the task and read out the instructions.
- Students plan their review by making notes on the points given and any other things they would like to include. You can set the writing task for homework.

**2**

- Students write their review, using their notes from Ex 1. Remind them to use linking words, qualifiers and phrasal verbs if possible.
- Take in the reviews. Stick them on the classroom walls. Students walk around and read the reviews, making a note of the place they think is the worst. <u>Alternatively</u>, ask students to read out their reviews to the class.
- Students vote for the worst place.

---

### Revision activities

**1) Wordlist activity**

- Revise vocabulary from this Unit by choosing a Wordlist activity from Teaching tips 'Reviewing and revising' on pages 21–22.

**2) Find your group**

- Divide the class into four groups.
- Assign one of these categories to each group: *phrasal verbs, types of transport, verbs that take -ing, verbs that take the infinitive.* Each person in the group writes a word or phrase for their category on a piece of paper.
- A student collects the pieces of paper and mixes them up in a hat or basket. Students take a piece of paper from the hat.
- Students walk around the class and say their word. When they meet somebody with a word from the same category, they stay together.
- Students continue until the four groups have collected all their members.
- Students in each group say their words. They should all be from the same category.

---

# Extra practice

Students complete the Extra practice material on page 89 either in class, or for homework.

### Extra practice answers

**1**
| | |
|---|---|
| 1 to have | 7 to come back |
| 2 to be | 8 taking / to take |
| 3 writing | 9 pretending |
| 4 to stay | 10 to fit |
| 5 to give | 11 trying |
| 6 carrying | 12 to see |

**2**
| | |
|---|---|
| 1 off | 5 on |
| 2 up for | 6 out off, down |
| 3 off | 7 off |
| 4 up | 8 down |

**3** 4, 8, 6, 1, 2, 7, 5, 3

**4** Transport: bus, car, taxi, train, tram
Phrasal verbs: cope with, put off, get in, get out, get on, get off, pick up, drop off, queue up for, flag down
Word from the text: sustainable
Phrase from the text: beaten track

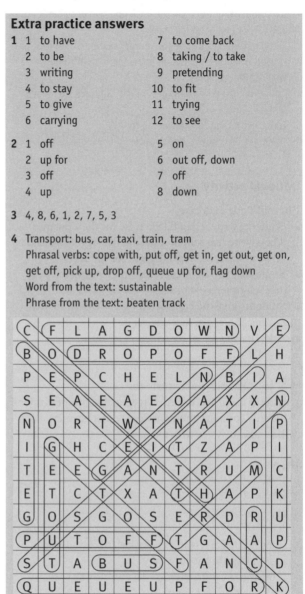

# References

Grammar reference: Coursebook page 91
Wordlist: Coursebook page 92
Photocopiable resources: Teacher's Book pages 94–95
Test: Teacher's Book pages 149–150

# CD-ROM

Unit 4 Globetrotting
Language exercise: Travel and tourism
Vocabulary activity: Journey across town
CEF-linked exercise: I can read an interview for general and specific information
Game: The big squeeze

# UNIT 5
# Review

Before starting this unit, ask students to read the Grammar reference on pages 90–91 and study the Wordlist on page 92 in the Coursebook.

---

**Ideas for preparation**
- Holiday brochures or holiday realia (see Warmer p85)
- Counters for the *Guess the word* game (see Vocabulary Ex 1 p85)
- Small prizes for the winners of the board game (see Vocabulary Ex 1 p85)

---

**Warmer**
- Show the class some realia connected with your next holiday (eg walking boots and pullover). Ask: *What do you think I'm going to do on my next holiday? Where do you think I'm going?* Students guess what you're going to do and where you're going. If they can't guess, tell them.
- Ask: *Have you got any holiday plans? Where are you going to go? Why have you chosen that place? What are you going to do there?*

---

## Lead-in

**1**
- Ask students to open their books on page 82. Read out the task and the questions.
- Students work in pairs or small groups and discuss the questions.
- Ask some students to tell the class about their partner's ideas.

## Language study

**1**
- Look at the two emails with the class. Ask: *What is the topic of both of them?* (holidays). Refer students to the first email. Ask: *Who is the mail from?* (Cathy), *Where did she go two weeks ago?* (Andalucia), *Did she have good weather?* (yes, it was very hot). Refer students to the second email. Ask: *Who's it from?* (Patrick), *Where is he?* (Turkey), *Is he staying in a hotel?* (no, in a rented villa).
- Read out the task. Correct the first mistake with the class as an example.
- Students work individually or in pairs. They correct the mistakes in the two emails.
- Check the answers with the class. Revise any problematic structures or refer students back to the appropriate Grammar reference.

---

**Answers**

| | |
|---|---|
| 1 went | 10 and |
| 2 was | 11 spending |
| 3 doing | 12 traditional, old, white |
| 4 had been | 13 absolutely / quite |
| 5 So | 14 hired |
| 6 relaxed | 15 were driving |
| 7 huge, blue, swimming | 16 beautiful, turquoise |
| 8 absolutely / quite | 17 but |
| 9 too | 18 quite |

---

**2**
- Explain the task
- Students work individually. They complete the sentences with true statements about holidays they've been on.
- Students compare their sentences with a partner.
- Ask students to read out a sentence each to the class.

## Vocabulary

**1**
- 🔊 **11** Tell students they are going to play a game called *Guess the word*. First look at the list of words with the class. Ask different students to read out a line of words each. Students say if they have forgotten any meanings and another student gives a definition.
- Read the rules of the game with the class. Check students have understood how to play.
- Students listen to the example.

**2**
- Students work in groups and play the game.
- Present the winner in each group to the class and give out small prizes.

**Listening script 11**
(A–D = game players)
A: OK, my turn. I've thought of a word.
B: Is the word a noun?
A: No. One.
C: Erm ... Is it an adjective?
A: Yes. Two.
D: Is it a material for clothes?
A: No. Three.
B: Is it a colour?
A: Yes. Four.
C: Is it khaki?
A: No. Five.
D: Is it turquoise?
A: Yes. Six. Your turn.
D: OK. I've chosen one ...

## Speaking: giving a presentation

**1**

- Explain the task. Students read through the information in each step. Check that they have understood everything.
- Students work in small groups. They choose their holiday and discuss the questions in Step 1.
- Students prepare their presentation according to the instructions in Step 2.
- Students practise their presentations.
- Students give their presentations to the class in turn. The class listens and asks questions if necessary.
- Students vote for the best holiday.

## Song

**1**

- Look at the photo of Dido with the class. Ask: *Do you know the singer Dido? What sort of music does she sing? Do you like her songs?*
- Read out the task and the questions.
- Students read the factfile about Dido and answer the questions.
- Check the answers with the class.

**Answers**

1   British.
2   No, she started to study law and then got involved in the music business.
3   She became famous when Eminem used part of her song *Thank you* in his hit song *Stan*.

**2**

- Explain the task. Read out the words in the box and check that students understand them.
- Students work in pairs. They predict the content of the song from the words in the box.
- Students report back to the class. Discuss their ideas.

**3**

- 🔘 **12**  Students listen to the song, read the words and check their predictions.
- Discuss if students predicted correctly.

**4**

- Read out the task.
- Students work individually. They read the song again and choose the correct alternatives.
- Check the answers with the class. Ask students to read out the part of the song that gives the answer.

**Answers**

1 a    2 b    3 c

---

**Optional activity**

**End of book quiz**

Test students on the contents of the Student's Book.

- Read out the questions below.
- Students work in pairs and write answers to the questions.
- Check the answers with the class.

Questions (and answers)

1   In which sport is Vladimir Kramnik world champion? (chess)
2   What does 'to be bullied at school' mean? (to be teased or attacked by other pupils)
3   In what year did Charles Lindbergh become the first person to fly solo across the Atlantic? (1927)
4   What is a 'trial'? (a court case)
5   What is a terraced house? (a house joined to other houses)
6   What is a tenant? (somebody who rents a flat)
7   In Britain, at what age can you drive a car? (17)
8   If you studied physics, what are you? (a physicist)
9   What is 'an only child'? (a child without brothers and sisters)
10  What does 'affectionate' mean? (showing love for somebody)
11  Who can be put on 'probation'? (people who have committed crimes)
12  What is 'a slob'? (an untidy, lazy person)
13  What does 'to fall out with somebody' mean? (to stop being friendly after an argument)
14  What countries make up the United Kingdom? (England, Scotland, Wales, Northern Ireland)
15  In Northern Ireland, are nationalists mainly Catholic of Protestant? (Catholic)
16  Who sang 'When a man loves a woman'? (Percy Sledge)
17  Which football team did David Beckham begin his career with? (Manchester United)
18  Which Olympic event was Carl Lewis famous for? (100 metres)
19  What is a 'sketch'? (a picture drawn with pencil)
20  Who is Basher? (an artist)
21  Do you use 'absolutely' or 'very' with the word 'wonderful'? (absolutely)
22  What is Romero Bryan's job? (fashion designer)
23  What's a shopaholic? (someone who can't stop shopping / buying things)
24  What does 'globetrotting' mean? (travelling the world)
25  Where does Dido come from? (Britain)

## References

Module 3 test: Teacher's Book pages 151–153

# Additional material

## Photocopiable resources

## Photocopiable tests

# UNIT 1
# Street life

**1**   Read the text quickly and answer these questions.

   1    How much does Louis earn each week?

   2    What is different about Beatrice and Juliette?

   3    Does Louis want to change his job?

> Hi, my name is Louis (pronounced Loo eee) and I sing and play guitar for a living. Sometimes I get paid quite well but sometimes not so well, it depends. It's a strange kind of job and some people don't really think it's a job at all. I don't have a salary, I don't have regular hours
> 5  and I don't pay tax. I work when I want to and for how long I want to; it all depends on what bills I have to pay, and how hungry I am.
>
> I'm a busker and my job is to entertain. I play and you pay. Pay what you want; pennies, pounds, cheques, stamps, gift vouchers, lottery tickets, whatever you think I deserve or whatever you think you can
> 10  afford.
>
> Most of my friends are buskers too; Sophie and Alice play steel drums, Charlie plays mandolin, Rhys plays flute, Anna plays xylophone and Beatrice and Juliette dance. Sometimes, usually on someone's birthday, we all get together and play in the park.
>
> 15  It's a good life most of the time but occasionally you get some people who don't like what you do. Sometimes they laugh, sometimes they shout abuse. Last week a group of teenagers spat at me, and a few weeks ago Sophie and Alice's steel drums were filled with beer.
>
> 20  I can't imagine doing anything else. Maybe one day I'll have to find a more normal job. It's a bit of a shame really, because the only thing I'm good at and happy with is singing songs and playing guitar.

**2**   Are these statements true or false?

   1    Louis doesn't have a nine-to-five job.

   2    Louis only accepts cash from his audience.

   3    Most people like Louis and his friends.

   4    It will be easy to find a normal job.

   5    Louis is generally happy and positive about his current lifestyle.

**3**   In a recent survey, over two hundred people were asked about their attitudes towards street entertainers. Read their comments and choose two which are similar to your own views.

'They should go out and find a proper job.'

'I don't mind them, so long as they don't do it in my street.'

'Dirty, lazy, talentless … put them in the army.'

'This town used to be beautiful until these ********* arrived!'

'I love 'em, even the ones who aren't very good.'

'If you give them money, they just go and spend it on alcohol and drugs.'

'I think they're great. Good luck to them.'

'They probably earn more than I do.'

**4**   Work with a partner. Discuss these statements.

   1    There is no difference between begging and busking.

   2    Each city should make special areas for beggars and buskers.

   3    Beggars and buskers are criminals.

   4    Society has a responsibility to house, clothe and feed people who live on the streets.

**5**   Work in a group of three and discuss these questions.

   1    What are the attractions of an unconventional job like busking?

   2    What other unconventional jobs can you think of?

   3    Would you like a job like this?

# UNIT 1
# My life's work

**1** Use the words in the box to find the names of the eight jobs shown in the pictures.

| | | | |
|---|---|---|---|
| motor | detective | war | cleaner |
| street | surgeon | football | |
| mechanic | rat | planner | |
| forensic | catcher | wedding | |
| referee | plastic | correspondent | |

**2** Work with a partner.

1 Make a list of four to six adjectives to describe the character of a person who would be good at the jobs in Ex 1. Give reasons for your choices.

2 How many of these qualities do you and your partner have?

3 Choose two of the jobs in Ex 1 that your partner would be good at. Does your partner agree with your choices? Why? / Why not?

4 Which of these jobs would you / wouldn't you do? Why?

**3** Write the jobs in the table and rank them, first in order of social importance and then in order of danger.
(1 = least important, 8 = most important;
1 = least dangerous, 8 = most dangerous).
Explain your choices.

| job | importance | danger |
|---|---|---|
| | | |
| | | |
| | | |
| | | |
| | | |
| | | |
| | | |
| | | |

**4** Work with a partner. Compare your lists.

**5** Choose one of the jobs and think about what a typical day is like. Write a description of a day in the life of the person. Read it out to the class and see if they can guess which job you have written about.

# UNIT 2
# The public eye

**1** It is common to divide celebrities into the A-list (major international film stars, rock stars etc), the B-list (people who are very famous nationally but less well-known abroad) and the C-list (people who are famous, but perhaps only for a while, and definitely only in one country / region).

Can you think of any examples? Write their names in the table.

| A-list | B-list | C-list |
|--------|--------|--------|
|        |        |        |
|        |        |        |
|        |        |        |
|        |        |        |

**2** C-list celebrities are often desperate to be more famous, or to keep the fame they have. How can they do this?

**3** What do you know about these people?

Angelina Jolie    David Beckham

Kylie Minogue    Venus Williams

Bill Gates    Michael Jackson

Tiger Woods    Jackie Chan

**4** Some celebrities try to use their fame to make the world better, while others only seem to be interested in making money or improving their own lives.

1 Are there any 'bad' celebrities in the list in Ex 3?

2 Can you think of any more 'good' celebrities?

**5** A recent survey asked school children what they wanted to be when they grew up; over half said they wanted to be famous. Which would you rather be? Why?

1 rich and famous

2 wealthy, but unknown

3 successful and respected in your profession

4 an ordinary person, living an ordinary life

**6** Work with a partner and discuss these suggestions. Use the language in the box to help you. What would you do to become famous?

1 appear on a reality TV programme (like *Big Brother*)

2 start a relationship with a famous person

3 finish a relationship with a famous person and sell your story to a newspaper

4 allow a TV documentary to be made about your family

5 appear on a TV game show

6 talk about your private life on a TV talk show (like *Jerry Springer*)

7 film your daily life and put it on the internet

8 sing a song on TV

**Useful language**
I'd really like to …
I'd never …
I'd think about … *-ing*
I wouldn't … if you paid me.
I wouldn't really want to …
I might consider … *-ing* if …

**7** Choose a political or social issue that is important to you. Imagine you are organising an event to publicise your cause. Think of a celebrity who could give you publicity and write a short letter to him / her. In your letter, you need to:

- explain the issue
- say what the event is
- tell the celebrity about the event
- invite him / her to support you.

She was born on 27 August 1910 in the city of Skopje.

As a child, she knew she wanted to work as a missionary.

After leaving school, she went to Ireland and became a Catholic nun.

She went to India after her training, where she started teaching at a high school.

While working there, she became aware of the terrible poverty around her.

So in 1948 she decided to stop teaching and work amongst the poor of Calcutta.

She started her own school in the city, where she taught children from the slums.

Her school was outside because she had no money to buy a building.

Volunteers joined her and she began to receive money from people who admired her work.

In 1950 she started an order of nuns to look after the poor.

Her organisation now works in countries in Asia, Africa, Europe and South America.

There, they not only work with the poor but also help the victims of natural disasters, such as floods and earthquakes.

Her nuns also help people who are sick, or who are refugees or homeless.

She died on 5 September 1997.

UNIT 3
# Sob story

A TV company has developed a new game show. Each week, the winner of the game receives £50,000. Each contestant has to explain why he / she should win. A jury listens to their stories and chooses which contestant should receive the money. The only problem is ... the contestants may not be telling the truth!

This week you are the jury, and four of your classmates are the contestants. They are:

A

Name: _____
Age: 29
Job: Nurse

B

Name: _____
Age: 78
Job: Retired

C

Name: _____
Age: 29
Job: Unemployed

D

Name: _____
Age: 35
Job: Teacher

**1** Work with a partner. Discuss who needs the money most, and who you would like to give it to.

**2** Listen to the contestants' reasons for wanting the money. Decide with your partner who you think should win.

**3** Work in a group of four. Discuss your choices. You must all agree on one winner. Speak to the contestants individually.

**4** Tell the class who your group decided on, and why.

**5** Ask questions of the four contestants to help your group make a final decision.

**6** As a class, choose a winner.

## Role cards

**A** Age: 29

Job: Nurse

You want the money as a deposit to buy a flat. You live in an expensive town, and can't afford to buy a place to live on a nurse's salary. Rent is very expensive, and if you can't buy somewhere you may have to move away.

**B** Age: 78

Job: Retired

Tell the jury that you want the money to study as you left school at 14 and never had the chance of an education. Decide what course you want to study, and why.

BUT you really want the money to go on a round-the-world cruise. You hope to find a new husband. Try to keep this secret from the jury.

**C** Age: 29

Job: Unemployed

You do voluntary work with poor children. You would use the money to take your group on an adventure holiday, and to decorate and buy equipment for the youth centre you work in. Think about why it is so important to take the children away, and what you would buy for the centre.

**D** Age: 35

Job: Teacher

Tell the group that you want the money to put your elderly mother into an old people's home. Explain how difficult your life is, and how much better it would be for your mother in the home.

BUT you really want the money to pay for a luxury wedding for you and your boyfriend. Try to keep this secret from the jury.

Move Intermediate Teacher's Book © Macmillan Publishers Limited 2006 **Photocopiable**

# Comparison hat trick

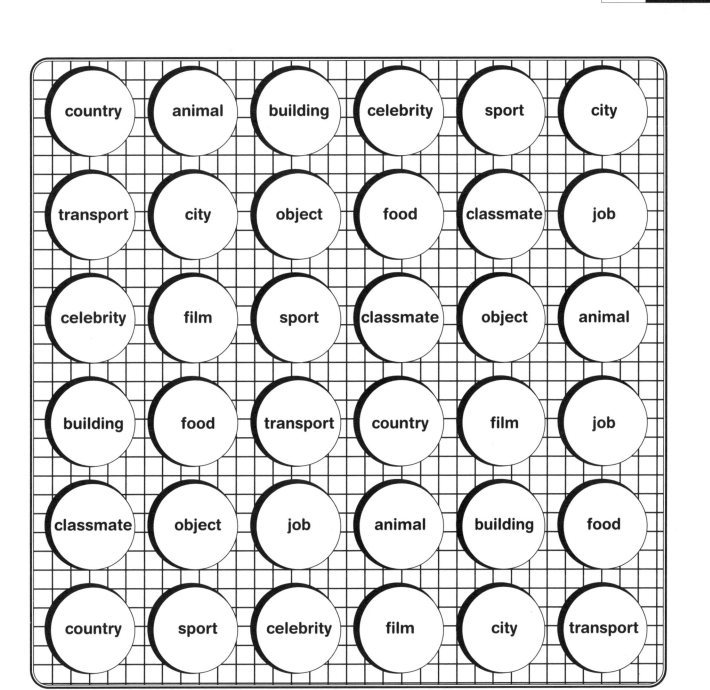

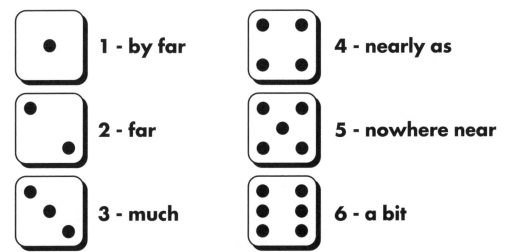

1 - by far

2 - far

3 - much

4 - nearly as

5 - nowhere near

6 - a bit

# Tied to the apron strings

**1** Mark on the scale:

1 the best age to leave home (ie stop living with your parents);

2 the most normal age to leave home in your country.

| Under 16  16  17  18  19  20  21  22  23  24  25  26  27  28  29  30  over 30 |

3 If there is a difference, why do you think this is?

4 Is it different for men and women? If so, why?

**2** Which of these opinions is closest to how you feel?

**Katie (20), UK**

I couldn't wait to move out; I left at 18 when I went to university. OK, I live in a horrible bedsit, and I never have any money, but I have my independence. Anyway, it's important to learn to stand on your own feet. I love my mum, but I wouldn't want to live there again. I see her at Christmas and sometimes in the holidays.

What's wrong with living at home? If I had my own flat, it'd be really expensive. I'd have to do all my washing and cooking myself. At home I've got all the things I need. Anyway, my mum would miss me. I'll probably move out when I get married.

**Roberto (25), Italy**

I'd love to move out. It drives me crazy living with my parents. My dad still treats me like a little girl and my little brother is always getting in the way when I'm trying to work. But there aren't any flats that I can afford and it's impossible to get a job while I'm studying. I know one or two people who live alone, but they get money from their parents.

I moved into a university residence when I started studying, as the university is too far away from my home town, but I go home every holiday, and I visit my parents once or twice a month. I'll probably go back when I finish studying, until I get a job.

**Marion (21), Germany**

**Maria (22), Poland**

**3** Group A: think of the advantages of leaving home early (18 or 19).

Group B: think of the advantages of staying at home.

Compare your ideas.

**4** Read the article. Does it mention any of the advantages you discussed?

**5** How would you feel if you were a parent in the situation in the article? What do you think parents could / should do?

## Boomerang Kids: chicks come back to the nest

For twenty or more years you work to give your children a good life. You spend most of your money on fashionable clothes (for them), on computers and books (for them), on family holidays (you go somewhere they will like). You spend all your time cooking, cleaning up after them and washing their clothes. You stay at home to look after them in the evenings and at weekends; then, when they're older, you can't go out because they've borrowed the car.

Finally the glorious day comes when you can wave goodbye as they leave for university or their first job. Of course you miss them and worry, and the house seems too big, but soon you get used to the freedom and enjoy the extra space. You discover that you can spend time with *your* friends, go on holiday where *you* want (and *when* you want). You begin to spend your money on eating out, fashionable clothes for *you* and computers and books for *you*. Perhaps you even think about moving to a smaller house, to release some extra cash.

Everything is perfect; then the phone call comes: 'Mum, Dad, I'll be moving back home for a while …'.

Your world collapses. You're happy to have them, of course, but suddenly there are extra people in the house, big people, with big and noisy friends. They eat everything in the fridge, borrow money, borrow the car and are always on the phone or the internet. And they are costing you a fortune.

This is the situation an increasing number of parents are finding themselves in. Expensive housing and unemployment are causing more and more 'boomerang children' to move back in with their parents and 'a while' can be months or even years.

This is not only a lifestyle problem though; having children at home for longer can affect parents' plans for retirement too.

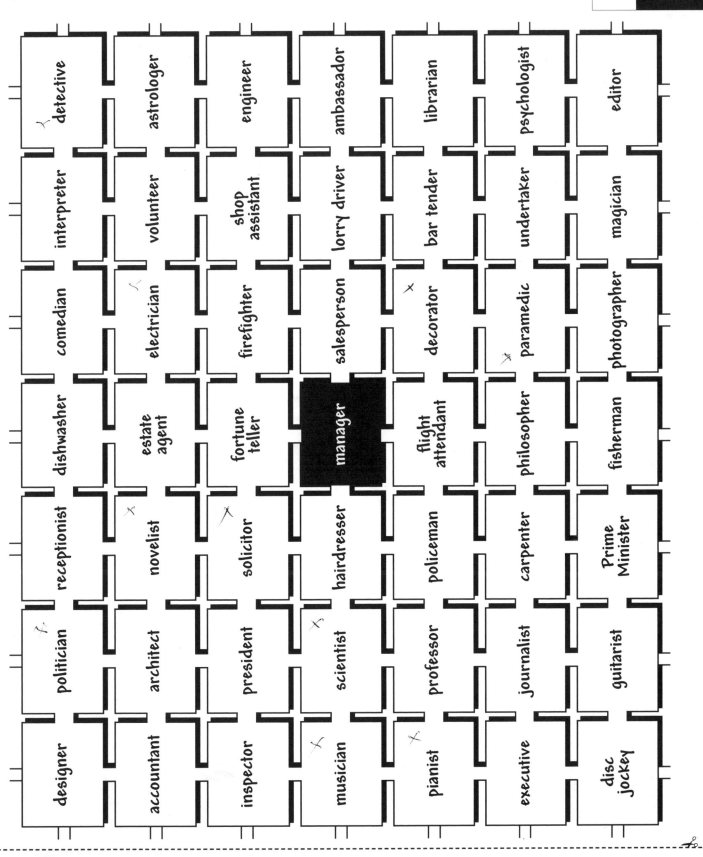

**Directions**

| Stress | or | Stress | – | Move |
|--------|-----|--------|---|------|
| ● ● ● | or | ● ● ● ● | – | Left |
| ● ● ● | or | ● ● ● ● | – | Right |
| ● ● ● | or | ● ● ● ● | – | Straight on |

**1** Put these words into two groups, *honest* and *dishonest*. Use your dictionary to help you.

| | | | |
|---|---|---|---|
| blunt | candid | deceitful | diplomatic |
| direct | frank | insincere | open |
| polite | rude | sincere | straightforward |
| tactful | truthful | untruthful | |

1 Put a (+) by words that have a positive meaning and a (−) by words which have a negative meaning.

2 Which three of the words best describe you?

**2** Is it ever good to lie or bad to tell the truth?

**3** Read these situations and decide if you would lie or tell the truth.

**4** Work with a partner and discuss these questions.

1 Which of the people in the box would you tell the truth to about the situations in Ex 3?
2 Why wouldn't you tell the truth?
3 What would you say?

**People**

your mum    your boss    your best friend
a colleague    your school friend    your teacher
a waiter    your brother    your sister
your ex-boyfriend    your ex-girlfriend
your dad    your boyfriend    your girlfriend

**5** Work in two groups.
**Group A:** you are one of the characters in the People box.
**Group B:** you are one of the characters in Ex 3. Choose one of the people from the People box and roleplay telling the truth about your situation to him / her.

1 You're feeling depressed; you're asked 'How are you?'
2 You accidentally scratch the paint on a car.
3 You think a new haircut looks stupid.
4 You're asked about a newspaper story by someone who has very different political opinions from you. You know you'll disagree.
5 You lose £100 in the street.
6 You drop a mobile phone and break it.
7 You make a big mistake at work / school; someone else is blamed and punished.
8 You're using a computer and you accidentally infect it with a virus.
9 You have a hangover and don't want to go to work.
10 You're invited to dinner with some people you don't like.
11 You forget to do some work / homework.
12 You're on a bus but you don't have a ticket. An inspector gets on.

Move Intermediate Teacher's Book © Macmillan Publishers Limited 2006    **Photocopiable**

### Architect: grandchild

**ambitious:** 'I want to design the tallest building in the world and I want to be the most famous architect ever.'

**successful:** 'I've won a lot of prizes for my designs and I own a very large company.'

**rebellious:** 'I hate traditional architecture. I like designing buildings that shock people.'

**Find someone who is:**
- self-motivated
- bad-tempered
- vain

### Teacher: second cousin

**self-motivated:** 'I don't need a boss to tell me what to do. I love my job and do everything myself.'

**independent:** 'I like working alone in the classroom.'

**confident:** 'I love speaking in front of strangers and meeting new people. I never get nervous.'

**Find someone who is:**
- responsible
- hard-working
- arrogant

### Librarian: cousin

**self-motivated:** 'I don't need a boss. I know what I have to do and I do it myself.'

**hard-working:** 'I love my job and I work 50 hours a week.'

**bad-tempered:** 'I often shout at people who talk in the library. They make me really angry.'

**Find someone who is:**
- confident
- cautious
- rebellious

### Firefighter: great grandchild

**obedient:** 'The most important thing is to follow orders. I always follow orders.'

**risk-taking:** 'I don't ever feel scared. I will always do dangerous things to save lives.'

**desperate:** 'I really, really want to have children more than anything else in the world.'

**Find someone who is:**
- self-motivated
- risk-taking
- arrogant

### Hairdresser: cousin

**confident:** 'I like meeting people and never feel shy or embarrassed when I meet someone new.'

**risk-taking:** 'I like to invent new hairstyles that nobody's ever seen before, but my career could fail if nobody likes what I do.'

**vain:** 'I spend all my time thinking about my hair and what it looks like.'

**Find someone who is:**
- responsible
- cautious
- successful

### Journalist: grandchild

**ambitious:** 'I want to be the editor of a big national newspaper and have my own TV show.'

**confident:** 'I meet lots of people in my job and I never feel shy or embarrassed when I meet someone new.'

**arrogant:** 'I'm one of the best journalists in the world. All my colleagues think so.'

**Find someone who is:**
- independent
- rebellious
- obedient

### Doctor: niece / nephew

**cautious:** 'I only prescribe medicine when I'm absolutely sure I know what's wrong with the patient.'

**reliable:** 'I'm never late for work and have never had a day off.'

**responsible:** 'The decisions I make can mean the difference between life and death.'

**Find someone who is:**
- confident
- hard-working
- miserable

### Musician: great grandchild

**successful:** 'I've sold over ten million CDs and played all over the world.'

**rebellious:** 'I've always wanted to be different and not do a normal job like work in a bank.'

**vain:** 'Do you think my hair looks good? I've just spent lots of money on a new hairstyle – I'm always changing my hair.'

**Find someone who is:**
- ambitious
- independent
- bad-tempered

### Bus driver: son / daughter-in-law

**obedient:** 'I never break the law. I respect all the traffic laws.'

**hard-working:** 'I work 10 hours a day and 6 days a week.'

**bad-tempered:** 'I always shout at motorists who don't drive well. They make me really angry.'

**Find someone who is:**
- ambitious
- generous
- reliable

### Businessman / woman: nephew / niece

**generous:** 'I give 10% of the company's profits to charity.'

**responsible:** 'I'm in charge of over a thousand people who work in my company.'

**arrogant:** 'I believe I am a very good boss and a fantastic businessman / woman.'

**Find someone who is:**
- ambitious
- reliable
- miserable

### Scientist: son / daughter-in-law

**cautious:** 'I don't take risks when I do experiments. The laboratory can be a very dangerous place.'

**miserable:** 'I'm not happy. I'm divorced and I don't think I'll ever fall in love again.'

**desperate:** 'I don't think I can live another day without a husband / wife. The situation is really bad.'

**Find someone who is:**
- obedient
- successful
- ambitious

### Psychologist: second cousin

**independent:** 'I like working by myself and not having a boss.'

**miserable:** 'I'm really depressed at the moment. I'm just never happy with anything.'

**reliable:** 'I'm always on time and if I make a promise I always keep it.'

**Find someone who is:**
- risk-taking
- vain
- generous

UNIT 2
# Number 35

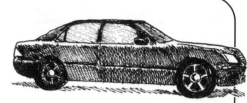

**1** Four different people have lived at number 35 during the last four years. Before you read the text, make a list of reasons why they might have decided to leave.

I've lived at number 37 for the last four years and during this time I've had four different neighbours at number 35.

When I first moved in, there was Duncan; he was
5 about my age – 27 – and said he was a law student. Whenever I saw him, he was carrying ancient-looking books and scrolls of paper. His bedroom light always seemed to be on and every Friday night he listened to opera. The last time I saw him was when the
10 police came and took him away. He left me the contents of his fridge, which included a bottle of champagne, three duck eggs and a bag of cherries.

Zoë was next. She always dressed in black. She drove a black car with black tinted windows and had
15 a black cat called Blackie. At least once a week she knocked on my door to borrow candles or playing cards. The postman often left her parcels outside her door. She seemed to disappear rather than leave. She didn't say goodbye and I don't think she
20 took her cat as I often hear it miaowing late at night.

Stuart was next and he stayed for nearly two years. A nurse used to visit him every Wednesday at eight in the morning and during those two years he
25 lost a lot of weight.

We became quite good friends and the night before he left he invited me round to help him make dinner for some friends. We ate everything he had, but I never found out what was in the box in his freezer
30 that had 'DO NOT EAT' written on it.

Melly moved in four months ago. I have no idea what she does but I hear a lot of banging and shouting and she has the occasional bonfire. I've never seen any visitors go to her door.

**2** Work with a partner and discuss these questions.

1 Why do you think the police came to take Duncan away?

2 What kind of films did Zoë most enjoy watching?

3 Why didn't Zoë say goodbye?

4 What do you think happened to Stuart?

5 What was in his box marked 'DO NOT EAT'?

6 What does Melly do?

7 Who lives at number 39?

8 Do you think the person at number 37 is a nosey neighbour? Why?

**3** In Britain there are groups called Neighbourhood Watch, in which people in a community are encouraged to keep their eye on their neighbours and report any suspicious activity to the police. The intention is to reduce the amount of crime and create a community spirit.

1 Think of five advantages and five disadvantages of this scheme.

2 Do you have similar schemes in your country?

3 Do you think such schemes work? Why?

4 How would you feel if a neighbour installed CCTV in their garden so that it could record visitors arriving at and leaving your house?

**4** Suggest three ways for communities to make their neighbourhoods:

• safer

_____

• cleaner

_____

• livelier

_____

# UNIT 2
# Landlord's choice

**1**  Create a new personality! Use your imagination and complete the profile.

Name _____     Age _____

Occupation _____

Personality adjectives – positives and negatives     My ideal home would have …

_____

_____

_____     A good landlord is someone who …

_____

_____

_____

Two things that irritate you     A good tenant is someone who …

_____

_____

Two things that make you laugh     I don't like neighbours who …

_____

_____

**2**  Introduce yourself to a partner. Try to remember your details from your profile.

**3**  Work in two groups. Choose one of these roles and use your new personality from Ex 1.

**Landlords:** you are looking for a suitable tenant for a flat you own near the city centre. Write questions you would ask the people who come to look at the flat in the space provided. Remember, you want an honest and reliable tenant.

**Tenants:** you are looking for a flat near the city centre. Imagine the questions a landlord might ask you, and write possible answers in the space provided. You may have to tell some white lies to convince the landlord that you are the right person for the flat.

**4**  **Landlords:** choose three tenants and interview them.

Who will you offer the flat to?

Move Intermediate Teacher's Book © Macmillan Publishers Limited 2006

# UNIT 3
# Modern love

**1** If you are / were single, would you consider any of these options to help you find a partner? Why / Why not?

1 going on a blind date (organised by friends)

2 using a dating agency

3 visiting an internet dating site

4 going to a speed dating night

5 joining a singles club

**2** Read the article from the web.

1 Do people use the same methods to find a partner in your country?

2 Is this is a problem, or just a part of modern life?

## Desperately seeking ... someone?

They're young, professional, attractive and successful. They have new cars, laptop computers and the latest thing in mobile phones and PDAs. But in the rush between the office, the Pilates class and the expense-account lunch they seem to have forgotten something. When they go home to their loft-style apartment they are greeted only by the cat. When they go to bed, they have only the pillow to hold.

More and more people in their 20s and 30s are finding the pressures of a busy lifestyle are leaving them with no time, or no opportunity, to meet a partner so they are turning to professional help to find that special someone.

Only twenty years ago most people would rather have died than say that they used a dating agency; nowadays it's not only acceptable, it's fashionable. And there is a huge variety of methods to meet a partner, from the traditional newspaper column or introduction agency, through the specialist agencies, to dinner clubs, the internet, speed dating, even dating-in-the-dark.

'Sure you meet some strange people,' said one dater at a club singles night, 'but since I started coming here two months ago, I've had more dates than I had in the year before that, and you're going to get lucky sooner or later. Anyway, it's fun. My social life's better than it's ever been.'

**3** Imagine you had a friend who was single and finding it difficult to meet someone. What advice would you give him / her?

**4** Read these advertisements from a lonely hearts column and answer these questions.

1 What do the abbreviations M; F; GSOH; n/s; ltr; WLTM mean?

2 How many other shortened words can you find?

3 Which person would you be most interested in?

**a** Intelligent, attract. F, 33, currently climbing the walls. Likes gardening, walking and eating out, WLTM grown-up M, with GSOH to bring me back down to earth.

**b** Profess. M, 29, tall and reasonably good looking, seeks sim. F for quiet nights in and wild nights out.

**c** I've kissed so many frogs my lips hurt. F, 24, seeks intelligent, profess. Prince Charming, for happy ending.

**d** Warm, straightforward M, 30-something, WLTM F, 20s / 30s for talk, laughter and more?

**e** Slim, romantic F 30s. WLTM witty, cultured n/s M, under 45, for fun times and possible ltr.

**f** Fat, ugly, stupid man, smoker, no money, terrible SOH, WLTM slim, attractive, wealthy F who values honesty, to take me to the pub.

**g** Walking in the wood, lying on the beach. Active outdoorsy F n/s, 36, seeks M 30–40 who thinks he can keep up with me.

**5** Write an advertisement to describe yourself in this box.

**6** Look at the advertisements your classmates have written.

1 Choose the one you like best.

2 Write a short note introducing yourself and suggesting a place to meet.

# Noughts and crosses

## Answers

*NB the object can change position, eg I did my coat up / I did up my coat.*

*I've finally given up smoking.

The aeroplane took off.

We don't get on.

We have run out of sugar.

I've fallen out with my girlfriend.

*I'm going to the airport to pick up my mum.

*I'm going to drop my wife off at the airport.

The concert was called off.

*I took up tennis last year.

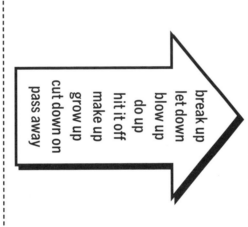

## Answers

*NB the object can change position, eg I did my coat up / I did up my coat.*

*I did up my coat.

I need to cut down on drinking wine.

He passed away three years ago.

*The bomb blew up the station.

She really let me down.

My boyfriend and I have broken up.

*He made up the story.

I grew up in Oxford.

We hit it off straight away.

## Answers

*NB the object can change position, eg I did my coat up / I did up my coat.*

I bumped into my friend yesterday.

*Can you turn on the TV, please?

I went out with her for 2 years.

Can you speak up? I can't hear you.

He turned up three hours late.

My car broke down on the way to work.

*Please fill in the form.

*I put off doing the washing up.

I need to get away for a while.

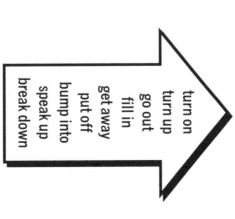

**1** Work with a partner and discuss these questions.

 1 Do you or your family own a gun? What type? Why?

 2 How common is it to own a gun in your country?

 3 How common is gun-related crime in your country?

 4 Would you know where to get a gun? Is it expensive?

 5 How easy is it to get a gun? Do you think it's too easy, about right, or too difficult?

**2** Read these opinions about gun control. Which is closest to your own point of view?

> Guns don't kill people, people kill people. If someone really wants to kill, they don't need a gun.

> Guns make it much easier to kill or seriously hurt someone.

> I hope I never have to use it, but I live alone and I just don't feel safe.

> People kill with knives. Do you want to ban knives as well?

> Everybody has the right to protect themselves, and the criminals carry guns.

> I'm not a criminal. I have a gun for hunting and I don't see why I should have to give up because some people are idiots.

> If you've got a gun in the house you're much more likely to kill a member of the family or a friend than an intruder.

**3** Work with a partner. Can you think of arguments **against** these points of view?

**4** Read these Case studies and discuss the questions.

## Case study 1

In August 1999 Tony Martin shot at two young men who were burgling his farm, wounding one and killing the other. Martin was arrested and charged with murder and possessing an illegally-held shotgun. In April 2000 he was convicted of murder, and sentenced to life in prison. In November 2000 the surviving burglar and the getaway driver were sentenced to three years in prison, but they were released in August / September 2001. Two months later, the getaway driver was back in prison.

On appeal, Tony Martin's conviction was reduced to manslaughter, and he was released, having been in prison for 3½ years.

● The man who was killed was only 16. He was shot in the back. The burglars weren't carrying guns and they did not attack Martin. Do you think murder or manslaughter was the right verdict?

● The burglars spent less than a year in prison, despite being career criminals. Martin was in jail for 3½ years. Does this seem fair?

● English law allows the use of reasonable force to defend yourself or your property. Do you think people should be allowed to kill to protect their property?

● Would gun control have changed this story? How?

## Case study 2

In March 1996, in Dunblane, Scotland, Thomas Hamilton walked into the local primary school. He was a member of a gun club and had three legally-held sporting handguns with him. He shot three members of staff and 28 pupils. Then he killed himself. One teacher and 16 children were killed.

After this, a law was passed in Britain that made it illegal to own any kind of handgun, for any reason, including pistols like Hamilton had used.

● Opponents of the British ban said that it would not stop a psychopath getting a gun, and anyway, someone crazy enough would find another way to kill. Do you agree?

● Those who supported the ban said that there was no good reason for a person to have a handgun. Their only purpose is to kill. Can you think of a good reason for owning a handgun?

● Would gun control have helped in this situation? How?

**5** Is there anything good that can come of owning a gun?

# What's the preposition?

**Game board squares:**

- **Finish**
- 47 to recover
- 46 typical
- 45 to shout
- 44 to escape
- 43 Move back 2 spaces
- 42 to agree
- 41 disappointed
- 40 to protest
- 39 bad
- 38 to argue
- 37 guilty
- 36 Move forward 3 spaces
- 35 to think
- 34 jealous
- 33 to succeed
- 32 to insist
- 31 to protect
- 30 Miss a turn
- 29 to depend
- 28 satisfied
- 27 suitable
- 26 to speak
- 25 to complain
- 24 to hear
- 23 to feel guilty
- 22 famous
- 21 to approve
- 20 to belong
- 19 to prepare
- 18 Miss a turn
- 17 upset
- 16 to apologise
- 15 to boast
- 14 responsible
- 13 to cover
- 12 Move forward 3 spaces
- 11 similar
- 10 bored
- 9 to waste money
- 8 Move back 2 spaces
- 7 married
- 6 to dream
- 5 to deal
- 4 Miss a turn
- 3 to worry
- 2 angry
- 1 to react
- **Start**

## Referee's answers

to agree with sb / about / on sth
angry at / with sb / about sth
to apologise to sb / for sth
to approve of sb / sth
to argue with sb / about sth
bad at sth / bad for sb
to belong to sb / sth
to boast about / of sth
bored with sb / sth
to complain to / about sb / about sth
to cover with / in sth
to deal with sb / sth
to depend on sb / sth
disappointed in / with sb / about / at / by / with sth
to dream about / of sb / sth
to escape from sb / sth
famous for sth
to feel guilty about sth
guilty of sth
to hear of / about sb / sth
to insist on sth
jealous of sb / sth
married to sb
to prepare for sth
to protect sb from / against sb / sth
to protest at / about / against / over sth
to react to / with sth
to recover from sth
responsible for / to sb / for sth
satisfied with sth
to shout at / to sb
similar to sb / sth
to speak of / to / with sb / about sth
to succeed in sth
suitable for sb / sth
to think about / of sb / sth
typical of sb / sth
upset about / by / over sth / with sb
to waste money on sth
to worry about sb / sth

Move Intermediate Teacher's Book © Macmillan Publishers Limited 2006

# UNIT 1
# Football in violence?

**1**  Work with a partner. Discuss these questions.

1   Is football hooliganism a problem in your country? Does hooliganism happen in other sports?

2   Do you think hooliganism exists because of football? Would it exist without football?

3   How does the behaviour of spectators affect the behaviour of the players?

4   Is the behaviour of some players worse than that of the spectators?

**2**  Put the these actions in order of how bad they are, starting with the worst. Compare your list with another pair.

1   Football fans throwing objects like coins and bottles onto the pitch during the game.

2   Football fans shouting racist insults when certain players have the ball.

3   Football fans booing the opposing team whenever they have the ball.

4   Football fans booing during the national anthem of the opposing team.

5   Football fans making chants about individual players.

6   Football fans invading the pitch to celebrate scoring a goal or winning a match.

7   Football fans throwing objects at the opposing team's supporters.

8   Football fans chanting insults about the opposing team's supporters.

**3**  Read the three newspaper articles and discuss these questions with a partner.

1   In your opinion, whose actions were the worst?

2   Whose actions were 'provoked'?

3   What punishments do you think are appropriate for these players?

## Diouf Spitting Row

Scottish police are investigating striker El-Hadji Diouf after he spat at the crowd during his side's 1–1 draw with Celtic. He reacted when a Celtic supporter patted his head in an apparently friendly gesture, as he went into the crowd to pick up the ball. The fans started booing Diouf whenever he touched the ball, so he was substituted before the end of the match.

## Cantona Attacks Fan

Eric Cantona attacked a spectator after being sent off when Manchester drew 1–1 with Crystal Palace several seasons ago. Cantona was dismissed after a foul on Palace's Shaw. As he was leaving the pitch, a spectator stood up and shouted abuse at the Frenchman. Cantona's reaction was to aim a kick at the fan. Manchester players ran over to break up the pair.

## Bowyer and Dyer: 'Sorry' for Fight

In their match with Aston Villa, Newcastle lost at home 3–0. After Villa scored their third goal, a fight started between two Newcastle players, Bowyer and Dyer. Several of their team-mates and Villa players separated them. Neither player was hurt, but Bowyer's shirt was ripped.

**4**  Read the actual punishments that were given. Match the punishment to the player.

1   He was banned for three games.

2   He was banned for two matches and dropped from the team for the next match. He was also fined two weeks' wages.

3   He was banned from football for eight months, fined £20,000 and given two weeks in prison; this was reduced to 120 hours community service.

4   He received a seven-match ban. His club fined him £200,000 and gave him a final warning.

**5**  Do you think the punishments were severe enough to stop players behaving this way again?

**6**  Work with a partner. Suggest five ways to reduce violent behaviour in players and fans.

# UNIT 1
# Sport for all

**1** In school playgrounds around the world, children play games that have been played for centuries. Listen to your teacher describe a childhood game and ask questions about it.

**2** Describe games you played at school.

   1   What were their names?

   2   Can you translate them into English?

**3** You are going to invent a new game and present it to the class. The sports are:

**Bigball**           **Hoop hoop**

**Throw back**      **Chicken run**

**Runaround**

**4** Make notes in the table to help you with your presentations.

**5** Vote on which new sport sounds the most enjoyable.

| | |
|---|---|
| How many players are there? Do they play in teams? | |
| What equipment do they need? | |
| Where is the sport played? Describe the layout of the area. | |
| How do you score points? | |
| Are there any things you are not allowed to do? | |
| How long does the game last? How does the game end? | |
| How do you know who has won? | |
| Any other information? | |

UNIT 2
# Look at this

**1**   Read these situations 1–7. On the scale, mark your reaction (0 = not at all offended, 5 = extremely offended).

◀ **not offended**      **very offended** ▶

| | 0 | 1 | 2 | 3 | 4 | 5 |
|---|---|---|---|---|---|---|

1   A bridge you cross on your way to work has been covered with graffiti.

2   You visit an art gallery with your parents while you're on holiday. The main exhibition consists of large animals, like cows and horses, which have been cut up and preserved in a display case.

3   Your best friend visits you and proudly shows you a tattoo of a lion that covers his / her whole back.

4   You switch on the TV and find a badly-drawn animated film that involves a lot of violence and swearing, and makes fun of poor and disabled people, as well as celebrities, but that your friends find extremely funny.

5   You go to a sculpture exhibition to find that many of the works are made out of frozen human blood.

6   You go to a friend's new house. He / she has decorated the walls of the living room with black and white photographs of naked men and women. On a shelf in one corner of the room is a small statue of a naked couple kissing.

7   You open the newspaper and see large colour photographs of a city that has been badly damaged by an earthquake. In the photos, you can clearly see dead bodies and badly injured people, as well as people who are shocked and upset by what has happened.

**2**   Work with a partner and discuss your reactions.

**3**   Interview your partner using these questions.

1   Have you ever seen any of the images mentioned above? How did you react?

2   Do you think that there should be any control over images that we see in public places, like art galleries? What do you think those controls should be?

3   What images do you find shocking or upsetting?

**4**   Imagine it is 2016. Your country is bidding to hold the Olympic Games in 2024. You have invited four artists to present their ideas for designs for a piece of artwork that will be displayed in the hotel where the Olympic Committee will meet to discuss the bid and that will be the basis for the 2024 logo.
The four artists are: a photographer, a painter, a graffiti sprayer, and a sculptor.

1   Listen to each presentation. Ask each artist questions about:

- his / her previous work
- his / her ideas for this project
- his / her influences
- what he / she plans to do with the work once the Olympics have finished.

2   When you have enough information, vote for a winner.

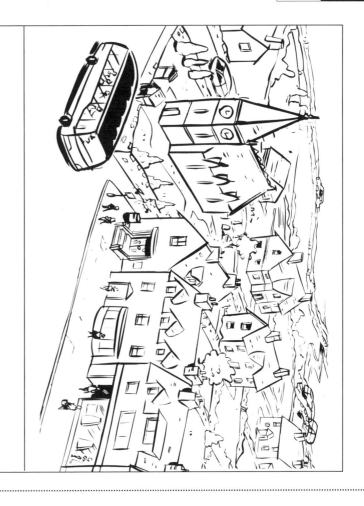

# Fashion fakes

**1** Work in groups and discuss these questions.

1 How many brand names can you find in the classroom?

2 Do you look for particular brands when you are shopping?

3 What are your favourite brands?

**2** Read *Faking it*. What is the problem it describes?

**3** Work with a partner and discuss these questions.

1 Is this a problem in your country?

2 Which of the two women in the article do you think has a better reason for buying fakes?

3 Are the companies right to be angry?

4 Have you ever bought a designer fake?

5 If you couldn't afford the real thing would you buy a fake:
- expensive designer watch
- pair of the latest sunglasses
- CD of computer software
- fashionable shirt
- bag
- perfume
- pop music CD

6 Are there any fakes you would buy to save money even if you could afford the real thing?

7 Is there anything wrong with producing designer fakes if people are willing to buy them?

# Faking it

**Oxford Street, London. A young man opens his suitcase and says, 'Designer perfumes, guaranteed stolen, £15 each, two for £20, come along ladies.'**

In the case are boxes of perfume, all with names you find in every fashion store. A couple of women pick up bottles, sniff them and hand over more than £40 each. Soon there are more women. The man looks around nervously as he takes their money. He spots a policeman's helmet in the crowd, stuffs the cash in his pocket, closes his case and runs into the nearby underground station. He isn't running because the perfume is stolen, but because it's fake. And the first two women to buy from him are, of course, his girlfriend and his sister.

It's a common sight on any city street around the world, and as designer labels become more important, so does the trade in designer fakes. Everything from Viagra to watches, from suitcases to sportswear can be bought on markets and out of the back of vans; all with the familiar logos, and all completely fake.

Designers spend thousands of pounds every year to fight the fraudsters, but it seems to be a losing battle while we are happy to buy them. But who are the customers?

'Karen' is a single mother, with four children. She has a part-time job working in a supermarket. 'It's for the children really,' she says. 'All the other kids at school have designer gear, but I can't afford the real stuff and I don't want my boys to be laughed at.'

'Juliet' works in the City of London. She also buys designer fakes for her children, but her reasons are different. 'I spend a fortune on designer stuff for myself and I always get the genuine article; the quality is better. But kids grow so quickly. If you buy designer clothes for them, they're too small in six months. So I get fakes.'

# Designer bombs?

Walk around any open-air market or visit any internet auction site and you will find an amazing number of designer goods at amazingly low prices. Anyone who wants to buy a copy of a designer handbag is only buying themselves part of a dream lifestyle that is splashed all over the pages of celebrity magazines. It doesn't harm anyone, right?

Wrong. Think about who made that handbag. Do you imagine men and women in a small factory, smiling as they work, having an hour lunch-break, and spending their wages in the same way as you, at a market on Saturday afternoon? Think again. Experts are now warning us that the trade in fake goods relies on sweatshops with terrible working conditions, including child labour. Money goes into terrorism and organised crime, not paying wages. Notorious terrorist groups have started faking designer clothing because the money is good, and if they're caught, the penalties are low – sometimes just a fine, not prison. And if you think that the money can't be that good, read the report that said last year British business lost over £6 billion to the counterfeiters. And that amount is still growing.

So next time you want to buy a fake designer suit, think about who you're giving your money to. It's certainly not the guy at the market who sells you the clothes.

**4** Read *Designer bombs?* What reasons does it give to stop buying fakes?

**5** Work in a group of four and discuss these questions.

1 Does this article change your mind about fake products?

2 What can countries / companies do to stop the trade in fake designer goods?

# UNIT 3
# Clothing families

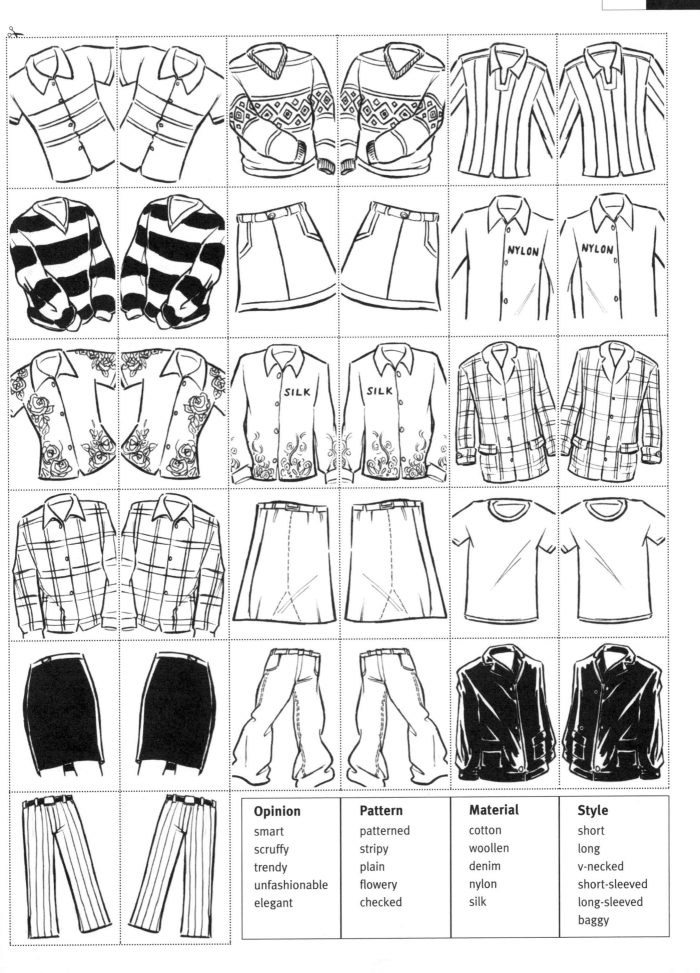

| Opinion | Pattern | Material | Style |
|---|---|---|---|
| smart | patterned | cotton | short |
| scruffy | stripy | woollen | long |
| trendy | plain | denim | v-necked |
| unfashionable | flowery | nylon | short-sleeved |
| elegant | checked | silk | long-sleeved |
| | | | baggy |

# UNIT 4
# See the world

**1**   Work with a partner and answer these questions.

   1   Do tourists visit your town regularly?

   2   What do the local people think of them?

   3   What are the benefits of tourists visiting?

**2**   Read this quote by a human rights activist and answer these questions.

   1   According to Mr Rajendra:

      1   Do tourists bring benefits to the countries they visit?

      2   How do tourists affect the culture of a country?

      3   Can a culture recover from the impact of tourism?

   2   How far do you agree with Mr Rajendra's view?

> *Today the tourist is a consumer. The raw material of the tourist industry is the flesh and blood of people and their cultures, thus its long-term effect on a country whose main income is derived from tourism can be devastating. Once a people or culture has been exploited and subverted to the needs of the tourist industry it can never be replaced.*
>
> Cecil Rajendra, lawyer and human rights activist, Malaysia

**3**   Work in a group of three and discuss the possible problems associated with tourism.

   1   Make notes and be ready to tell the class what you thought.

   2   Think about local examples or places you have visited.

**Land use: building and infrastructure**

_____

_____

_____

_____

**Local traditions and culture**

_____

_____

_____

_____

**Resources: water, fuel**

_____

_____

_____

_____

**Human rights**

_____

_____

_____

_____

**The environment: local and global pollution**

_____

_____

_____

_____

**Effect on the local economy**

_____

_____

_____

_____

**4**   People who are worried about the problems caused by tourism often try to be ethical tourists. The motto of ethical tourism is *Take only photographs, leave only footprints*. How do you think an ethical holiday would be different from a normal one?

**5**   Your group is going to prepare a list *Guidelines for ethical tourism*. Think about the problems you identified above, and make a poster to encourage tourists to behave responsibly.

**6**   Display your posters around the classroom and look at the other groups' work. Which poster do you think is most effective?

**A**
hope

practise

remind someone

attempt

learn

finish

manage

expect

keep

choose

survive

don't mind

agree

**D**

fancy

**B**
risk

enjoy

feel like

seem

persuade someone

fail

promise

pretend

can't afford

decide

prepare

want

can't stand

give up

suggest

plan

delay

offer

no point

refuse

**C**

miss

agree + infinitive
attempt + infinitive
can't afford + infinitive
can't stand + *-ing*
choose + infinitive
decide + infinitive
delay + *-ing*
don't mind + *-ing*
enjoy + *-ing*
expect + infinitive
fail + infinitive
fancy + *-ing*
feel like + *-ing*
finish + *-ing*
give up + *-ing*
hope + infinitive
keep + *-ing*
learn + infinitive
manage + infinitive
miss + *-ing*
no point + *-ing*
offer + infinitive
persuade someone + infinitive
plan + infinitive
practise + *-ing*
prepare + infinitive
pretend + infinitive
promise + infinitive
refuse + infinitive
remind someone + infinitive
risk + *-ing*
seem + infinitive
suggest + *-ing*
survive + *-ing*
want + infinitive

# Teacher's resource notes

## Module 1

### Unit 1   Street life

**Lead-in**

Say: *Look at the picture. Who is this?* to elicit vocabulary connected with busking and begging.

**Procedure**

1   Students read the text and answer the questions. Check the answers with the class.
2   Students read the comments and decide on the two which are most similar to their own views. Students work in pairs to compare their attitudes. Encourage them to add their own opinions and explain why they hold their views.
3   Students work in pairs to discuss the four statements. Say: *Talk about the first point until I give you a signal to move on to questions 2, 3 and 4.*
4   Students work in groups of three to answer the questions.

**Answers**
1 1 it varies (line 2), 2 they're dancers (line 13), 3 no, he doesn't (line 20); 2 1 T, 2 F, 3 T, 4 F, 5 T

**Vocabulary**

busker, beggar, to deserve, gift voucher, abuse, to spit

### Unit 1   My life's work

**Lead-in**

Ask: *What is your dream job?*

**Procedure**

1   Focus students' attention on the pictures and ask: *What jobs are shown here?*
2   Students check their ideas by using the words in the box to make the names of the eight jobs.
3   Students work in pairs to list character adjectives for each job and to decide which job from Ex 1 would most suit their partners, and the jobs they wouldn't do. Make sure students discuss reasons for their choices.
4   Students complete the table by writing in the jobs and ranking each one for danger and social importance. They compare their lists with a partner and discuss any differences.
5   Students write about a typical day at work for one of the jobs. Make sure they write in a way that makes it difficult for the other students to guess which jobs they are writing about.

**Answers**
motor mechanic, rat catcher, war correspondent, forensic detective, street cleaner, wedding planner, football referee, plastic surgeon

**Vocabulary**
jobs, occupations, character adjectives

### Unit 2   The public eye

**Lead-in**

If you have pictures of celebrities from magazines / the internet, ask: *Who is this?* Find out what students know about them.

**Procedure**

1   Students brainstorm Ex 1 individually and compare notes in small groups.
2   Students note as many ways as possible to stay famous. Write a list of suggestions on the board.
3   Students work in groups to discuss the famous people listed. Encourage them to expand on anything they know about the celebrities' private lives or other work. Remix the groups to discuss which celebrities use their fame 'well'.
4   Ask: *Would you like to be famous? What for?* Discuss Ex 5 with the class.
5   Discuss ways to become famous without having an obvious talent. Drill the sentence frames in the box with examples.
6   Students write a letter to a celebrity to help them campaign on an issue that is important to them.

**Vocabulary**

wealthy, issue, event, to publicise

### Unit 2   Who is it?

**Lead-in**

Give each student one strip and ask: *Can you guess whose story this is?* (A: Mother Teresa of Calcutta). Accept suggestions without comment.

**Procedure**

1   Students memorise the sentence on their strip of paper.
2   Say: *Stand up!* Students leave their strips of paper on their seats.
3   Students decide on the correct order of the story by reciting the sentence on their strip and listening to the other students' sentences. They stand in the same order as the story. If they forget their part, they can return to their seat to refresh their memory but must not carry their strip of paper with them. Note: the initial organisation can take some time but do not interfere. Nominate stronger students to act as directors.
4   Students recite the story when they have the correct order.
5   Elicit or confirm the identity of Mother Teresa.
6   Follow up: students write the story from memory.

**Vocabulary**

volunteer, poverty, slum, flood, refugee

## Unit 3  Sob story

### Lead-in
Ask: *Have you ever won a prize in a competition?*

### Procedure
1  Choose four creative / confident students. Set Ex 1 for the rest of the class while you give the four contestants their role cards, and take them aside to prepare. Encourage the contestants to add details to their stories.
2  Contestants argue why they should receive the money. The class listen, but do not ask questions.
3  Students work in groups of four. They discuss which contestant should get the money.
4  Say: *You can now ask the contestants any questions you want*. Remind the class that the contestants may not be telling the truth about the reasons they want the money. Set a time limit for each group to ask their questions.
5  Signal when the time is up and allow students to ask any final questions. Find out the groups' decisions.
6  The class vote for a winner. If you can, bring a fake cheque to present to the winner.
7  Contestants reveal what they are really going to do with the money, if the class has not already found out.

### Vocabulary
contestant, jury, deposit

## Unit 3  Comparison hat trick

### Procedure
1  Enlarge the board if possible. Students work in groups of four.
2  A student chooses a circle with a subject in it and rolls the dice. He / she must then make a sentence about the subject area in the circle, using the modifying phrase for that number as shown at the bottom of the worksheet. For example, sport and number one: *Football is by far the best sport*. If the other students agree that the sentence is correct, the player wins that circle and initials it.
3  The object for each player is to get three circles in a line. Lines can be horizontal, vertical or diagonal and other players should try to prevent others from making lines.
4  The winner is the player with the most lines at the end of the activity.

### Vocabulary
see Module 1, Unit 3 of the Coursebook

## Unit 4  Tied to the apron strings

### Lead-in
Ask: *What do you think 'tied to the apron strings' means?*

### Procedure
1  Students consider Ex 1 individually and give reasons for their choices. In monolingual groups, allow students to reach agreement on suggested ages. In multinational classes, explore reasons behind any differences.
2  Separate the pairs. Students consider the statements in speech bubbles individually. They form new pairs to discuss the opinions.
3  Students work in two groups. Ask them to think also about the parents' point of view, and what they think the advantages would be.
4  Students read the article and discuss what parents could do in the situation described.
5  Follow up: roleplay the conversation between parent and returning child.

### Vocabulary
bedsit, to stand on your own feet, to treat, to release, retirement

## Unit 4  Occupational stress

### Lead-in
Ask: *Which of these jobs would you like to do?*

### Procedure
1  Start at the centre of the board, *manager*. Students decide which stress pattern in the *Directions* box it matches.
2  Elicit that it matches the pattern Ooo, so they move left to *hairdresser*.
3  Students move through the maze by identifying the stress in the word and moving in the direction shown.
4  Make sure students are aware that left and right is relative to the direction they are moving so they should turn the paper in the direction they are travelling.
5  The object is to find the occupation which is the exit – *pianist*.
6  If possible, give feedback with the aid of an OHP.

### Answer
manager → hairdresser → policeman → professor → scientist → musician → inspector → president → architect → accountant → designer → politician → receptionist → novelist → estate agent → fortune teller → firefighter → electrician → comedian → interpreter → volunteer → astrologer → engineer → ambassador → lorry driver → bar tender → librarian → psychologist → undertaker → magician → photographer → paramedic → decorator → flight attendant → philosopher → carpenter → Prime Minister → guitarist → journalist → executive → pianist

### Vocabulary
jobs and occupations

# Module 2

## Unit 1  Liar

### Lead-in

Students organise the words in the box using dictionaries, then decide on positive / negative connotations.

### Procedure

1  Nominate a secretary to write suggestions for Ex 1 on the board. Correct when the class have placed and decided on all words.

2  Students work in pairs to discuss briefly whether always telling the truth is a good thing.

3  Students decide individually how they would react in the situations in the box.

4  Students work in pairs to compare ideas. Encourage them to explain their decisions.

5  Students work in pairs to consider whether they would tell the truth about the situations to the people in the box. They must suggest what they would say if they would not tell the truth in a particular situation.

6  Divide the class into two groups. Group A are the characters from the *People* box, Group B the guilty parties.

7  Group B choose a person they would tell the truth to and roleplay the conversation. Write useful language on the board, eg *I'm really sorry but …; I don't know how to tell you this, but …; You know …? Well, the thing is …*

8  When most students have done two or three roleplays, reverse the roles and repeat.

### Vocabulary

scratch, blame, hangover

## Unit 1  The birthday party

### Lead-in

Build the following scenario: *'It's your Great Aunt Mabel's 100th birthday party and you and lots of other relatives have been invited to a big party, but you don't know anyone there. You have to meet as many relatives as you can and get to know your extended family as well as possible.'*

### Procedure

1  Give students a role card each. If there are more than twelve students, use duplicates.

2  Allow students time to check vocabulary and think about how to introduce themselves at the party.

3  Make sure they understand that they will not find one person who fits all three characteristics at once.

4  The aim is to make small talk with other guests, while finding relatives who match the personality adjectives on their role cards. They should include the sentences on their cards that give clues to their own personality as naturally as possible in their conversations.

5  As soon as a student realises that the person he / she is speaking to doesn't have any of the characteristics on the card, he / she must take their leave politely and find another guest.

6  It is important students keep to their character adjectives. Encourage them to develop their personalities within these limits.

7  After the activity, check if the class identified people successfully.

### Vocabulary

personality adjectives

## Unit 2  Number 35

### Lead-in

Focus students' attention on the pictures and ask: *How do you think these items could be connected in a story?*

### Procedure

1  Students make a list of reasons why people move house, before they read the text.

2  Students work in pairs to discuss the questions that follow the text. Encourage them to use their imaginations and be creative!

3  Students work in groups to discuss the advantages and disadvantages of Neighbourhood Watch schemes. If necessary, play devil's advocate and promote an extreme opinion on Neighbourhood Watch schemes, either for or against.

4  Write suggestions on the board and invite comments on the ideas for making neighbourhoods better places to live.

### Vocabulary

ancient, scrolls, tinted, candles, parcels, to miaow, bonfire

## Unit 2  Landlord's choice

### Lead-in

Say: *Write down six objects you usually find in a kitchen; a living room; a bedroom.*

### Procedure

1  Students complete the profiles. Set a time limit that challenges them to think fast.

2  Encourage students to ask each other questions about their new identities.

3  Say: *You need to use the information from your profiles for your roles in the next part of the activity.* Divide the class into two groups, landlords and tenants, and ask them to prepare questions and answers for an interview. Model a few landlord questions, eg *How long do you intend to stay? Do you know how to look after a garden?* and elicit appropriate responses.

4  Ask if the landlords found suitable tenants. If pairs finish early, they could write a brief agreement between landlord and tenant for the flat.

### Vocabulary

houses, household goods

# Unit 3   Modern love

## Lead-in

Ask: *Have you ever been chatted up? What's the best / worst chat-up line you've ever heard?*

## Procedure

1   Students ask each other the questions in Ex 1.
2   Students read the web article and discuss whether the situation it describes exists in their own countries.
3   Students make a list of suggestions for their single friends. Play the lonely heart yourself and raise objections to students' suggestions to push them to more elaborate solutions.
4   Students read the advertisements and choose a suitable partner for themselves. Elicit reasons for their choices.
5   Students write an advertisement for themselves.
6   Pin up the adverts on a notice board so students can look at each other's advertisements and decide which they like best.
7   Tell students to write a short reply.

### Answers

M=male; F=female; GSOH=good sense of humour; WLTM=would like to meet; n/s=non-smoker; ltr=long-term relationship

## Vocabulary

Pilates, expense account, loft, pressure, wealthy, to keep up with, abbreviation

# Unit 3   Noughts and crosses

## Procedure

1   Students work in groups of three. Two of them play against each other, the third is the referee.
2   Players choose to be noughts or crosses and decide who will start.
3   Players take it in turns to reformulate the sentences in the grid using the correct phrasal verbs in the arrow. If they choose the correct phrasal verb and reformulate the sentence well enough to satisfy the referee, they win the square and write in a nought or a cross.
4   The first player to get three noughts or crosses in a horizontal, diagonal or vertical line is the winner.
5   When the game finishes, change the referee and start the next round. At the end of the activity, encourage students to look back at the unused boxes and guess the answers.

## Vocabulary

see Module 2, Unit 3

# Unit 4   Gun control

## Lead-in

Bring in newspaper headlines relating to any recent gun-related incident, if possible. Elicit what students know about it.

## Procedure

1   Give students 3–5 minutes to think about Ex 1. Discuss the questions with the class.
2   Students read the opinions in the speech bubbles and identify which opinion(s) most closely resemble their own.
3   Students work in pairs to think of reasons against the points of view in the speech bubbles.
4   Divide the class into two groups. Each group reads and discusses one case study.
5   Groups report back on their case study and invite comments and questions from the other group.
6   With the class, discuss whether owning a gun has any benefits.

## Vocabulary

to wound, to charge, to convict, to possess, getaway, appeal, manslaughter, reasonable, psychopath

# Unit 4   What's the preposition?

## Procedure

1   Students work in small groups. One student in each group is the referee.
2   Players take it in turns to roll the dice and move around the board by making a sentence using the word on the square they land on and the correct dependent preposition.
3   Players have two chances to get the preposition right. If the answer is correct, they stay on that square. If it isn't, then they have to return to their previous position.
4   It is essential that referees do not reveal correct answers unless a player gives the correct answer.
5   The winner is the first to reach the *Finish* square.

## Vocabulary

see Module 2, Unit 4

# Module 3

## Unit 1  Football in violence?

### Lead-in
Brainstorm the word *football*.

### Procedure
1  Students work in pairs to answer the questions in Ex 1.
2  Students rank the actions from worst to least worst and compare their ideas with their group.
3  Students read the articles and discuss the actions of the players.
4  Students suggest appropriate punishments for the players before they look at the actual punishments.
5  Students match the punishment to the players. Discuss whether the punishment was appropriate in each case.
6  Ask: *How can we reduce violent behaviour in players or spectators?* Elicit and discuss suggestions from the class.

### Answers
a Dyer b Diouf c Cantona d Bowyer (Note: his punishment was so severe because he had been in trouble for violent behaviour before).

### Vocabulary
insult, to boo, to chant, to invade, to investigate, spectator, to rip, apparently, ban, community service

## Unit 1  Sport for all

### Lead-in
Describe a game you used to play at school. If you are the same nationality as your students, use this description of a British game.

#### British Bulldog
Any number of people can play – the more the better! You need a large space, like a field. Choose a person to be 'it' (*the person who has to catch everyone*). 'It' stands in the middle of the field, with all the other players on one side. When 'it' shouts '*Go*', everyone runs to the other side of the field. 'It' tries to catch one (or more) of the other players, who then join him / her in the middle. The process repeats, with the number of people who are 'it' growing each time, until there is one person left to catch. The last person to be caught is the winner.

### Procedure
1  Students work in groups to describe their own playground games.
2  Change the groups. Students use their imagination to think what the names of the games might mean.
3  Make sure groups write notes in the grid, so that their presentations are well-structured.
4  Ask each group to the front of the class to give their presentations.
5  Students vote for the best game. They cannot vote for their own.

### Vocabulary
sport, including equipment, places and rules

## Unit 2  Look at this

### Lead-in
Ask: *What kinds of pictures did you draw when you were a child? Did your parents put them on the wall?*

### Procedure
1  Students read the seven situations and mark how offended they feel on the scale.
2  Students work in pairs to discuss their reactions.
3  Students work in pairs to interview each other.
4  Choose four students to take on the roles of the artists. They prepare a presentation and (if willing) a sketch of the work they will produce.
5  At the same time, the rest of the class discuss in small groups ideas that must be conveyed in the artwork, and prepare questions for the artists.
6  Invite the artists to present their ideas and designs, and take questions from the class.
7  Students choose a winner.

### Vocabulary
to preserve, to swear, naked, injured, to bid, influence

## Unit 2  Quick draw

### Lead-in
Students tell you to draw something on the board. Encourage them to make it difficult, and ask questions about what else is around the main subject, eg '*OK, what's behind the elephant?*'. Write on the board useful expressions for giving location, eg *in the background, (a little) to the left,* etc. Note: if your picture is rather bad, it will give confidence to students who are not very good at drawing.

### Procedure
1  Students work in pairs, so that they cannot see each other's work.
2  Give one picture to a student in each pair. Allow them a few minutes to prepare their instructions.
3  They describe the picture to their partner, who draws it.
4  When they have finished, give the second picture to the second student in each pair to describe.
5  Students work in pairs to compare their pictures.

### Vocabulary
background, foreground, underneath, above, etc

# Unit 3  Fashion fakes

### Lead-in

Ask a student to draw the logo of a well-known brand on the board. Elicit the name of the brand and its products.

### Procedure

1  Students look for brand names amongst bags and clothes around the classroom and work in pairs to discuss the questions in Ex 1.
2  Students work in groups to read the text and discuss the questions. Challenge them (gently) on the morality of buying fakes, putting the companies' case, if they are happy to buy fakes.
3  Ask students how they feel about the people who produce the fakes.
4  Introduce the second article. Ask: *Does this change your minds at all?*
5  Students suggest ways of preventing the trade in fakes.

### Vocabulary

trade, fraudster, to fight a losing battle, to spend a fortune on, sweatshop, penalty, counterfeit

# Unit 3  Clothing families

### Procedure

1  Students work in groups of four.
2  The object of the activity is to collect pairs of cards by asking other players for cards, using detailed descriptions of the clothes shown.
3  The cards are dealt and any pairs which a player has are put down and count as one point.
4  Player 1 begins by asking any of the other players for a card he / she needs to make a pair, eg *Maria, have you got an elegant pair of stripy tight nylon trousers?* If Maria does not have the card, the player on the left takes their turn to ask. If player 2 has the card player 1 is looking for, he / she must give it to player 1.
5  Students have to use four adjectives in the correct order when asking, including an adjective of opinion which they think is appropriate.
6  The winner is the player who has collected the most pairs of cards.

### Vocabulary

clothes, adjectives to describe clothes

# Unit 4  See the world

### Lead-in

Ask: *Where do you normally go on holiday? What do you like about the places you visit?*

### Procedure

1  Students work in pairs and tell each other about tourists that visit their towns / regions.
2  Students read the quote and discuss its implications.
3  Students make notes on possible problems with tourism.

4  Students consider how an ethical tourist differs from a 'normal' tourist, and how one might overcome the negative effects listed.
5  Each group produces a poster / advertisement to encourage tourists to behave responsibly.
6  Encourage students to comment on the items on their lists. Ask: *How realistic are the ideas? Can you think of occasions when tourists in your area have broken any of these rules?*

### Suggested answers

(some may be relevant to more than one category)
Land use: stay in smaller, local-run hotels; eat and drink local foods
Resources: use public transport or hire a bike; don't waste water
The environment: take your rubbish home with you
Local traditions and culture: find out about the country you are visiting; learn some of the local language; talk to local people; keep an open mind
Effects on the local economy: buy local goods

### Vocabulary

consumer, raw material, flesh and blood, devastating, infrastructure, income

# Unit 4  Infinitive or *-ing*?

### Procedure

1  Students play in groups of five, with one player as the referee.
2  Players each put a coin on a hexagon A, B, C, D in the corners. The players take it in turns to make a sentence that includes the verb on their hexagon.
3  The referee decides whether the sentence is correct. If it is, the player moves to an adjoining hexagon.
4  Players have to visit the letters in the other three corners, so A has to go to B, C and D before returning to A. The winner is the first player to return to their hexagon.
5  If a player gets the verb form wrong, he / she cannot move forward. With stronger groups, players move back one hexagon when they make a mistake. With weaker students, or limited time, reduce the number of letters a player has to visit, eg A only has to go to D and back.
6  Alternatively, organise the class into teams with the teacher as the referee and check answers on an OHP, if one is available.

### Vocabulary

see Module 3, Unit 4

# *Move* placement test

**Name:** _____

**Section 1 Language: Total** _____ / 50
**Section 2 Vocabulary: Total** _____ / 25
**Section 3 Writing: Total** _____ / 25
**Section 4 Speaking: Total** _____ / 25

**Total score:** _____ / _____

## Section 1 Language

(Circle) the correct alternative – *a, b or c.*

1   _____ a bank near here?
    a Is    b Is it    c Is there

2   Sam speaks English very _____.
    a good    b well    c bad

3   My mother is _____ teacher.
    a –    b a    c one

4   What _____?
    a Sam does want    b does Sam wants
    c does Sam want

5   We had _____ rain last night.
    a a lot    b a little    c a few

6   Sam is _____ than Dave.
    a more old    b more older    c older

7   _____ out last night?
    a Did you go    b Have you been
    c Have you gone

8   She's in the same class _____ me.
    a to    b like    c as

9   Who _____ this book?
    a gave you    b did give you    c did you give

10  _____ the newspaper.
    a I always read    b I read always    c Always I read

11  Where _____?
    a is Harry going    b Harry is going
    c is going Harry

12  This picture _____ by my friend.
    a painted    b was painting    c was painted

13  A: I love Indian food.   B: _____.
    a I do so    b So do I    c So I do

14  There's a no-smoking sign. You _____ smoke here.
    a don't have to    b don't must    c mustn't

15  If you're hot, I _____ the window.
    a 'll open    b am going to open    c open

16  I'm going out _____ some milk.
    a for get    b for to get    c to get

17  Try _____ late.
    a to not be    b to be not    c not to be

18  _____ here before.
    a I think I haven't been    b I don't think I've been
    c I don't think I haven't been

19  Someone _____ the meeting was cancelled.
    a said me    b told me    c told to me

20  If you _____ me your email address, I'll write to you.
    a will give    b give    c gave

21  Life would be easier if I _____ a bit more money.
    a would have    b have    c had

22  I'm late for school _____.
    a sometimes    b never    c always

23  I look forward _____ you next week.
    a seeing    b to see    c to seeing

24  He speaks with _____ strong accent.
    a –    b the    c a

25  I'm going to the hairdresser's _____.
    a to get my hair cut    b to get cut my hair
    c to cut my hair

26  I _____ in Rome since 2003.
    a 'm living    b 've lived    c live

27  Is it alright _____ I open the window?
    a –    b that    c if

28  We complained to the waiter _____ the food.
    a for    b of    c about

29  _____ it was raining we went for a walk.
    a However    b But    c Although

30  Sam was only pretending _____ upset.
    a be    b to be    c being

31  My parents never let me _____ computer games.
    a play    b to play    c playing

32  I _____ call you yesterday, but I didn't have time.
    a would    b would be going to    c was going to

33  Peter came out with us last night _____ feeling ill.
    a yet    b although    c despite

34  I was surprised _____ Tom at the party last night.
    a to see    b seeing    c for seeing

35  If you're tired, _____ to bed.
    a go    b you go    c you will go

36  Have you any idea where _____ ?
    a does she live    b she does live    c she lives

37  I wish I _____ to David yesterday.
    a had spoken    b would have spoken    c spoke

38  A: What does this word mean? B: Look _____ in the dictionary.
    a up    b it up    c up it

39  This time next week, I _____ on a beach in Greece.
    a 'm lying    b 'll lie    c 'll be lying

40  I could see a small road _____ into the distance.
    a disappearing    b was disappearing
    c disappeared

41  It _____ Pete who broke the window – he wasn't here at the time.
    a mustn't have been    b couldn't be
    c can't have been

42  This is the first time _____ Vietnamese food.
    a I've eaten    b I'm eating    c I eat

43  I can't give you a lift because my car is _____ .
    a still repairing    b still being repaired
    c still repaired

44  _____ , that everyone stayed indoors.
    a The weather such was    b Such was the weather
    c Such the weather was

45  Phone me when you _____ .
    a have arrived    b will arrive    c will have arrived

46  I'd rather you _____ in the house.
    a didn't smoke    b not smoke    c don't smoke

47  Nobody rang me, _____ ?
    a did anybody    b did he or she    c did they

48  _____ realised, I would've told you.
    a Had I    b Would I have    c If I would have

49  Sam doesn't work, _____ he always seems to have a lot of money.
    a whereas    b yet    c however

50  _____ all the questions, James felt quite pleased with himself.
    a Has finally answered    b Finally answering
    c Having finally answered

**Total mark _____ / 50**

# Section 2 Vocabulary

### Add the missing word.

1   I _____ born in Paris.

2   I _____ 21 years old.

3   My birthday is _____ July.

4   Last month, I went _____ the USA.

5   I stayed in New York _____ two weeks.

6   Did you _____ many photos on holiday?

7   What does Katy's new boyfriend look _____ ?

8   Did you _____ your homework last night?

9   It's a good idea to try _____ clothes before you buy them.

10  As _____ as I'm concerned, Internet shopping is a great idea.

11  Oxford is famous _____ its university.

12  Have you any _____ what time it is?

13  I get on really _____ with my brothers and sisters.

14  We went to lots of places last night, but we ended _____ in *Bar Soleil*.

15  Sue's new dress is very eye-_____ .

16  We used to be friends, but we lost _____ a few years ago.

17  I don't know how old he is, but he looks to be in _____ late-twenties.

18  The sea was very cold – in fact it was absolutely _____ .

19  Can you _____ a secret?

20  Lizzy has got a great _____ of humour.

21  After being off school for a week, he found it difficult to _____ up with the work he'd missed.

22  You're the only person I've told. No-one knows about it _____ from you and me.

23  The advantages far _____ the disadvantages.

24  Central Park in New York is a great place to while _____ a few hours.

25  She'll be very successful – she's a real go-_____ .

**Total mark _____ / 25**

This page contains guidance for teachers for
Section 3 Writing and Section 4 Speaking.

# Section 3 Writing

**Ask students to write about <u>one</u> of the following
topics. Write a maximum of 150 words.**

a    My family
b    My home town or city
c    My job / studies
d    My hobbies and interests

---
**Give a score out of 25**
out of 5 points for accuracy
out of 5 points for vocabulary use
out of 5 points for cohesion
out of 5 points for complexity of language used
out of 5 points for general impression
---

# Section 4 Speaking

**Choose from the following questions / instructions.
Within each section the questions become
progressively more challenging.**

## Home town / city

Where are you from?
How long have you lived there?
Can you tell me something about (student's home
town / city)?
How do you feel about living in (student's home
town / city)?

## Family and friends

Do you have a large or small family?
Tell me something about your family.
What kinds of things do you do together as a family?
Can you tell me something about your friends?
What kinds of things do you do with your friends?
What do you think are the important qualities of a good
friend?

## Work / study

Do you work or are you a student?
What do you do / study?
How long have you had this job / been a student?
Can you tell me something about your work / studies?
What do you enjoy most about you work / studies?
Is there anything you don't like?

## Leisure

Have you got any hobbies or interests?
Are you interested in sports / music / cinema / reading etc?
What's your favourite sport / kind of music / film / book etc?
What else do you like to do in your free time?
How did you become interested in (student's hobby or
interest)?
What do you generally do in the evenings and at weekends
in (student's home town / city)?

## Future plans

What do you hope to do in the next few years?
Do you have any long-term plans?
Where do you see yourself in ten years' time?

## Learning English

How long have you been studying English?
Why are you learning English?
How do you feel about learning English?
How important is English for you?

## What do you want to gain from this English course?

Which areas of English are the most important for you to
work on during this course?
– speaking
– writing
– reading
– listening
– grammar
– vocabulary
– pronunciation

---
**Give a score out of 25**
out of 5 points for accuracy
out of 5 points for vocabulary use
out of 5 points for cohesion
out of 5 points for complexity of language used
out of 5 points for general impression
---

**See page 154 for answers to Section 1 Language
and Section 2 Vocabulary.**

**Most students should be able to complete sections
1 and 2 in approximately 30 minutes.**

**Name** _____

**1** Put the adverbs in the box in the correct order.

| always   never   occasionally   often |
| ~~sometimes~~   ~~usually~~ |

a _____ → b usually → c _____ →
d sometimes → e _____ → f _____

**2** In four of these sentences the adverb is in an incorrect position. Put a ✓ (correct) or a ✗ (incorrect) in the boxes.

a   I usually go out with friends on Saturday. ☐

b   I visit usually my grandparents at the weekend. ☐

c   My grandparents always are pleased to see me. ☐

d   I cook never my own dinner. ☐

e   My housemate is usually happy to cook for us. ☐

f   Occasionally we have a take-away meal. ☐

g   Never I play football. ☐

h   Sometimes I watch football on TV. ☐

**3** Rewrite the four incorrect sentences in Ex 2 with the adverb in the correct position.

a   _____

b   _____

c   _____

d   _____

**4** Rewrite these sentences with the adverb in an appropriate position.

a   I get up at 7.30. (usually)
_____

b   I am late for school. (sometimes)
_____

c   I miss my lessons. (never)
_____

d   I do my homework. (always)
_____

e   I am asleep by midnight. (always)
_____

**5** Rearrange these words to make full sentences.

a   with friends / how often / you / go out / do ?
_____
_____?

b   once or twice / normally / go out together / we / a / week.
_____
_____.

c   you / go / do / usually / where ?
_____?

d   for a meal / sometimes / go / we
_____ , but …

e   go / we / to a bar or a club / usually
_____.

**6** Complete these sentences with the words in the box.

| couch potato   match   opponents   point   row |
| tournament   unwind |

a   The World Cup is the biggest football
_____ in the world.

b   England's _____ when they won the World Cup in 1966 were West Germany.

c   I've got a very busy day – I've got three meetings in a _____ this afternoon.

d   There's no _____ in taking the exam if you think you're going to fail it.

e   At the end of the day, I like to _____ by listening to some relaxing music with a glass of wine.

f   Did you see the _____ last night? I can't understand why Madrid didn't win the game – they played really well.

g   I'm a real _____ . I hate playing sport, but I can spend hours watching it on TV.

**7** Read the article. Are these statements true or false? Write T (true) or F (false) in the boxes.

a Britons spend at least 50% of their time sleeping, working and watching television. ☐

b British men normally sleep more than women each night. ☐

c Britons usually spend about 3½ hours at work each day. ☐

d Most people watch television at least once a day. ☐

e Britons watch on average 2½ hours of television a day. ☐

f Britons usually spend more time cleaning the house than watching television. ☐

g Only 1 in 10 regularly watches TV while they eat dinner. ☐

h British people spend more time watching sport on TV than actually doing sport. ☐

i Men usually do more physical exercise than women. ☐

j The people in the survey recorded what they were doing ten times a day. ☐

# Work, rest and TV for the average Briton

Work, sleep and watching television is the standard way of passing time in 21st century Britain, with these activities taking up more than half of our time. Sleeping takes up a third of each day, with women getting on average 8 minutes more than men each night.

Despite being at our place of work for an average of 8 hours a day, the survey revealed that we do only about 3½ hours actual work during this time.

9 out of 10 of us watch television at least once a day and the average person spends about 2½ hours of each day in front of the box. In contrast, only half an hour per day is spent cleaning the house and ¾ of an hour on personal care and hygiene. We spend just over an hour of each day eating and 75%

of us regularly watch television during our evening meal. Only 1 in 10 of us never eats in front of the television.

Britons surprisingly devote more time to doing sport than watching it. The survey revealed that we spend an average of 17 minutes each day doing some form of sport yet only 4 minutes watching it on TV. Men generally do 22 minutes of physical activity and watch 6 minutes of sport each day, whereas for women the figures are 13 minutes and 2 minutes.

In the survey, the biggest of its kind, 12,000 individuals recorded what they were doing every ten minutes over the course of the day.

| Exercise | Score |
|---|---|
| 1 Language | _____ / 4 |
| 2 Language | _____ / 8 |
| 3 Language | _____ / 4 |
| 4 Language | _____ / 5 |
| 5 Language | _____ / 5 |
| 6 Vocabulary | _____ / 14 |
| 7 Reading | _____ / 10 |
| Total: | _____ / 50 |
| | _____ % |

**Name:** _____

**1** Complete these sentences with *before* or *beforehand*.

   a  Let's go for a meal tonight – maybe we can go for a drink _____ .

   b  Shall we go for a drink _____ we go to the restaurant?

   c  I'll call for you sometime _____ 7 o'clock ...

   d  ... no, let's make that 8 – I need to do a bit of shopping _____ .

**2** Complete these sentences with *after* or *afterwards*.

   a  _____ spending a few days in Paris, we went to Bordeaux.

   b  I'm busy until 6.30, but I'll call you as soon as I can _____ .

   c  I've got a meeting immediately _____ lunch ...

   d  ... and I'm playing tennis _____ .

**3** Complete the second sentence with *beforehand* or *afterwards* to replace some of the words in the first sentence.

   a  We're going to the cinema and then we'll go for a drink after we have been to the cinema.

   We're going _____
   _____

   b  I'll see you later, but I need to speak to John before I see you.

   I'll _____
   _____

   c  Let's meet at 7. I'm seeing Jeff before I meet you and I'm having dinner with Sam after I meet you.

   Lets' meet at 7. I'm _____
   _____
   _____

**4** Look at the magazine feature about what famous people did before they were famous. Choose the correct alternative.

## Before they were famous

(a) *Before / Beforehand* they became two of the biggest names in Hollywood, Brad Pitt delivered refrigerators for a living and Jennifer Aniston, just like her character in the TV show *Friends*, was a waitress a few years *before / earlier*. They first met each other (c) *while / later* he was making a guest appearance in *Friends*. The got married in 2000, but broke up only 4 years (d) *after / later*.

(e) *Before / Beforehand* becoming Prime Minister of the UK in 1997, Tony Blair was a barrister. And (f) *before / earlier* that, (g) *while / earlier* he was studying law at Oxford University, he was the lead singer in a pop band called Ugly Rumours. He admitted (h) *after / afterwards* that his ambition at one point had been to be a rock star.

Tom Cruise first joined Hollywood's A-list (i) *after / afterwards* his role in *Top Gun* in 1985. In contrast to his all-action image of the time, he had (j) *earlier / before* spent a year studying theology and contemplating becoming a priest.

**5** Underline the stressed syllable in each word.
For example: *advantage*

   (a) pressure      (e) scientist      (i) electric
   (b) biography     (f) scientific     (j) energy
   (c) famous        (g) privacy        (k) guitarist
   (d) journalist    (h) terrific       (l) democracy

**6** Complete these sentences about aviator Charles Lindbergh with the words in the box.

   ┌──────────────────────────────────────────┐
   │ achievements   airborne   escape   kidnapped │
   │ ransom   runway   trial                    │
   └──────────────────────────────────────────┘

Charles Lindbergh is responsible for one of the greatest (a) _____ in aviation history. He was the first person to fly solo across the Atlantic.

After leaving New York on 20th May 1927, Lindbergh and his plane, *Spirit of St Louis*, finally landed on the (b) _____ at Le Bourget airport in Paris after being (c) _____ for thirty hours.

Lindbergh's fame however had tragic consequences. In 1932, his baby son was (d) _____ . The Lindberghs paid a (e) _____ of $50,000, but their son was not returned.

Two years later, a man was charged with the child's murder and after a six-week (f) _____ , the Lindberghs moved to Britain to (g) _____ the media attention.

**7** Complete the expressions with the words in the box.

| break up   bullied   drive   esteem   expectations |

a To be famous you need a strong _____ to succeed.

b The film didn't live up to my _____ .

c You'll never be a successful actor if you have low self- _____ .

d Are Brad and Jen still together or did they _____ ?

e She hated school because she was _____ .

**8** Read the article and choose the correct alternative.

1 The paparazzi are:
  a film characters
  b celebrity photographers
  c actors

2 Actor George Clooney led a campaign against the paparazzi because:
  a they refused to photograph him
  b they photographed him
  c they criticised his latest film

3 The paparazzi later protested against George Clooney by:
  a refusing to go to his next film premier
  b taking photographs of him and his girlfriend
  c refusing to take his photograph

4 The paparazzi claim:
  a celebrities are always happy to give something back to the public
  b celebrities are never 'off-duty'
  c celebrities need the publicity and enjoying posing for the cameras

5 Which of the following do the celebrities not claim:
  a the paparazzi help them become more famous
  b they have a right to privacy when 'off-duty'
  c the paparazzi can at times be too intrusive

# The fame game: celebrities and the paparazzi

The word 'paparazzi' is used to describe celebrity photographers and comes from the name of a character called Paparazzo in the 1960 film *La Dolce Vita*. The word 'paparazzi' literally means 'buzzing insects'.

In 1996, actor George Clooney led a campaign against the paparazzi after they took pictures of him and his girlfriend. A year later, at the premiere of his film *The Peacemaker* in New York, the paparazzi refused to take pictures of the actor to protest against his comments.

The paparazzi and their supporters claim that the stars need publicity to promote their image and to brand themselves and that most celebrities actually enjoy the attention while posing for the cameras. Another argument is that as it's the general public that makes them rich and famous, they should be happy to give something in return.

The main argument put forward by George Clooney and his supporters is that public figures deserve a right to privacy when 'off-duty'. They also fear that the paparazzi can sometimes be too intrusive, such as their alleged involvement in the death of Princess Diana in 1997. Other celebrities who have publicly spoken out against the paparazzi include Madonna, Tom Cruise, Nicole Kidman and Robert DeNiro.

| Exercise | Score |
|---|---|
| 1 Language | _____ / 4 |
| 2 Language | _____ / 4 |
| 3 Language | _____ / 4 |
| 4 Language | _____ / 10 |
| 5 Pronunciation and vocabulary | _____ / 6 |
| 6 Vocabulary | _____ / 7 |
| 7 Vocabulary | _____ / 5 |
| 8 Reading | _____ / 10 |
| Total: | _____ / 50 |
| | _____ % |

# UNIT 3
# Test

**Name** _____

**1** Complete these sentences comparing the two places or things. Use the comparative form of the adjective in brackets.

a Brazil (big) _____ the UK.

b Emails (popular) _____ letters these days.

c London (expensive) _____ Bangkok.

d Today (warm) _____ yesterday.

**2** Write sentences comparing the places and things in Ex 1 with *not as … as* and the adjective.

a _____

b _____

c _____

d _____

**3** Complete these sentences with the superlative form of the adjectives in the box.

| big   common   famous   small |

a 'The' _____ word in English.

b Ukraine _____ country in Europe.

c Pluto _____ planet in the solar system.

d The Beatles _____ band in the world.

**4** Write sentences comparing Thailand and the United Kingdom. Use the modifiers and adjectives in the boxes.

|                       | Thailand    | United Kingdom |
| --------------------- | ----------- | -------------- |
| Area (km²)            | 0.5 million | 0.25 million   |
| Population            | 61 million  | 60 million     |
| Average temperature   | 29°c        | 9°c            |

| twice   much   a bit | | hot   big   big |

a Thailand is _____ the United Kingdom.

b The population of Thailand is _____ the United Kingdom.

c Thailand is _____ the United Kingdom.

**5** ~~Cross out~~ one alternative which is not possible.

a The Pacific is *much / by far* the biggest ocean.

b Canada is *a bit / not quite* bigger than the USA.

c Pele and Maradonna are *far / by far* the best footballers ever.

d Football is *much / far / by far* more popular than cricket.

e Spain is *not quite / a bit / nearly* as big as France.

f The Taj Mahal is *much / nearly / far* older than Buckingham Palace.

**6** Complete the house types.

a
_____

b
_____

c
_____

d
_____

e
_____

f
_____

g
_____

h
_____

**7** Complete the advert with the words in the box.

| fully-equipped   furnished   inclusive   landlord location   parking   rent   share |

**Wanted:** Third person to (a) _____ a spacious three-bedroomed flat. Excellent (b) _____ – five minutes' walk from city centre. Flat is (c) _____ and (d) _____ with all kitchen appliances, telephone, TV, hi-fi etc and has off-street car (e) _____ . (f) _____ : £500 per month (g) _____ of all bills. **Contact Jim Smith, (h) _____ , on 07914 329409.**

# The world's most expensive house

Businessman Lakshmi Mittal has bought a central London house for the record-breaking price of £70 million.

The Indian steel magnate's new home has entered the Guinness Book of Records as the world's most expensive house. The house had previously belonged to Bernie Ecclestone, the Formula One racing boss, who had bought it for his wife three years before. She didn't like the house and the Ecclestones never moved in.

The 12-bedroom mansion located at the prestigious Kensington Palace Gardens is 55 times bigger than the average family home. The house, which was once the Egyptian Embassy, includes a ballroom, an art gallery, a swimming pool, whose ceiling is decorated with semi-precious stones, and underground parking for 20 cars.

Mittal, who in 2005 became the richest person in Britain with a personal wealth of £3.5 billion, began working in his father's steel factory in India as a teenager in the 1960s. The company he set up in 1975 is now by far the world's largest steel producer with over 175,000 employees and annual revenues of over $22 billion.

Mittal owns many more properties including a luxury flat overlooking Hyde Park and houses in Surabaya, Indonesia and Trinidad.

The previous record for the most expensive house was £62.7 million for a 1997 sale in Hong Kong.

8  Read the article and answer these questions.

a  Who owned the house before Lakshmi Mittal bought it?

_____

b  How long did the previous owner own the house?

_____

c  How long did the previous owner live in the house?

_____

d  Match the figures to what they refer to in the text.

(1) £70 million   (2) 12   (3) 55   (4) 20
(5) £3.5 billion   (6) 1960s   (7) 1975
(8) 175,000   (9) $22 billion   (10) £62.7 million

(a) previous record   (b) parking spaces
(c) price of the house   (d) times bigger
(e) employees   (f) personal wealth
(g) annual revenues   (h) started his company
(i) bedrooms   (j) started to work

1 _____       6 _____
2 _____       7 _____
3 _____       8 _____
4 _____       9 _____
5 _____       10 _____

| Exercise | Score |
|---|---|
| 1 Language | _____ / 4 |
| 2 Language | _____ / 4 |
| 3 Language | _____ / 4 |
| 4 Language | _____ / 3 |
| 5 Language | _____ / 6 |
| 6 Vocabulary | _____ / 8 |
| 7 Vocabulary | _____ / 8 |
| 8 Reading | _____ / 13 |
| Total: | _____ / 50 |
|  | _____ % |

**Name** _____

**1** Correct the grammar mistake in each sentence.

a    I'd like that I go out tonight.

I'd _____ go out tonight.

b    We're hoping go to the same university.

We _____ the same university.

c    I'm aiming that I'll finish my homework by 8.

I'm aiming _____ by 8.

d    The taxi due to arrive at 8.30.

The taxi _____ at 8.30.

e    I expect to back home before midnight.

I expect _____ before midnight.

f    I'm intending getting up early tomorrow morning.

I'm intending _____ tomorrow morning.

**2** Write complete sentences with these words.

a    I / due / finish university next year.

_____
_____ .

b    What / you / hope / do after university?

_____
_____ ?

c    I / hope / work in the music industry.

_____
_____ .

d    I / aim / be a millionaire by the time I'm 40.

_____
_____ .

e    I / hope / I'll / retire when I'm 50.

_____
_____ .

f    you / like / live abroad one day?

_____
_____ ?

g    Yes, / I / like / live in New York one day.

_____
_____ .

h    I expect / get a job / multinational company.

_____
_____ .

**3** Read the speech bubbles and complete the name of the job and the course.

a    I study science that deals with heat, light and other forms of energy

I treat people who are ill or injured

b    I prepare and check financial records

<u>physicist</u>  _____  _____

<u>physics</u>  _____  _____

c    I study how people's minds work and how this affects their behaviour

d    I study and speak a lot of languages

e    I treat people's injuries using special physical exercises

_____  _____  _____

_____  _____  _____

f    I give legal advice, write legal contracts and represent people in court

g    I prepare and sell medicines

_____  _____

_____  _____

**4** Underline the stressed syllable in the words in Ex 3.

**5** Complete these sentences with the missing particle *around, into, off, on* or *up.*

a    I grew _____ in Sheffield and I moved to Oxford to go to university when I was 18.

b    I did several jobs when I was younger, but in my late 20s I got _____ teaching English.

c    I taught English in several countries, but after a year or so, it was always time to move _____ .

d    I helped to set _____ an English language school in Japan.

e    I ended _____ living and working back in Oxford.

f    I took a year _____ from working two years ago and I travelled around the world.

g    I've been a teacher for long enough so I'm looking _____ for something else at the moment.

**6**   Read the weblogs. Who:

a   plans to go to university?

_____  _____  _____

b   wants to be a teacher?

_____  _____

c   would like to be an author?

_____

d   aims to set up his / her own business?

_____

e   wants to travel around the world?

_____  _____

f   is getting married soon?

_____

g   expects to get married one day?

_____  _____

h   intends to become rich?

_____  _____

i   has no real plans for the future?

_____

| Exercise | Score |
|---|---|
| 1 Language | _____ / 6 |
| 2 Language | _____ / 8 |
| 3 Vocabulary | _____ / 7 |
| 4 Pronunciation | _____ / 7 |
| 5 Vocabulary | _____ / 7 |
| 6 Reading | _____ / 15 |
| Total: | _____ / 50 |
| | _____ % |

# My future

I'm getting married next month.  I have no clue where we are going on our honeymoon – hopefully somewhere exotic. After I'm married, I intend to work as a teacher and then have 4 children.

**(Sam, 24)**

My future plans are to graduate from university, become very, very rich, see the world, marry the woman of my dreams and have a family!

**(Al, 21)**

When I grow up I'd like to be a teacher like my teacher Miss King. I want to be a teacher because it will be fun to teach kids what they don't know. But if they forget, I can teach them again.

**(Tania, 12)**

My most immediate plans are my vacation plans. I'm going to the Caribbean in March and to Europe in the summer. My longer-term plans are to study business at university and ultimately, I aim to have my own business, work for myself and retire at 50 a multi-millionaire.

**(Chad, 18)**

At this point in time, I have no idea where my future is heading. I have not yet chosen what to study, or even if I will study anything. I don't even know what I want to do next weekend. What I do know, though, is that I have plenty of time to make decisions.

**(John, 16)**

I don't see the point in going to university. I'm going to study gorillas in Africa. Then I will drive around the world making films and writing poetry.

**(Tim, 19)**

My future plan is to graduate from university and then start writing books. I'd like to become a children's book writer. When I find the right man, we will live together for at least a year. Then, we will get married and have 3 children. I hope to live a peaceful and happy life.

**(Laura, 15)**

# Module test

**Name** _____

**1** Rewrite these sentences with the adverb in brackets in an appropriate position.

a My brother is playing computer games. (always)

_____

_____

b Who do you go on holiday with? (usually)

_____

_____

c I am late for work. (often)

_____

_____

d I get my hair cut every six weeks. (usually)

_____

_____

e I read magazines about famous people. (occasionally)

_____

_____

**2** Choose the correct alternative.

a Do you want to go for a drink *after / afterwards* the lesson?

b I'll call you sometime *before / beforehand* 7.30.

c The meeting went on until 6.30. We all needed a drink *after / afterwards*.

d We met in 2000 and got married two years *after / later*.

e *After / Later* getting married, we moved to the USA.

**3** Choose the correct alternative.

a I'm *much / not nearly* as good at tennis as my brother.

b My brother is *far / by far* the best tennis player I know.

c My father is *far / by far* older than my mother.

d I'm *not quite / a bit* as tall as my sister.

e My English is *a bit / not quite* better than my French.

**4** Complete the second sentence using the word in brackets so the meaning is similar to the first sentence.

a The taxi should arrive in ten minutes. (due)

The taxi _____ in ten minutes.

b We would like to go to France this summer. (hoping)

We _____ to France this summer.

c We want to go to Paris. (like)

We _____ to Paris.

d I'm planning to leave work early today. (intend)

I _____ early today.

e I should be home at about 7.30. (expect)

I _____ at about 7.30.

**5** Choose the correct alternative.

> **Wanted:** Male or female student to (a) *divide / share* a (b) *semi-detached / half-detached* house with large garden. Excellent (c) *location / situation* – ten minutes' from the university. Flat is (d) *full-equipped / fully-equipped*. (e) *Hire / Rent*: £800 / month (f) *inclusive / included*.

**6** Complete the phrasal verbs by adding the correct particle.

a I was born in Manchester, but I grew _____ in London.

b I first got _____ music when I was in my early teens.

c I had several jobs, but I usually got bored and was constantly looking _____ for something else.

d I was always moving _____ from one job to another.

e I took a few months _____ from working and …

f … I decided to set _____ my own record company.

g I ended _____ being a millionaire before I was 30.

**7** Complete the newspaper headlines with the words in the box.

> airborne   drive   kidnapped   opponents
> ransom   row   runway

> **Plane catches fire on**
> **(a)** _____ **only seconds**
> **away from being (b)** _____ **.**

> **Business tycoon's son**
> **(c)** _____ **. $1million**
> **(d)** _____ **demanded.**

> **Chelsea's cup final**
> **(e)** _____ **are Real Madrid.**

> **Research shows woman have**
> **greater (f)** _____ **to**
> **succeed in business.**

> **Snow continues for tenth day in a**
> **(g)** _____ **.**

**8** 🔘 **03** Listen to a journalist talking about fame. Answer these questions.

1   How long has the journalist been writing about famous people?

_____

2   According to the journalist, what is the main reason why famous people feel good about themselves?

_____

3   Which of the following does the journalist <u>not</u> mention when talking about people who make a lot of money?
   a   sports stars
   b   actors
   c   fashion designers
   d   artists

4   Why do designers give their clothes to famous people for free?

_____

5   According to the journalist, famous people often meet interesting people because:
   a   they go out a lot
   b   they like to be with other famous people
   c   they generally meet more people
   d   people want to meet them

6   Which of the following does the journalist <u>not</u> mention when talking about the downsides of being famous?
   a   being followed by the paparazzi
   b   needing a lot of security
   c   living up to expectations
   d   having to go to every party

7   What would the journalist like to do for a month?

_____

8   Who does the journalist write for?
   a   newspapers
   b   a TV station
   c   a radio station
   d   magazines

9   Which of the following does the journalist not mention about famous people's problems?
   a   failure in exams
   b   low self-esteem
   c   not loved by their parents
   d   bullied at school

10   According to the journalist, most people have a desire to become famous because they want to:
   a   do better than their parents
   b   do better than they did at school
   c   show they are good at something
   d   become rich

## Fifties teenager –
### Books and radio and bed by 9 o'clock

Every morning, I get up at 7.30. I usually have porridge for breakfast and then I walk to school. It's about a mile and it takes me about 20 minutes.

At school there are a lot of strict rules. We all have to stand up when a teacher comes into the room and we can't sit down until they say so. If you don't do your homework, you are beaten. We don't study many different subjects – maths, English, history and geography are the main ones. I like history best of all. School finishes at 3pm.

After school, I get the bus home and do two hours of homework before dinner. All of us sit down for an evening meal. We usually have leftovers from my father's shop, who's a butcher, and occasionally we have some tinned meat or cheese for a treat.

My favourite things are my books and I like to read them after dinner. If I have been good, I am allowed to listen to the radio for a while before I go to bed at about 9 o'clock.

*Emily Jones, 16, Ipswich, UK*

## Noughties teenager –
### Surf the Net and text till midnight

Like most people my age, an alarm clock is not enough. So, at seven every weekday, my human alarm clock, my mother, wakes me up. I have a quick shower and sometimes I'll have a bite to eat.

At 8.35am, I take my place at the bus stop, which is about a minute's walk from my house. My school is 5 minutes' bus ride away.

My day consists of seven 45-minute lessons and we study many different subjects. At the moment I'm most into sociology and politics. My friends and I also work on our projects outside school through phone calls, emails and meetings. It's also a good excuse to go shopping and to do some socialising.

I spend the early evening watching soaps and talk shows. I generally eat my dinner on my knee in front of the TV. My favourite is pizza. Then I surf the net, download some new music and get and send my emails. My prized possession at the moment is my mobile phone. It's dead cool. My friends and I usually spend some time texting each other before bed. I'm generally in bed around midnight.

*Juanita Rosenior, 16, London, UK*

---

**9** Read the extracts about the typical day of a teenager in the 1950s and a teenager of today. Do these statements refer to Emily or to Juanita? Write E or J in the boxes.

a   She doesn't always have breakfast. ☐

b   She walks to school. ☐

c   Her journey to school takes five minutes. ☐

d   She has to stand up when a teacher comes into the classroom. ☐

e   Her school day consist of seven 45-minute lessons. ☐

f   Her favourite subjects are sociology and politics. ☐

g   She only studies a few subjects. ☐

h   She usually eats dinner at the table with her family. ☐

i   She is a bit of a couch potato. ☐

j   She sometimes listens to the radio in the evening. ☐

**10** Describe a typical day in your life. Write about 150 words.

| Exercise | Score |
|---|---|
| 1 Language | _____ / 5 |
| 2 Language | _____ / 5 |
| 3 Language | _____ / 5 |
| 4 Language | _____ / 5 |
| 5 Vocabulary | _____ / 6 |
| 6 Vocabulary | _____ / 7 |
| 7 Vocabulary | _____ / 7 |
| 8 Listening | _____ / 20 |
| 9 Reading | _____ / 20 |
| 10 Writing | _____ / 20 |
| Total: | _____ / 100 |
| | _____ % |

**Name** _____

**1** Complete the lists with the time expressions in the box

| last year   two weeks ago   since 2004   yesterday |
| this year   recently   for the last ten minutes |
| when I was a child |

| 'Completed' time | Time 'up to now' |
|---|---|
| in 2005 | already |
| last night | never |
| 3 months ago | so far |

a _____   e _____

b _____   f _____

c _____   g _____

d _____   h _____

**2** ~~Cross out~~ one alternative which is not possible.

a I've lived in London *since 2004 / for a few years / a few years ago.*

b I moved to the UK *since 2004 / in 2004 / a few years ago.*

c I haven't seen my parents *for weeks / since January / last week.*

d I got married *since last year / last year / six months ago.*

**3** Complete these sentences with the present perfect or the past simple form of the verbs.

I (a) _____ (speak) to Sam on the phone last week, but I (b) _____ (not / see) him since his birthday.

I (c) _____ (never / be) to Australia. But I (d) _____ (go) to New Zealand when I was a child.

I (e) _____ (move) to London just after I (f) _____ (finish) at university. So, I guess I (g) _____ (be) here for over six years now.

I (h) _____ (already / have) lunch. I (i) _____ (have) a pizza from the new Italian place that (j) _____ (open) last week.

I (k) _____ (work) late every day this week so far. Yesterday, I (l) _____ (not / get) home until eight o'clock.

**4** Complete the character adjectives with the missing vowels (*a, e i, o, u*).

a My parents are very c__nv__nt__ __n__l and traditional …

b … but my brother and I are quite r__b__ll__ __ __s and often break the rules.

c I think my parents are too n__rr__w - m__nd__d and won't listen to other people's opinions.

d But they are very r__l__ __bl__ I suppose – always there if you need them.

e My brother is very b__d - t__mp__r__d and often gets angry for no reason ...

f … and he thinks he's the best at everything. He's so __rr__g__nt sometimes.

g My little sister is very __ff__ct__ __n__t__. She's always hugging and kissing us.

h My boyfriend is very g__n__r__ __s – always buying me presents and paying for things when we go out.

**5** Find eight character adjectives in the word snake.

ambitiouscautiousconfidenthard-workingindependentsociablematureresponsible

a _____   e _____

b _____   f _____

c _____   g _____

d _____   h _____

**6** Complete these sentences with the words in the box.

| approach   claim   status   rebels |

a Research has shown that women are more _____ conscious than men.

b Only 60% of British adults _____ they have never broken the law.

c Most people choose a partner with similar interests and a similar _____ to life as themselves.

d Many women say that they are attracted to men who are _____ , but the relationships don't last long.

# TV Families part 4:
# The Osbournes

In 2002, the chaotic home life of ageing heavy metal icon Ozzy Osbourne and his family seemed a strange subject for a TV show. But *The Osbournes*, which followed the ups and downs of the family's daily life, proved an instant hit with viewers and turned Ozzy's wife Sharon and their rebellious children, Kelly and Jack, into celebrities. The show has been broadcast in over 100 countries and at its peak was MTV's most watched show.

Ozzy was surprised by its popularity, saying: 'I guess people enjoy watching a crazy family like us make total fools of ourselves every week'.

And it was true. America loved them and wanted to see more of them. As a result, Kelly has now started a pop career, Sharon got her own talk show and Jack has made various appearances in films and TV shows.

The show has been so successful that many other celebrities have tried to copy the idea. Hollywood legend Liza Minnelli and model Anna Nicole Smith are just two celebrities that invited cameras into their homes to follow their lives for TV. Unfortunately, neither received the same success, mainly because their lives were pretty normal and uninteresting compared to the Osbournes.

TV commentators believe the show's ground-breaking status is secure. As well as setting a completely new standard for fly-on-the-wall reality TV, *The Osbournes* has given us an insight into one of the most unusual celebrity families in America.

---

**7** Read the article. Are these statements true or false? Write T (true) or F (false) in the boxes.

a   Ozzy Osbourne was famous before the show started.   ☐

b   The show was popular from the very beginning.   ☐

c   Sharon Osbourne was famous before the show started.   ☐

d   Liza Minnelli and Anna Nicole Smith have made their lives into a film.   ☐

e   The show has been shown in over 100 countries.   ☐

f   Ozzy doesn't think his family is crazy.   ☐

g   Jack and Kelly have begun pop careers.   ☐

h   Sharon became a talk show host.   ☐

i   Other shows that copied *The Osbournes* have been equally as successful.   ☐

j   *The Osbournes* created a new approach to fly-on-the-wall reality TV.   ☐

| Exercise | Score |
|---|---|
| 1 Language | _____ / 8 |
| 2 Language | _____ / 4 |
| 3 Language | _____ / 12 |
| 4 Vocabulary | _____ / 8 |
| 5 Vocabulary | _____ / 4 |
| 6 Vocabulary | _____ / 4 |
| 7 Reading | _____ / 10 |
| Total: | _____ / 50 |
| | _____ % |

**Name** _____

**1** Choose the correct alternative.

a *Will / Would* you mind if I turned the music down?

b I *was / am* wondering if you *will / would* show me how to use the photocopier?

c Is it alright if I *make / made* a coffee?

d I'd be grateful if you *would / will* help me.

**2** Rewrite these sentences to make them more polite and / or formal. Begin with the words given.

a Can I open the window?

Is it alright _____ ?

b Can I use the phone?

Would you mind _____ ?

c Will you do me a favour?

I was wondering _____ ?

d Can you help me for a minute?

I'd be grateful _____ .

e Can I watch the football on TV.

I was wondering _____ ?

f Can I get a lift into town?

Is it possible _____ ?

**3** Rearrange these words to make apologies.

a sorry / 'm / we've got no milk left / but / I

_____

_____

b for / apologise / I / arriving late this morning

_____

_____

c that / I / afraid / I can't make it to your party / 'm

_____

_____

d actually / busy / I / this weekend / Well / am / really

_____

_____

**4** Match the character adjectives in the box to the definitions. One of the adjectives is not used.

bad-tempered   bossy   cheerful   forgetful
generous   mature   selfish   unreliable   untidy

a behaving in a happy and friendly way

_____

b giving people more of your time or money than is usual or expected _____

c made annoyed or angry very easily _____

d often unable to remember things _____

e thinking only about yourself and not caring about other people _____

f someone who cannot be depended on

_____

g someone who is annoying because they keep telling other people what to do _____

h behaving like an adult _____

**5** Choose the correct alternative in the newspaper stories.

A man (a) *obsessed / convicted* with supermodel Cindy Campbell has been arrested and charged with (b) *obsession / harassment*. He was caught (c) *singing / swearing* and shouting outside her home after she refused to reply to his daily love letters.

Pop star Robbie Gallagher is (d) *suing / convicting* a national newspaper for printing a story which claimed that he has previously had a (e) *conviction / probation* for shoplifting.

Bank of England thief, Ronnie Smalls, was yesterday released on (f) *potential / probation* after serving 15 years of his 20-year sentence. 'He is still a (g) *potential / obsessed* danger to the public', commented the judge.

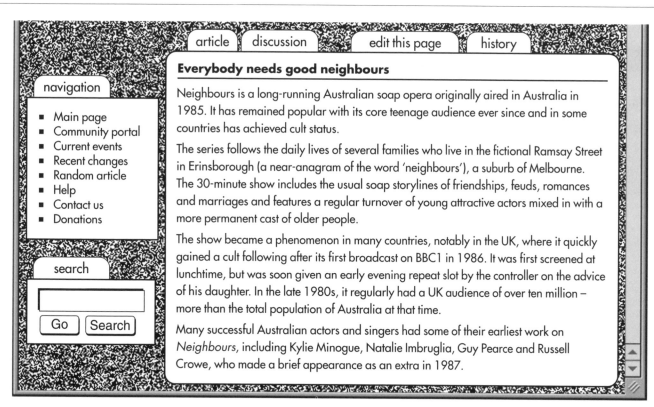

**Everybody needs good neighbours**

article · discussion · edit this page · history

navigation
- Main page
- Community portal
- Current events
- Recent changes
- Random article
- Help
- Contact us
- Donations

search

Go Search

Neighbours is a long-running Australian soap opera originally aired in Australia in 1985. It has remained popular with its core teenage audience ever since and in some countries has achieved cult status.

The series follows the daily lives of several families who live in the fictional Ramsay Street in Erinsborough (a near-anagram of the word 'neighbours'), a suburb of Melbourne. The 30-minute show includes the usual soap storylines of friendships, feuds, romances and marriages and features a regular turnover of young attractive actors mixed in with a more permanent cast of older people.

The show became a phenomenon in many countries, notably in the UK, where it quickly gained a cult following after its first broadcast on BBC1 in 1986. It was first screened at lunchtime, but was soon given an early evening repeat slot by the controller on the advice of his daughter. In the late 1980s, it regularly had a UK audience of over ten million – more than the total population of Australia at that time.

Many successful Australian actors and singers had some of their earliest work on Neighbours, including Kylie Minogue, Natalie Imbruglia, Guy Pearce and Russell Crowe, who made a brief appearance as an extra in 1987.

**6** Read the article and answer these questions.

a Neighbours is only shown in Australia. True or false?

_____

b What age are the majority of Neighbours viewers?

_____

c Ramsay Street exists in real life. True or false?

_____

d Which actors change more frequently – the younger or older ones?

_____

e Neighbours' popularity grew slowly in the United Kingdom. True or false?

_____

f At what time of day was Neighbours first shown in the United Kingdom?

_____

g Why was Neighbours repeated in the early evening in the UK?

_____

h In the 1980s, what was the UK audience bigger than?

_____

i Lots of famous people made guest appearances on Neighbours. True or false?

_____

j Actor Russell Crowe had a major role in Neighbours. True or false?

_____

**7** Match the figures to what they refer to in the text.

(1) 1985  (2) 1986  (3) 1987  (4) 30
(5) 1  (6) over ten million

(a) BBC  (b) Russell Crowe
(c) length of the show  (d) viewers
(e) first show  (f) first UK show

1 _____

2 _____

3 _____

4 _____

5 _____

6 _____

| Exercise | Score |
|---|---|
| 1 Language | _____ / 5 |
| 2 Language | _____ / 6 |
| 3 Language | _____ / 8 |
| 4 Vocabulary | _____ / 8 |
| 5 Vocabulary | _____ / 7 |
| 6 Reading | _____ / 10 |
| 7 Reading | _____ / 6 |
| Total: | _____ / 50 |
| | _____ % |

**Name** _____

**1** Complete the phrasal verbs with the words in the box.

| away   down   off   on   out   over   together up   with |
|---|

a   We went out _____ each other for about 5 years.

b   We met at university and hit it _____ immediately.

c   We got _____ a few weeks later.

d   We got _____ really well at first …

e   … but I soon started to feel that the relationship was taking _____ my whole life …

f   … and we started arguing and falling _____ all the time.

g   I realised I had to get _____ from it. I needed more freedom in my life.

h   We broke _____ last month.

i   I hope we can stay friends, but he feels that I really let him _____ .

**2** Rearrange these words to make full sentences which give advice.

a   I'm tired.

go / should /You / to bed

_____.

b   I forgot my girlfriend's birthday yesterday.

you, / were / I / buy her some flowers / I / If /'d

_____

_____.

c   My boyfriend needs to improve his English.

join / he / an English course / Maybe / could

_____

_____.

d   I don't get on with my new boss.

about / might /You / a new job / think / looking for

_____

_____.

e   I've got no money.

should / on computer games /You / n't / spend so much

_____

_____.

**3** Read the web forum postings on the next page and answer these questions.

1   Whose dilemma is whether or not to …

a   sell something

_____

b   pay something

_____

c   talk to someone

_____

d   return something

_____

e   claim something

_____

2   Are these statements true or false according to the web forum postings? Write T (true) or F (false) in the boxes.

a   Dave bought a camera for £50.                 ☐

b   Donna is getting married next month.          ☐

c   Simona found a lottery ticket.                 ☐

d   Simona has mentioned the lottery ticket to her parents' friend.          ☐

e   Alex thinks one of his classmates is a cheat.          ☐

f   Alice used to like the necklace.               ☐

g   The necklace is worth over £500.              ☐

# Your dilemma.com

**a** Posted by: **Dave**

I asked my friend to drive me to the shops. While I was there he moved the car and waited in a no-parking area. He was caught on camera and later received a £50 fine. He wants me to pay the fine as it was because of me that he was there. What should I do – pay all, half or none?

**b** Posted by: **Donna**

My boyfriend and I have recently broken up. We were due to be married next month, but he met someone else. He wants me to return the engagement ring to him. Do I give it back to him or keep it?

**c** Posted by: **Simona**

After a visit from a wealthy friend of my parents, I noticed a lottery ticket down the side of the chair he had been sitting in. I later discovered that the ticket had won £1000. The man hasn't mentioned the lost ticket and the money must be claimed in two weeks. Should I claim the money for myself?

**d** Posted by: **Alex**

A guy in my class constantly gets high marks because his mother is a professor (at a different university) and she helps him with all his assignments. I think it is unfair that he has this advantage over his classmates. It's cheating. Should I tell one of our professors?

**e** Posted by: **Alice**

An elderly aunt, who I see only once a year at most, has given me an old necklace. She remembered that I used to like it as a small child, but I didn't and I will never wear it. A jeweller has valued it at over £500. If I sold it, my aunt would never know. What should I do?

---

**4** Complete the responses to the dilemmas with the correct missing words *think, should, would* and *were*.

**1** Posted by: **Erin**

You (a) _____ definitely keep it. And then sell it and use the money to treat yourself to something special.

**2** Posted by: **Hannah**

Return it to its rightful owner. But if you don't, you might (b) _____ about giving the winnings to charity.

**3** Posted by: **Hank**

Sell it. Your aunt will never know.

**4** Posted by: **Steve**

If I (c) _____ you, I (d) _____ talk to your classmate first. Maybe you can get him to tell the teacher.

**5** Posted by: **Sally**

Tell your friend that as he chose where to park, he is the one to pay it. And maybe you (e) _____ choose your friends more carefully in the future.

**5** Match the responses in Ex 4 to the dilemmas in Ex 3.

1 _____
2 _____
3 _____
4 _____
5 _____

| Exercise | Score |
|---|---|
| 1 Vocabulary | _____ / 18 |
| 2 Language | _____ / 10 |
| 3 Reading | _____ / 12 |
| 4 Language | _____ / 5 |
| 5 Reading | _____ / 5 |
| Total: | _____ / 50 |
| | _____ % |

Move Intermediate Teacher's Book © Macmillan Publishers Limited 2006

**Name** _____

**1** Choose the correct alternative.

a I need to speak *about* / *to* you *about* / *to* the arrangements for the party.

b My brother and I get on well and generally agree *with* / *on* each other *with* / *on* most things.

c We complained *about* / *to* the waiter *about* / *to* the food.

d The restaurant manager apologised *for* / *to* us *for* / *to* the terrible service.

e A: Have you heard the news *about* / *from* William?
B: No, I haven't. In fact I haven't heard *about* / *from* William for ages – no phone calls, no emails, nothing.

f A: Have you heard *of* / *from* Tim Jones? He's that new comedian on TV. He's really funny, everyone loves him!
B: No I've heard nothing *about* / *from* him.

g A: You're being quiet – what are you thinking *about* / *of*?
B: Oh, Harry and I are thinking *about* / *of* going away at the weekend. I was just wondering where we could go.

**2** Add the missing prepositions to these newspaper headlines.

a **Thousands protest _____ tax increases.**

b **Asylum seekers fight _____ right to stay in UK.**

c **Footballer reads _____ his fiancée's affair in local paper.**

d **Millions dream _____ end to war.**

e **£20 billion wasted _____ Moon base.**

f **'Stick _____ me' says President to voters.**

**3** Match the words in the box to the definitions.

attack  daft  grudging  slap  startled  stick with

a done in an unwilling way
_____

b suddenly feeling frightened or surprised
_____

c use violence against a person or place
_____

d put something on a flat surface quickly and noisily
_____

e to stay close to someone
_____

f not sensible or reasonable
_____

**4** Complete these sentences with the words in the box in Ex 3.

a Everyone was completely _____ by the explosion.

b Even though I don't like Manchester United, I suppose I do have a _____ admiration for them.

c Don't be _____ . That's a crazy idea – it'll never work.

d The soldiers planned to _____ the enemy during the night.

e All you need to do is clean the place, _____ a bit of paint on the walls, get some nice furniture, and you're ready to move in.

f Don't worry, just _____ me and you'll be fine.

**5** Complete these sentences with *passive, aggressive* or *assertive*.

a Rachel doesn't handle arguments too well, she always starts shouting. She's too _____ .

b Emma's great when it comes to conflict. She's calm and rational, but always manages to get her opinion across. She's very _____ .

c Katia hates confrontations. She just stands there without saying a word. And she always takes the blame. She is so _____ .

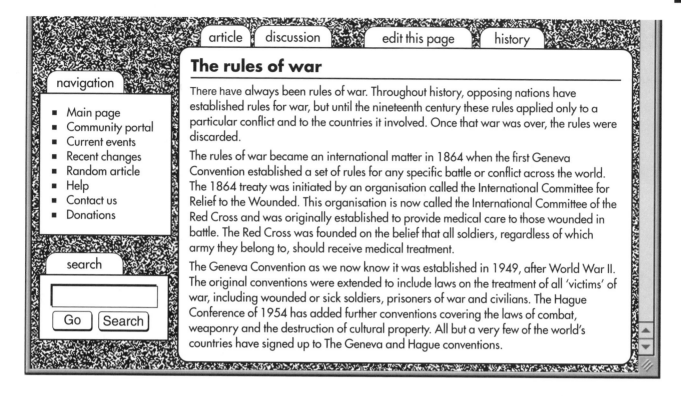

article | discussion | edit this page | history

## The rules of war

There have always been rules of war. Throughout history, opposing nations have established rules for war, but until the nineteenth century these rules applied only to a particular conflict and to the countries it involved. Once that war was over, the rules were discarded.

The rules of war became an international matter in 1864 when the first Geneva Convention established a set of rules for any specific battle or conflict across the world. The 1864 treaty was initiated by an organisation called the International Committee for Relief to the Wounded. This organisation is now called the International Committee of the Red Cross and was originally established to provide medical care to those wounded in battle. The Red Cross was founded on the belief that all soldiers, regardless of which army they belong to, should receive medical treatment.

The Geneva Convention as we now know it was established in 1949, after World War II. The original conventions were extended to include laws on the treatment of all 'victims' of war, including wounded or sick soldiers, prisoners of war and civilians. The Hague Conference of 1954 has added further conventions covering the laws of combat, weaponry and the destruction of cultural property. All but a very few of the world's countries have signed up to The Geneva and Hague conventions.

**navigation**
- Main page
- Community portal
- Current events
- Recent changes
- Random article
- Help
- Contact us
- Donations

**search**

[ Go ] [ Search ]

**6** Read the article and choose the correct alternative.

1 Originally, the rules of war:
   a lasted only as long as each conflict
   b were opposed by different nations
   c were established in the nineteenth century

2 What is the Geneva Convention?
   a a battle
   b a way of treating wounded soldiers
   c a set of rules for war

3 Why was the Red Cross originally established?
   a to produce the rules of war
   b to treat wounded soldiers
   c to make sure the rules of war were followed

4 The Red Cross believe that medical treatment:
   a should only be given to your own army
   b should only be given to seriously wounded soldiers
   c should be given to soldiers from all armies

5 Today, which of the following is <u>not</u> covered by the conventions of war?
   a the size of armies
   b the weapons which can be used
   c the destruction of cultural property

6 The Geneva and Hague Conventions have been:
   a rejected by most of the world's countries
   b accepted by most of the world's countries
   c produced by most of the world's countries

7 What happened in:
   a 1864?

   _____

   b 1949

   _____

   c 1954

   _____

| Exercise | Score |
|---|---|
| 1 Language | _____ / 14 |
| 2 Language | _____ / 6 |
| 3 Vocabulary | _____ / 6 |
| 4 Vocabulary | _____ / 6 |
| 5 Vocabulary | _____ / 3 |
| 6 Reading | _____ / 15 |
| Total: | _____ / 50 |
| | _____ % |

# Module test

**Name** _____

**1** Match the halves to make adjectives that describe character.

| | | | | |
|---|---|---|---|---|
| a | bad- | 1 | taking |
| b | narrow- | 2 | motivated |
| c | hard- | 3 | tempered |
| d | risk- | 4 | minded |
| e | self- | 5 | working |

**2** Match the character adjectives in the box to the descriptions.

> ambitious   arrogant   forgetful   rebellious
> reliable

a Sam often doesn't remember things.

_____

b You can depend on Anne. She's always there if you need her. _____

c Harry often breaks the rules and doesn't do what he should. _____

d Barry always thinks he's the best at everything.

_____

e Alice really wants to be successful and get an important, well-paid job. _____

**3** Choose the correct alternative.

a Sam and I went *on* / *out* with each other for two years.

b We met at a friend's party and hit it *off* / *on* immediately.

c We got *off* / *on* really well for the first year.

d But then we started falling *down* / *out* all the time.

e We broke *up* / *out* about three months ago.

**4** Complete the newspaper headlines with the words in the box.

> attack   claim   protest   sue   waste

a
> **1000s of motorists _____ against increase in petrol prices.**

b
> **Family _____ they were abducted by aliens.**

c
> **Prince to _____ newspaper for printing picture of new girlfriend.**

d
> **NASA and ESA _____ £500 million on failed space mission.**

e
> **Rebels _____ army base – 30 dead.**

**5** Complete these sentences with the pairs of prepositions in the box.

> about / from   to / for   to / about   to / about

a I'd like to speak _____ you _____ your work.

b We complained _____ the waiter _____ the food.

c He apologised _____ us _____ being late.

d I heard _____ the accident _____ Dave. He told me when I saw him yesterday.

**6** Complete the dialogues with the present perfect or the past simple form of the verbs.

A: (a) _____ (you / see) David recently? I (b) _____ (not / see) him for ages.

B: Yes, I (c) _____ (see) him a few days ago actually – Tuesday I think. We (d) _____ (go) for a drink.

A: Sorry I (e) _____ (not / call) you yesterday – I just (f) _____ (not / can) find the time. I (g) _____ (be) so busy for the past few days.

B: Don't worry. I (h) _____ (be) out for most of the day anyway.

**7** Rearrange these words to make full sentences.

a Is if I the TV alright on put it?

_____

b used if Would phone you mind I the?

_____

c I was if I could your computer for a few use minutes wondering?

_____

d I'd be if you help me for grateful could a minute.

_____

**8** Complete the advice with the words in the box.

| 'd should shouldn't think were |
|---|

a If you need to improve your English, you _____ join an English course.

b If I _____ you, I _____ find someone to have English conversation with.

c You might _____ about spending some time in an English speaking country.

d You _____ speak your own language so much in class.

**9** 🔘 **15** Listen to Amanda talking about the people she is close to. Are these statements true or false? Write T (true) or F (false) in the boxes.

a Amanda lives with her mother. ☐

b She has known her boyfriend for about a year. ☐

c Amanda and her boyfriend live close to each other. ☐

d Amanda sees Kerri once a week. ☐

e Amanda is not as close to Adam as she used to be. ☐

f Adam doesn't ring his girlfriend very often. ☐

g Amanda and her sister are similar ages. ☐

h Amanda sees Helen about twice a year. ☐

**10** Choose the correct names.

a Amanda's boyfriend is:

Adam / Helen / Kerri / Laura / Nick

b Amanda's friends are:

Adam / Helen / Kerri / Laura / Nick

c Amanda's sisters are:

Adam / Helen / Kerri / Laura / Nick

**11** Who does Amanda describe using these words? Choose from the people in the box.

| Adam   Kerri   Laura   Nick |
|---|

a generous

_____

b affectionate

_____

c cheerful

_____

d irritating

_____

e selfish

_____

f insensitive

_____

g good fun

_____

# The disappearing generation gap

A RECENT STUDY has produced an interesting picture of today's parent–child relationships. It has revealed that many of today's parents and children dress the same, listen to the same music, have similar interests and attitudes and are in fact best friends. And there is now a much greater tolerance and understanding between generations than ever before.

Although the generation gap hasn't disappeared completely, it is getting smaller all the time. Today it is very common for parents and their children to share their clothes, make-up, music and other possessions. Conversations that were unthinkable a generation ago, on subjects such as relationships, sex and drugs are now comfortable and common. And many parents and children regularly spend much of their leisure time together.

Katy and William Evans of London, UK go out with their children and their children's friends once or twice a week. 'We have been doing this for a few years now. We go to restaurants and cafes, we do sports together and we quite often go to gigs and go clubbing with them. We talk about all kinds of things, from pop music to TV soaps to boyfriend and girlfriend trouble. I'd say there's nothing that we can't talk about. We're definitely part of the gang', Mrs Evans says. 'And our children have become our best friends. Also, we have changed the way we discipline our children. We now discuss things with them as friends and equals and we always allow them to decide what to do. Some may say it's quite radical and too soft, but it works for us.'

---

**12** Read the article about parent–child relationships. Are these statements true or false? Write T (true) or F (false) in the boxes.

a   The study was about the relationship between parents and their children. ☐

b   Many parents and children are best friends. ☐

c   Parents and children tolerate each other much more than in previous generations. ☐

d   The generation gap has disappeared. ☐

e   Many parents and children wear the same clothes. ☐

f   Most parents and children still don't talk about topics such as sex and drugs. ☐

g   It is uncommon for parents and children to spend their leisure time together. ☐

h   Katy and William Evans regularly go out with their children and their friends. ☐

i   Katy Evans believes she can talk to her children about anything. ☐

j   The Evans family have a traditional and conventional approach to disciplining their children. ☐

**13** Imagine you were asked to be part of a survey similar to the one mentioned in the article in Ex 9. Write about 150 words describing your relationship with either (i) your parents, (ii) your brothers and sisters or (ii) your friends.

| Exercise | Score |
|---|---|
| 1 Vocabulary | _____ / 5 |
| 2 Vocabulary | _____ / 5 |
| 3 Vocabulary | _____ / 5 |
| 4 Vocabulary | _____ / 5 |
| 5 Language | _____ / 4 |
| 6 Language | _____ / 8 |
| 7 Language | _____ / 4 |
| 8 Language | _____ / 4 |
| 9 Listening | _____ / 8 |
| 10 ·Listening | _____ / 5 |
| 11 Listening | _____ / 7 |
| 12 Reading | _____ / 20 |
| 13 Writing | _____ / 20 |
| Total: | _____ / 100 |
| | _____ % |

**Name** _____

**1** These icons contain the wrong captions. Correct the captions.

a
Javelin
_____

b
Long jump
_____

c
Relay
_____

d
Rowing
_____

e
Gymnastics
_____

f
Sailing
_____

g
Basketball
_____

**2** Match the words in the box to the definitions.

| bloke  calm down  go for  own up  swear rage |

a  begin to feel more relaxed _____

b  attack someone _____

c  a man (British informal) _____

d  a very strong feeling of anger _____

e  admit you have done something bad _____

f  use words that are offensive _____

**3** Complete these newspaper headlines with the correct form of the words in Ex 2.

a
**Footballer Wade Moody fined £50,000 after _____ at referee.**

b
**'We all make mistakes – I'm a normal _____' says Beckley after penalty miss.**

c
**'Don't panic' – Head coach asks fans to _____ after latest 4−0 defeat for United.**

d
**Goalkeeper banned for 12 months as he _____ to deliberately not saving last-minute penalty.**

e
**Angry demonstration against United's new owner – fans show their _____.**

f
**Mass fight as players _____ each other during Cup final.**

**4** Read about football legend Pele and complete the sentences with the past simple, past continuous or past perfect form of the verbs.

Brazilian football legend Pele was born Edson Arantes do Nascimento on 23 October 1940.

From the age of five, he was coached by his father, who (a) _____ (be) an excellent professional football player himself until a knee injury (b) _____ (end) his career early.

While he (c) _____ (play) schoolboy football, Pele was discovered by one of Brazil's top players, Waldemar de Brito. De Brito (d) _____ (take) Pele to meet the directors of the Sao Paulo club Santos and (e) _____ (tell) them 'This boy will be the greatest soccer player in the world.' At the time, the 11-year-old Pele (f) _____ (work) as a shoe-shiner to earn extra money for his family.

Pele (g) _____ (sign) for Santos and (h) _____ (score) on his professional debut aged 16. By the end of the season he (i) _____ (become) the league's top scorer.

In 1958, he (j) _____ (win) his and Brazil's first World Cup after scoring six goals, including two in the final. He instantly (k) _____ (became) a hero. By the time he retired from international football, he (l) _____ (play) in four World Cups, winning again in 1962 and 1970.

When Pele finally (m) _____ (retire) from the game in 1977, he (n) _____ (play) in 1,363 professional games and (o) _____ (score) a world record 1,281 goals. In addition to being a great footballer Pele (p) _____ (publish) several autobiographies, starred in documentary films and composed numerous musical pieces.

# Who is the greatest sportsman ever?

**Posted by:** Alison, UK

The greatest sportsmen take a sport to another level. Pele, Muhammed Ali and Tiger Woods have all done just this. But in terms of pure success at winning things, Tiger has done the most in the shortest time. So he gets my vote.

**Posted by:** Ronan, Ireland

To be the best at any sport takes talent, discipline, courage and determination. Muhammed Ali showed all these characteristics and more. He is simply the best.

**Posted by:** Sanjit, India

I think that the title 'The Greatest Sportsman ever' itself is an extremely stupid title. There is no way anyone can compare two sportsmen competing in different games or in the same sport in a different age.

**Posted by:** Sally, Australia

The greatest are those who dominated their sports by the biggest margin and for the longest. Sergei Bubka, Ed Moses, Michael Jordan, Pete Sampras, Lance Armstrong and Michael Schumacher all fit the bill. But the greatest has to be rower Steve Redgrave. He won five gold medals in successive Olympics. Say no more.

**Posted by:** Tom, USA

It's not often that people get called a 'living legend', but we have one in basketball player Michael Jordan. Whenever he was playing, something magic was bound to happen. He is simply the most exciting attacking athlete ever.

**Posted by:** Carlos, Spain

It's not about longevity or domination, it's about impact. And for that reason I choose Pele. The greatest player of the world's greatest game.

**Posted by:** Clive, UK

I would suggest Muhammed Ali, closely followed by Pele and Tiger Woods as the best sportsmen ever. Their total domination of their chosen sports, and not necessarily in terms of titles or medals they won, makes them the best by a mile.

**5**   Read the online poll and answer these questions.

a   Which two sportsmen are mentioned the most?

_____ and _____

b   Which two people mentioned the same sportsmen?

_____ and _____

c   Which two people thought that domination of their sport was the most important factor?

_____ and _____

d   Which of the following does <u>not</u> describe Sanjit's view?
You can't compare people:
1   of different ages.
2   competing at different times.
3   competing in different sports.

e   Who believes that winning is not a key factor in deciding who is the greatest?

_____

f   Who did each person chose as the greatest sportsman ever?

Alison   _____

Ronan   _____

Sanjit   _____

Sally   _____

Tom   _____

Carlos   _____

Clive   _____

| Exercise | Score |
|---|---|
| 1 Vocabulary | _____ / 8 |
| 2 Vocabulary | _____ / 6 |
| 3 Vocabulary | _____ / 6 |
| 4 Language | _____ / 15 |
| 5 Reading | _____ / 15 |
| Total: | _____ / 50 |
|  | _____ % |

**Name** _____

**1** Match the gradable adjectives to their ungradable equivalents.

| | | | |
|---|---|---|---|
| a | good | 1 | tiny |
| b | bad | 2 | fantastic |
| c | big | 3 | terrible |
| d | small | 4 | huge |

**2** Complete these sentences with *very* or *absolutely*.

a  The party last night was _____ fantastic.

b  The other guests were _____ nice.

c  And I spoke to some _____ interesting people.

d  The music was _____ perfect.

e  And the food was _____ good.

f  All in all, it was _____ wonderful.

**3** In these sentences does *quite* mean the same as *a bit* or *absolutely*?

a  The film wasn't as good as the book. I suppose it was quite good though.

_____

b  The view from the top of the Empire State Building is quite amazing.

_____

c  The news about William and Harry is quite extraordinary.

_____

d  The new restaurant is quite nice, but nothing special.

_____

**4** Complete the colours with the missing vowels (*a, e, i, o, u*).

a)  b___ ___g___      d)  p___rpl___

b)  kh___k___      e)  sc___rl___t

c)  n___vy      f)  t___rq___ ___ ___s___

**5** Match the colours in Ex 4 to the definitions.

a  bright red _____

b  very light brown _____

c  between red and blue _____

d  green-brown _____

e  very dark blue _____

f  bright green-blue _____

**6** Complete these sentences with the words in the box.

> commercial   contemporary   distinctive   emotional   flexible

a  Van Gogh's art is very _____. As soon as you see it, you can tell immediately that it's by him.

b  The Millennium Dome in London, which was opened in 2000, didn't make any money at all – it was a _____ disaster.

c  I sometimes get quite _____ when I listen to the music of Debussy. It's so deep and moving.

d  Damien Hirst is one of the most well-known _____ artists in the world.

e  The hotel is very _____. We can stay as many nights as we like.

**7** Rearrange the words to make full sentences.

a  This picture is terrible. *just / It's / joke / a*

This picture is terrible.

_____.

b  I know lots of people like listening to opera, but *me / for / boring / quite / it's*.

I know lots of people like listening to opera, but

_____.

c  This sculpture *if / as / looks* it was made by a child.

This sculpture _____ it was made by a child.

d  Every time I watch the film Brief Encounter, *to / it / makes / want / me* cry. It's so sad.

Every time I watch the film Brief Encounter, _____ cry. It's so sad.

e  I know you like country music, but *nothing / it / me / does / for*.

I know you like country music, but

_____.

article<tab/>discussion<tab/>edit this page<tab/>history

## The Mona Lisa

navigation

- Main page
- Community portal
- Current events
- Recent changes
- Random article
- Help
- Contact us
- Donations

search

[          ]

[ Go ] [ Search ]

Leonardo Da Vinci's Mona Lisa is widely recognized as the most famous painting of all time. She has aroused admiration, curiosity and suspicion for over 500 years. She can provoke a reaction known as the Mona Lisa Syndrome: the viewer is enchanted by her legendary smile, which becomes increasingly enigmatic the more you look at it.

Mona Lisa is believed to be Lisa Gherardini del Giocondo, who was about 24 years old when Leonardo painted her. The portrait was commissioned by her wealthy husband. Her legendary features were achieved by 'sfumato', a style of painting invented by Da Vinci that blended light and shade to create blurred outlines. He did this to the corners of Mona Lisa's mouth and eyes, which explains her unfathomable smile and why she may look different from different angles.

After spending four years completing the painting, Da Vinci carried the Mona Lisa with him all around Italy, impressing other painters with his mastery of style.

The painting was moved from Italy to France at the beginning of the 1500s and was bought by the King of France. In 1797, the painting moved to the Louvre, which was an old royal residence, and has remained there ever since. One of the very few occasions when it has left the Louvre was in 1911 when it was stolen by an employee, who walked out of the museum with it under his coat.

As it will never be sold, the Mona Lisa is priceless, although for insurance reasons it is believed to be valued at anything up to $1 billion.

**8**   Read the article. Are these statements true or false?
Write T (true) or F (false) in the boxes.

a   The Mona Lisa was painted over 500 years ago. ☐

b   Mona Lisa's smile becomes more mysterious the more you look at it. ☐

c   Mona Lisa is believed to be Leonardo Da Vinci's wife. ☐

d   Mona Lisa sometimes looks different depending on where you stand when you look at her. ☐

e   Some of the techniques used to paint the Mona Lisa were new at the time. ☐

f   The Mona Lisa was moved to a museum in 1797. ☐

g   The painting has only left the Louvre once since 1797. ☐

| Exercise | Score |
|---|---|
| 1 Language | _____ / 4 |
| 2 Language | _____ / 6 |
| 3 Language | _____ / 4 |
| 4 Vocabulary | _____ / 6 |
| 5 Vocabulary | _____ / 6 |
| 6 Vocabulary | _____ / 5 |
| 7 Vocabulary | _____ / 5 |
| 8 Reading | _____ / 14 |
| Total: | _____ / 50 |
| | _____ % |

**Name** _____

**1** Add the adjectives in the correct order.

a A _____ shirt.

   *multicoloured / disgusting*

b A _____ cat.

   *lovely / black and white*

c _____ boots.

   *football / cool / silver and red*

d A _____ ring.

   *wedding / gold / traditional*

e A _____ coat.

   *grey / thick / woollen*

f A _____ car.

   *sports / red / tiny*

**2** Complete these sentences with the words in the box.

| as a result   so   because |
|---|

a It was raining, _____ we took an umbrella.

b We took an umbrella _____ it was raining.

c It was raining. We got completely wet _____ .

**3** Complete these sentences with the words in the box.

| also   and   too |
|---|

a We went shopping _____ we went for a coffee.

b We went shopping. We _____ went for a coffee.

c We went shopping. We went for a coffee _____ .

**4** Complete these sentences with the words in the box.

| although   but   however |
|---|

a I like the style _____ I don't like the colour.

b _____ I like the style, I don't like the colour.

c I like the style. I don't like the colour _____ .

**5** Complete these sentences with an appropriate linking word.

a I'm learning English _____ I need it for my job.

b I'm studying English _____ I can get a better job.

c _____ I'm studying English, I don't speak it very well.

d I'm studying English and I'm _____ studying French.

e I'm studying English. I hope to study French _____ .

f _____ I study hard, I won't pass my exams.

**6** Match the words in the box to the pictures.

| checked   floral   plain   stripy |
|---|

a _____   b _____

_____   _____

c _____   d _____

_____   _____

**7** Match the words in the box to the definitions.

| eye-catching   natural   outrageous overwhelming   trendy   unexpected   versatile |
|---|

a unusual and likely to shock people _____

b something you notice very easily _____

c fashionable _____

d surprising _____

e existing in nature _____

f making you feel a strong emotion that you cannot control _____

g able to be used in many different ways _____

**8**  ~~Cross out~~ one alternative which is not possible.

a  He's got a *natural / trendy* talent for design.

b  A shopaholic is usually *vain / trendy / unexpected*.

c  She was wearing an *overwhelming / eye-catching / outrageous* dress.

d  The news was *unexpected / overwhelming / eye-catching*.

e  Her new jacket is very *versatile / trendy / natural*.

f  He always wears *eye-catching / trendy / unexpected / outrageous* clothes.

# Coco Chanel – biography

Gabrielle 'Coco' Chanel was one of the most influential women in the history of fashion. Her success was accomplished primarily due to hard work and a determined desire for fame. Along the way she pioneered new styles, gave the world its most famous perfume and invented 'the little black dress'.

Gabrielle Chanel was born in Saumur, France in 1883. In 1895, her mother died and the remaining part of Gabrielle's childhood was spent in an orphanage.

When Gabrielle turned twenty, she got a job as a shop assistant in a small clothes shop. It was during this time that she acquired the nickname 'Coco', after a dog in a song that she regularly sang. In 1913, she opened her own shop. Her clothes were uniquely loose, casual and in darker shades with an emphasis on jewellery and other accessories. They were an instant success. By 1915, Coco had opened two more fashion houses in Paris and Biarritz. She also started a perfume company and in 1920 brought out her signature perfume Chanel No. 5.

By the late 1930s, Coco's businesses were beginning to lose money, in part due to her very public relationship with a Nazi officer, and in 1939 she was forced to close all her shops and sell her perfume company. In 1954, however, aged 71, she made a successful comeback and reopened her shop in Paris. Coco died in Paris of natural causes on 10 January 1971.

**9**  Read the article and answer these questions.

1  Which of the following is <u>not</u> given as one of the main reasons for Coco Chanel's success?
   a  working hard
   b  wanting to be famous
   c  creating new styles

2  Her nickname 'Coco' was the name of:
   a  a shop
   b  a dog
   c  a song

3  Which of the following does <u>not</u> describe her own original designs?
   a  dark-coloured
   b  informal
   c  formal

4  By mid-1915, she had:
   a  two shops
   b  three shops
   c  four shops

5  In what year did Coco Chanel:
   a  start to live in an orphanage? _____
   b  start to work as a shop assistant? _____
   c  start to sell her own clothes? _____
   d  go back into business? _____

| Exercise | Score |
| --- | --- |
| 1 Language | _____ / 6 |
| 2 Language | _____ / 3 |
| 3 Language | _____ / 3 |
| 4 Language | _____ / 3 |
| 5 Vocabulary | _____ / 6 |
| 6 Vocabulary | _____ / 4 |
| 7 Vocabulary | _____ / 7 |
| 8 Vocabulary | _____ / 6 |
| 9 Reading | _____ / 12 |
| Total: | _____ / 50 |
| | _____ % |

**Name** _____

**1** Complete the email with the infinitive or *-ing* form of the verbs in brackets.

Send Now  Send Later  Save as Draft  Add Attachments  Signature  Contacts  Check Names

Account: Default Set ⬦   Priority: Normal ⬦
To:
Cc:
Bcc:
Subject:

Size Medium ⬦   B I U T — ≣ ≣ ≣ ≣ ≣ ≣ ≣ ▮

Hi Anna,

Here I am in New York and I'm having a fantastic time. Sorry I haven't managed (a)_____(write) to you sooner - I wanted (b)_____(email) you when I first arrived, but I've just been so busy.

Anyway, I'm having such a great time that I've decided (c)_____(stay) a little longer. I'm going to spend a few weeks (d)_____(travel) around the country with my friend Jane. First, we're hoping (e)_____(go) to California to spend a few days (f)_____(lie) on the beach. I'm really going to enjoy (g)_____(do) nothing for a few days! We're going to stay in a cheap hotel she knows in Los Angeles and some friends of hers have offered (h)_____(lend) us their car. I guess I'll have to learn how (i)_____(drive) on the wrong side of the road!

Anyway, I promise (j)_____(email) you again soon and I'll see you in a few weeks.

Take care and lots of love,

Sally xxx

**2** Complete the second sentence so the meaning is similar to the first sentence. Use the infinitive or *-ing* form of the <u>underlined</u> verb.

a  It took me two hours to <u>cook</u> dinner.

   I spent two hours _____

b  It's important that I <u>see</u> Toni later today.

   I need _____

c  I'll <u>help</u> you if you like.

   I don't mind _____

d  Fred <u>wasn't</u> really upset.

   Fred was only pretending _____

e  I last <u>smoked</u> five years ago.

   I gave up _____

f  John wouldn't <u>lend</u> me any money.

   John refused _____

g  I've made a decision – I'll <u>have</u> pizza.

   I've decided _____

**3** Complete these sentences with the words in the box.

> chatting   end up   off the beaten track
> passing through   sustainable

a  When I go travelling, I like having no plans. It's exciting not knowing where I'll _____ .

b  I really like to get _____ – somewhere where there are no other tourists.

c  I love just sitting around in restaurants and hotel lobbies _____ to people.

d  I've occasionally done a bit of work, like teaching English, in foreign countries while I was _____ .

e  I live in a popular tourist town and am very keen to encourage eco-friendly, _____ tourism here.

**4** Complete the phrasal verbs in the dialogues.

Tom:   You're late – what kept you?

Sam:   Sorry about that – I got (a) _____ the bus OK, but I got (b) _____ at the wrong stop and had to walk.

Alice:  Should we queue (c) _____ for a taxi here?

Liz:    Let's walk down the road a bit and try to flag one (d) _____ .

Sarah:  I'll give you a lift to the city centre if you like. Get (e) _____ the car.

Bill:   Great, thanks.

Sarah:  I just need to pick Anna (f) _____ on the way. It'll only take a couple of minutes.

Bill:   No worries.

Sarah:  Where do you want me to drop you (g) _____ ?

Bill:   I don't mind – I can get (h) _____ anywhere in the centre. Whatever's easiest for you.

Mike:   We've been sitting on this plane for ages.

Jenny:  I know, we were supposed to take (i) _____ forty minutes ago.

# France heads top ten tourist destinations

France remains the world's most visited country. The country has headed the rankings since the World Tourist Organisation's annual survey began in 1950. Paris is the country's top attraction. Touted as the city of romance and culture, the Louvre, the Arc de Triomphe, Montmartre, Notre Dame, le Métro, and the latest Parisian summer craze, Paris Beach, are just a few of the capital's notable attractions. The Eiffel Tower tops the list.

Spain, the United States, Italy and China are the second, third, fourth and fifth most visited

destinations. All four are becoming more popular every year, with China consistently seeing the greatest increase in the number of visitors. It is forecast that China will become the world's top tourist destination by the year 2020.

Although the order of the ranking has been fairly constant over recent years, not all destinations have grown at the same pace. The biggest increases are in the number of visitors to Asian countries while European countries, particularly Spain and France, show the most consistent

figures. For American visitors, the top five destinations tend to remain unchanged as Mexico, Canada, the United Kingdom, France and Germany.

The top 10 tourism destinations account jointly for almost half of the three-quarters of a billion annual arrivals reported worldwide. With this number of people travelling, international tourism generates over half a trillion dollars per year.

**5** Read the article and answer these questions.

a   How long has France been recorded as the most visited country?

_____

b   Which is the most visited attraction in Paris?

_____

c   Which country is predicted to become the top destination by 2020?

_____

d   The rankings haven't changed much over recent years. True or false?

_____

e   Which two countries have the most consistent number of visitors?

_____

f   Where do almost 50% of all tourists visit?

_____

| Exercise | Score |
| --- | --- |
| 1 Language | _____ / 10 |
| 2 Language | _____ / 14 |
| 3 Vocabulary | _____ / 5 |
| 4 Vocabulary | _____ / 9 |
| 5 Reading | _____ / 12 |
| Total: | _____ / 50 |
| | _____ % |

# Module test

**Name** _____

**1**   Choose the correct alternative.

a   You get *on* / *in* the bus outside the shops and get *off* / *out of* it opposite the library.

b   We can either queue *up* / *down* for a taxi here or walk a bit further and try to flag one *up* / *down*.

c   I'll pick you *out* / *up* at your house and I can drop you *off* / *out* in the town centre.

**2**   Do these words describe pattern, colour or shade? Write P (pattern), C (colour) or S (shade) in the boxes.

a   checked   ☐

b   light   ☐

c   stripy   ☐

d   turquoise   ☐

e   beige   ☐

f   bright   ☐

g   khaki   ☐

h   scarlet   ☐

i   stripy   ☐

j   navy   ☐

k   dark   ☐

l   floral   ☐

**3**   Complete the Olympic sports with the missing vowels (*a, e, i, o, u*).

a   b_ sk_ tb_ ll

b   j_ v_ l_ n

c   r_ l_ y

d   l_ ng j_ mp

e   r_ w_ ng

f   s_ _ l_ ng

**4**   Complete these comments with the words in the box.

| boring   joke   looks   makes   nothing |
| --- |

a   It's just a _____ .

b   For me it's quite _____ .

c   It _____ as if it was drawn by a child.

d   It _____ me want to cry.

e   It does _____ for me.

**5**   Choose the correct alternative.

a   Our holiday was *very* / *absolutely* fantastic.

b   We met some *very* / *absolutely* interesting people.

c   The hotel was *very* / *absolutely* nice.

d   But the rooms were *very* / *absolutely* tiny.

e   The food was *very* / *absolutely* wonderful.

f   And the weather was *very* / *absolutely* perfect.

**6**   In these sentences does *quite* mean the same as *a bit* or *absolutely*?

a   The museum wasn't what I expected. I suppose it was quite interesting though. _____

b   But the Van Gogh exhibition was quite amazing. _____

c   The concert was quite good, but nothing special. _____

d   The light show was quite extraordinary. _____

**7**   Add the adjectives in the correct order.

a   A _____ table.
   *beautiful* / *dining* / *wooden*

b   A _____ cottage.
   *stone* / *tiny* / *white*

c   _____ shoes.
   *leather* / *black and gold* / *eye-catching*

d   A _____ mobile phone.
   *huge* / *old* / *plastic*

**8** Choose the correct alternative

a   It was a lovely day, *so / because* we went for a walk.

b   We went to the park. We *too / also* went for a coffee.

c   The cafe was nice. The food was terrible *although / however*.

d   We'll go again *unless / if* the weather's bad.

**9** Complete the sentences with the infinitive or *-ing* form of the verbs in brackets.

a   I'd like _____ (live) abroad for a while.

b   I can't stand _____ (play) computer games.

c   I really should give up _____ (smoke).

d   I forgot _____ (do) my homework last night.

e   I finally managed _____ (finish) my work.

f   I really enjoy _____ (study) English.

**10** Complete the dialogues with the past simple, past continuous or past perfect form of the verbs.

A:  (a) _____ you _____ (see) Robert at the party on Saturday?

B:  No, he (b) _____ (already / leave) when we (c) _____ (arrive).

A:  I (d) _____ (see) you last night – you (e) _____ (get) out of a taxi with Tom and Bill.

B:  Yes, we (f) _____ (just / come) back) from the theatre.

A:  Sorry I (g) _____ (not / come out) with you last night.

B:  No worries. We (h) _____ (not / do) anything special.

**11** 🔘 **08** Listen to Claire talking about clothes. Choose the correct alternative.

1   Claire buys clothes:
   a   not very often
   b   sometimes
   c   as often as possible

2   Claire describes her fashion style as:
   a   outrageous
   b   unique
   c   fashionable

3   Claire learns about fashion by:
   a   looking at what other people are wearing
   b   watching TV
   c   reading fashion magazines

4   Claire's favourite trousers are:
   a   smart
   b   casual
   c   versatile

5   Claire admires Cameron Diaz because:
   a   everybody else does
   b   she is confident
   c   she knows what fashion is about

6   Claire likes a man that:
   a   looks like he has made a big effort to look good
   b   looks like he hasn't made a big effort to look good
   c   looks scruffy and has made no effort to look good

**12** Listen again and answers these questions.

a   How often does Claire wear make-up?
   _____

b   Why are clothes important to Claire?
   _____
   _____

c   Is she a follower of the latest fashion trends?
   _____

d   Why doesn't she wear short skirts?
   _____
   _____

# Van Gogh – the man behind the paintings

**Vincent van Gogh was born in the Netherlands on 30 March 1853 and died in France at age 37. Vincent painted some of the most famous paintings of our time, but sold only one in his own lifetime.**

In 1869, aged 16, Vincent left school and began to work for an art dealer company. This career lasted for seven years and took him all over Europe. He went on to try various other vocations such as teaching and the priesthood. In 1880, Vincent took the advice of his brother Theo and went to Brussels to begin to study art.

Despite his fame today, Vincent received little recognition for his work while he was alive. During his lifetime he sold only one painting. Vincent was not a rich man. The little money he had he often chose to spend on art supplies rather than food.

Vincent was very close to his Brother Theo, who encouraged and supported him financially with his painting. They even lived together in Paris for a while where Theo, who was an art dealer, introduced Vincent to famous artists such as Gauguin and Pissaro.

In 1888, Vincent started to suffer from epilepsy and severe depression, and later admitted himself to a psychiatric clinic after cutting off a part of his left ear. During his stay at the clinic, Vincent painted one of his most famous paintings, *Starry Night*. It was painted solely using his imagination.

On 27 July 1890, feeling like a failure, Vincent van Gogh shot himself in the chest. He died two days later, with his brother Theo by his side. Theo, ill and unable to live without his brother, died six months later.

---

**13** Read the biography of Vincent van Gogh. Are these statements true or false? Write T (true) or F (false) in the boxes.

a   At age 15, he began to study art. ☐

b   He was an art dealer for seven years. ☐

c   He worked as a teacher and trained to be a priest. ☐

d   His brother Theo believed Vincent should study art. ☐

e   He became rich from selling his paintings. ☐

f   He lived with artists Gauguin and Pissaro. ☐

g   He had mental health problems later in life. ☐

h   He cut off his own ear. ☐

i   The painting *Starry Night* is a view from the asylum where he was staying. ☐

j   He committed suicide. ☐

**14** Write a brief biography of either (i) a famous person, (ii) someone you know or (iii) yourself. Write about 150 words.

| Exercise | Score |
|---|---|
| 1 Vocabulary | _____ / 6 |
| 2 Vocabulary | _____ / 6 |
| 3 Vocabulary | _____ / 3 |
| 4 Vocabulary | _____ / 5 |
| 5 Language | _____ / 3 |
| 6 Language | _____ / 4 |
| 7 Language | _____ / 2 |
| 8 Language | _____ / 4 |
| 9 Language | _____ / 3 |
| 10 Language | _____ / 4 |
| 11 Listening | _____ / 12 |
| 12 Listening | _____ / 8 |
| 13 Reading | _____ / 20 |
| 14 Writing | _____ / 20 |
| Total: | _____ / 100 |
| | _____ % |

# Placement test answers

## Section 1 Language

(One point for each correct answer)

| | |
|---|---|
| 1 | c |
| 2 | b |
| 3 | b |
| 4 | c |
| 5 | b |
| 6 | c |
| 7 | a |
| 8 | c |
| 9 | a |
| 10 | a |
| 11 | a |
| 12 | c |
| 13 | b |
| 14 | c |
| 15 | a |
| 16 | c |
| 17 | c |
| 18 | b |
| 19 | b |
| 20 | b |
| 21 | c |
| 22 | a |
| 23 | c |
| 24 | c |
| 25 | a |
| 26 | b |
| 27 | c |
| 28 | c |
| 29 | c |
| 30 | b |
| 31 | a |
| 32 | c |
| 33 | c |
| 34 | a |
| 35 | a |
| 36 | c |
| 37 | a |
| 38 | b |
| 39 | c |
| 40 | a |
| 41 | c |
| 42 | a |
| 43 | b |
| 44 | b |
| 45 | a |
| 46 | a |
| 47 | c |
| 48 | a |
| 49 | b |
| 50 | c |

## Section 2 Vocabulary

(One point for each correct answer)

| | |
|---|---|
| 1 | was |
| 2 | am |
| 3 | in |
| 4 | to |
| 5 | for |
| 6 | take |
| 7 | like |
| 8 | do |
| 9 | on |
| 10 | far |
| 11 | for |
| 12 | idea |
| 13 | well / badly |
| 14 | up |
| 15 | catching |
| 16 | touch / contact |
| 17 | his |
| 18 | freezing |
| 19 | keep |
| 20 | sense |
| 21 | keep / catch |
| 22 | apart |
| 23 | outweigh |
| 24 | away |
| 25 | getter |

## Score banding

| | |
|---|---|
| 0–30 | Elementary |
| 31–40 | Pre-intermediate |
| 41–50 | Intermediate |
| 51–60 | Upper-intermediate |
| 61–75 | Advanced |

# Unit test answers

**(One point for each answer unless stated otherwise)**

## Module 1 Unit 1

**1**
a always
b (usually)
c often
d (sometimes)
e occasionally
f never

**2**
a ✓     e ✓
b ✗     f ✓
c ✗     g ✗
d ✗     h ✓

**3**
a I usually visit my grandparents at the weekend. / I visit my grandparents at the weekend usually. / Usually I visit my grandparents at the weekend
b My grandparents are always pleased to see me.
c I never cook my own dinner.
d I never play football.

**4**
a I usually get up at 7.30. / I get up at 7.30 usually. / Usually I get up at 7.30.
b I am sometimes late for school. / I am late for school sometimes. / Sometimes I am late for school.
c I never miss my lessons.
d I always do my homework.
e I am always asleep by midnight.

**5**
a How often do you go out with friends?
b We normally go out together once or twice a week. / Normally we go out together once or twice a week. / We go out together once or twice a week normally.
c Where do you usually go?
d We sometimes go for a meal. / Sometimes we go for a meal. / We go for a meal sometimes.
e We usually go to a bar or club. / Usually we go to a bar or club. We go to a bar or club usually.

**6** (Two points each)
a tournament
b opponents
c row
d point
e unwind
f match
g coach potato

**7**
a T     f F
b F     g F
c F     h F
d T     i T
e T     j F

## Module 1 Unit 2

**1**
a beforehand
b before
c before
d beforehand

**2**
a After
b afterwards
c after
d afterwards

**3** (Two points for c)
a We're going to the cinema and then we'll go for a drink afterwards.
b I'll see you later, but I need to speak to John beforehand.
c Let's meet at 7. I'm seeing Jeff beforehand and I'm having dinner with Sam afterwards.

**4**
a before     f before
b earlier     g while
c while     h afterwards
d later     i after
e before     j earlier

**5** (Half point each)
a pressure
b biography
c famous
d journalist
e scientist
f scientific
g privacy
h terrific
i electric
j energy
k guitarist
l democracy

**6**
a achievements
b runway
c airborne
d kidnapped
e ransom
f trial
g escape

**7**
a drive
b expectations
c esteem
d break up
e bullied

**8** (Two points each)
1 b     4 c
2 b     5 a
3 c

## Module 1 Unit 3

**1**
a is bigger than
b are more popular than
c is more expensive than
d is warmer than

**2**
a The UK is not as big as Brazil.
b Letters are not as popular as emails.
c Bangkok is not as expensive as London.
d Yesterday was not as warm as today.

**3**
a is the most common
b is the biggest
c is the smallest
d is / are the most famous

**4**
a Thailand is **twice as big as** the United Kingdom.
b The population of Thailand is **a bit bigger than the population of** the United Kingdom.
c Thailand is **much hotter than** the United Kingdom.

**5**
a ~~much~~ / by far
b a bit / ~~not quite~~.
c ~~far~~ / by far
d much / far / ~~by far~~
e not quite / ~~a bit~~ / nearly
f much / ~~nearly~~ / far

**6**
a  flat
b  terraced house
c  semi-detached house
d  cottage
e  windmill
f  warehouse
g  bungalow
h  narrow boat

**7**
a  share
b  location
c  furnished
d  fully-equipped
e  parking
f  Rent
g  inclusive
h  landlord

**8**
a  Bernie Ecclestone, the Formula One racing boss.
b  Three years.
c  They never moved into the house.
d  1  c      6  j
   2  i      7  h
   3  d      8  e
   4  b      9  g
   5  f     10  a

# Module 1 Unit 4

**1**
a  I'd **like to** go out tonight.
b  We're **hoping to go to** the same university.
c  I'm aiming **to finish my homework** by 8.
d  The taxi **is due to arrive** at 8.30.
e  I expect **to be back home** before midnight.
f  I'm intending **to get up early** tomorrow morning.

**2**
a  I'm due to finish university next year.
b  What do you hope / are you hoping to do after university?
c  I hope / 'm hoping to work in the music industry.
d  I aim / 'm aiming to be a millionaire by the time I'm 40.
e  I hope / 'm hoping I'll retire when I'm 50.
f  Would you like to live abroad one day?
g  Yes, I'd like to live in New York one day.
h  I expect to get a job with / in a multinational company

**3**  (Half point each)
a  doctor  medicine
b  accountant  accountancy
c  psychologist  psychology
d  linguist  linguistics
e  physiotherapist  physiotherapy
f  solicitor  law
g  pharmacist  pharmacy

**4**  (Half point each)
a  <u>do</u>ctor  <u>me</u>dicine
b  a<u>cc</u>ount<u>ant</u>  a<u>cc</u>ountancy
c  psy<u>cho</u>logist  psy<u>cho</u>logy
d  <u>lin</u>guist  lingu<u>is</u>tics
e  physio<u>the</u>rapist  physio<u>the</u>rapy
f  so<u>li</u>citor  law
g  <u>phar</u>macist  <u>phar</u>macy

**5**
a  up       e  up
b  into     f  off
c  on       g  around
d  up

**6**  (One point for each correct name, in any order)
a  Al, Chad, Laura
b  Sam, Tania
c  Laura
d  Chad
e  Al, Tim
f  Sam
g  Al, Laura
h  Al, Chad
i  John

# Module 2 Unit 1

**1**
a – d, in no particular order:
last year, two weeks ago, yesterday, when I was a child
e – h, in no particular order:
since 2004, this year, recently, for the last ten minutes

**2**
a  since 2004 / for a few years / ~~a few years ago~~.
b  ~~since 2004~~ / in 2004 / a few years ago.
c  for weeks / since January / ~~last week~~.
d  ~~since last year~~ / last year / six months ago.

**3**
a  spoke
b  haven't seen
c  've never been
d  went
e  moved
f  finished
g  've been
h  've already had
i  had

j  opened
k  've worked
l  didn't get

**4**
a  conventional
b  rebellious
c  narrow-minded
d  reliable
e  bad-tempered
f  arrogant
g  affectionate
h  generous

**5**  (Half point each)
a  ambitious
b  cautious
c  confident
d  hard-working
e  independent
f  sociable
g  mature
h  responsible

**6**
a  status
b  claim
c  approach
d  rebels

**7**
a  T       f  F
b  T       g  F
c  F       h  T
d  F       i  F
e  T       j  T

# Module 2 Unit 2

**1**  (Two points for b)
a  Would
b  was  would
c  make
d  would

**2**
a  Is it alright **if I open the window?**
b  Would you mind **if I use(d) the phone?**
c  I was wondering **if you would do me a favour?**
d  I'd be grateful **if you could help me for a minute.**
e  I was wondering **if I could watch the football on TV?**
f  Is it possible **to get a lift into town?**

**3**  (Two points each)
a  I'm sorry but we've got no milk left.
b  I apologise for arriving late this morning.
c  I'm afraid that I can't make it to your party.
d  Well, actually I am really busy this weekend.

**4**
a cheerful
b generous
c bad-tempered
d forgetful
e selfish
f unreliable
g bossy
h mature

**5**
a obsessed
b harassment
c swearing
d suing
e conviction
f probation
g potential

**6**
a False.
b Teenagers.
c False.
d Younger.
e False.
f Lunchtime.
g The controller's daughter advised it.
h The population of Australia at the time.
i False.
j False.

**7**
| | | | |
|---|---|---|---|
| 1 | e | 4 | c |
| 2 | f | 5 | a |
| 3 | b | 6 | d |

## Module 2 Unit 3

**1** (Two points each)
a with
b off
c together
d on
e over
f out
g away
h up
i down

**2** (Two points each)
a You should go to bed.
b If I were you, I'd buy her some flowers.
c Maybe he could join an English course.
d You might think about looking for a new job.
e You shouldn't spend so much on computer games.

**3** 1
a Alice
b Dave
c Alex
d Donna
e Simona

2
a F          e T
b F          f F
c T          g T
d F

**4**
a should
b think
c were
d would
e should

**5**
1 b
2 c
3 e
4 d
5 a

## Module 2 Unit 4

**1** (One point for each correct preposition)
a to about
b with on
c to about
d to for
e about from
f of about
g about of

**2**
a about
b for
c about
d of
e on
f with

**3**
a grudging
b startled
c attack
d slap
e stick with
f daft

**4**
a startled
b grudging
c daft
d attack
e slap
f stick with

**5**
a aggressive
b assertive
c passive

**6** (Two points for 1–6)
1 a
2 c
3 b
4 c
5 a
6 b
7 a The (first) Geneva Convention was established.
b The (present) Geneva Conventions (as we now know them) were established.
c The Hague Conference (added further conventions covering the rules of combat, weaponry and the destruction of cultural property).

## Module 3 Unit 1

**1**
a basketball
b gymnastics
c javelin
d long jump
e relay
f rowing
g sailing

**2**
a calm down
b go for
c bloke
d rage
e own up
f swear

**3**
a swearing
b bloke
c calm down
d owns up
e rage
f go for

**4**
a had been
b ended
c was playing
d took
e told
f was working
g signed
h scored
i had become
j won
k became
l had played
m retired
n had played
o (had) scored
p published

**5** (Two points for a, b and c)
  a   Pele, Muhammed Ali
  b   Alison, Clive
  c   Sally, Clive
  d   1
  e   Clive
  f   Alison – Tiger Woods
     Ronan – Muhammed Ali
     Sanjit – no-one
     Sally – Steve Redgrave
     Tom – Michael Jordan
     Carlos – Pele
     Clive – Muhammed Ali

## Module 3 Unit 2

**1**  a   2
  b   3
  c   4
  d   1

**2**  a   absolutely
  b   very
  c   very
  d   absolutely
  e   very
  f   absolutely

**3**  a   a bit
  b   absolutely
  c   absolutely
  d   a bit

**4**  a   beige
  b   khaki
  c   navy
  d   purple
  e   scarlet
  f   turquoise

**5**  a   scarlet
  b   beige
  c   purple
  d   khaki
  e   navy
  f   turquoise

**6**  a   distinctive
  b   commercial
  c   emotional
  d   contemporary
  e   flexible

**7**  a   It's just a joke
  b   for me it's quite boring
  c   looks as if
  d   it makes me want to
  e   it does nothing for me

**8** (Two points each)
  a   T
  b   T
  c   F
  d   T
  e   T
  f   F
  g   F

## Module 3 Unit 3

**1**  a   disgusting, multicoloured
  b   lovely, black and white
  c   cool, silver and red football
  d   traditional, gold wedding
  e   thick, grey, woollen
  f   tiny, red sports

**2**  a   so
  b   because
  c   as a result

**3**  a   and
  b   also
  c   too

**4**  a   but
  b   Although
  c   however

**5**  a   because
  b   so
  c   Although
  d   also
  e   too
  f   Unless

**6**  a   stripy
  b   checked
  c   plain
  d   floral

**7**  a   outrageous
  b   eye-catching
  c   trendy
  d   unexpected
  e   natural
  f   overwhelming
  g   versatile

**8**  a   natural / ~~trendy~~
  b   vain / trendy / ~~unexpected~~
  c   ~~overwhelming~~ / eye-catching / outrageous
  d   unexpected / overwhelming / ~~eye-catching~~
  e   versatile / trendy / ~~natural~~
  f   eye-catching / trendy / ~~unexpected~~ / outrageous

**9** (Two points for 1–4)
  1   c
  2   b
  3   c
  4   b
  5   a   1895
     b   1903
     c   1913
     d   1954

## Module 3 Unit 4

**1**  a   to write
  b   to email
  c   to stay
  d   travelling
  e   to go
  f   lying
  g   doing
  h   to lend
  i   to drive
  j   to email

**2** (Two points each)
  a   I spent two hours **cooking dinner.**
  b   I need **to see Toni later today.**
  c   I don't mind **helping you if you like.**
  d   Fred was only pretending **to be upset.**
  e   I gave up **smoking 5 years ago.**
  f   John refused **to lend me any money.**
  g   I've decided **to have pizza.**

**3**  a   end up
  b   off the beaten track
  c   chatting
  d   passing through
  e   sustainable

**4**  a   on
  b   off
  c   up
  d   down
  e   in
  f   up
  g   off
  h   out
  i   off

**5** (Two points each)
  a   Since 1950.
  b   The Eiffel Tower.
  c   China.
  d   True.
  e   Spain and France.
  f   The top ten tourist destinations.

# Module test answers

**(One point for each answer unless stated otherwise)**

## Module 1

**1**  a  My brother is always playing computer games.

  b  Who do you usually go on holiday with? / Who do you go on holiday with usually? / Usually, who do you go on holiday with?

  c  I am often late for work. / Often, I am late for work. / I am late for work often.

  d  I usually get my hair cut every six weeks. / Usually, I get my hair cut very six weeks. / I get my hair cut every six weeks usually.

  e  I occasionally read magazines about famous people. / Occasionally I read magazines about famous people. / I read magazines about famous people occasionally.

**2**  a  after
  b  before
  c  afterwards
  d  later
  e  After

**3**  a  not nearly
  b  by far
  c  far
  d  not quite
  e  a bit

**4**  a  The taxi **is due to arrive** in ten minutes.
  b  We **are hoping to go** to France this summer.
  c  We**'d like to go** to Paris.
  d  **I'm intending to leave** early today.
  e  I **expect to be home** at about 7.30.

**5**  a  share
  b  semi-detached
  c  location
  d  fully-equipped
  e  Rent
  f  inclusive

**6**  a  up
  b  into
  c  around
  d  on
  e  off
  f  up
  g  up

**7**  a  runway
  b  airborne
  c  kidnapped
  d  ransom
  e  opponents
  f  drive
  g  row

**8**  (Two points each)
  1  20 years
  2  they've got to the top of their tree/reached the top of their profession
  3  d
  4  it's (great) free advertising
  5  b
  6  d
  7  be famous
  8  d
  9  a
  10  c

**9**  (Two points each)
  a  J
  b  E
  c  J
  d  E
  e  J
  f  J
  g  E
  h  E
  i  J
  j  E

**10**  Give a score out of 20
  5 points for accuracy
  5 points for vocabulary range
  5 points for organisation and cohesion
  5 points for content (appropriacy)

## Module 2

**1**  a  3
  b  4
  c  5
  d  1
  e  2

**2**  a  forgetful
  b  reliable
  c  rebellious
  d  arrogant
  e  ambitious

**3**  a  out
  b  off
  c  on
  d  out
  e  up

**4**  a  protest
  b  claim
  c  sue
  d  waste
  e  attack

**5**  a  to / about
  b  to / about
  c  to / for
  d  about / from

**6**  a  Have you seen
  b  haven't seen
  c  saw
  d  went
  e  didn't call
  f  couldn't
  g  've been
  h  was

**7**  a  Is it alright if I put the TV on?
  b  Would you mind if I used the phone?
  c  I was wondering if I could use your computer for a few minutes?
  d  I'd be grateful if you could help me for a minute.

**8**  a  should
  b  were  'd
  c  think
  d  shouldn't

**9**  a  F
    b  T
    c  F
    d  F
    e  T
    f  F
    g  F
    h  T

**10**  (One point for each name)
    a  Nick
    b  Adam, Kerri
    c  Helen, Laura

**11**  a  Nick
    b  Nick
    c  Kerri
    d  Adam
    e  Laura
    f  Laura
    g  Nick

**12**  (Two points each)
    a  T
    b  T
    c  T
    d  F
    e  T
    f  F
    g  F
    h  T
    i  T
    j  F

**13**  Give a score out of 20
    5 points for accuracy
    5 points for vocabulary range
    5 points for organisation and
    cohesion
    5 points for content
    (appropriacy)

# Module 3

**1**  (Two points each)
    a  on  off
    b  up  down
    c  up  off

**2**  (Half point each)
    a  P
    b  S
    c  P
    d  C
    e  C
    f  S
    g  C
    h  C
    i  P
    j  C
    k  S
    l  P

**3**  (Half point each)
    a  basketball
    b  javelin
    c  relay
    d  long jump
    e  rowing
    f  sailing

**4**  a  joke
    b  boring
    c  looks
    d  makes
    e  nothing

**5**  (Half point each)
    a  absolutely
    b  very
    c  very
    d  absolutely
    e  absolutely
    f  absolutely

**6**  a  a bit
    b  absolutely
    c  a bit
    d  absolutely

**7**  (Half point each)
    a  beautiful, wooden, dining
    b  tiny, white, stone
    c  eye-catching, black and
       gold, leather
    d  huge, old, plastic

**8**  a  so
    b  also
    c  however
    d  unless

**9**  (Half point each)
    a  to live
    b  playing
    c  smoking
    d  to do
    e  to finish
    f  studying

**10**  (Two points each)
    a  Did (you) see
    b  had already left
    c  arrived
    d  saw
    e  were getting
    f  had just come back
    g  didn't come out
    h  didn't do

**11**  (Two points each)
    1  c
    2  b
    3  a
    4  c
    5  b
    6  b

**12**  (Two points each)
    a  Rarely.
    b  They are part of her
       appearance.
    c  No.
    d  Because she hates her legs.

**13**  (Two points each)
    a  F
    b  T
    c  T
    d  T
    e  F
    f  F
    g  T
    h  T
    i  F
    j  T

**14**  Give a score out of 20
    5 points for accuracy
    5 points for vocabulary range
    5 points for organisation and
    cohesion
    5 points for content
    (appropriacy)